KU-695-531

The Savage Visit

THE BERKELEY SERIES IN BRITISH STUDIES

Mark Bevir and James Vernon, University of California, Berkeley, editors

The Savage Visit

New World People and Popular Imperial Culture in Britain, 1710-1795

KATE FULLAGAR

LIS LIBRARY

Date 19.7.13 Fund i-che

WITHDRAWN

Order No 2428386

University of Chester

Global, Area, and International Archive
University of California Press

BERKELEY   LOS ANGELES   LONDON

The Global, Area, and International Archive (GAIA) is an initiative of the Institute of International Studies, University of California, Berkeley, in partnership with the University of California Press, the California Digital Library, and international research programs across the University of California system.

University of California Press, one of the most distinguished university presses in the United States, enriches lives around the world by advancing scholarship in the humanities, social sciences, and natural sciences. Its activities are supported by the UC Press Foundation and by philanthropic contributions from individuals and institutions. For more information, visit www.ucpress.edu.

University of California Press
Berkeley and Los Angeles, California

University of California Press, Ltd.
London, England

© 2012 by The Regents of the University of California

Library of Congress Cataloging-in-Publication Data

A catalog record for this book is available from the Library of Congress

Manufactured in the United States of America

21 20 19 18 17 16 15 14 13 12
10 9 8 7 6 5 4 3 2 1

The paper used in this publication meets the minimum requirements of ANSI/NISO Z39.48–1992 (R 1997) (*Permanence of Paper*).

To Iain

[T]here is a long, continuous, though not invariant history of Eurocentrism that needs frequent retelling; but we understand it better, though we do not mitigate its effects, if we keep in mind that the concepts Europeans have used to relegate and repress others are at the same time those they have used to understand and even criticise themselves.

J. G. A. POCOCK, *Barbarism and Religion IV*

Contents

Illustrations

Acknowledgments

This book was based on research undertaken at the University of California, Berkeley. I am grateful to the Department of History and the Graduate Division at Berkeley, as well as the Andrew W. Mellon Foundation, for supporting that work. I am especially grateful to the people who helped me turn it into a book. Thomas Laqueur was an inspiring adviser whose inimitable way of interrogating both the qualitative and the quantitative—"so what *was* an indigenous person in the eighteenth century?" and "how many of these guys are we talking about anyway?"—will stay with me always. James Vernon was my closest reader and most steadfast supporter. His professional example and ribald humor has kept me afloat in academia more often than he knows. I would also like to acknowledge the guidance of David Lieberman and Thomas Metcalf, whose grace and enthusiasm respectively sealed my fate as a student of the eighteenth century. For hospitality and/or wise counsel during these years (and later), I thank John Byron, Dipesh Chakrabarty, James Chandler, the late Greg Dening, Alastair MacLachlan, Jon Mee, Donna Merwick, Philip Pettit, Simon Schaffer, and Frances Whistler. For the opportunity to air and/or publish some initial iterations, I thank John Brewer, Ann Curthoys, Jocelyn Hackforth-Jones, Robert Markley, Paul Pickering, Peter Read, and Paul Turnbull.

My colleagues at the University of Sydney while I was a postdoctoral fellow made all the difference for turning the thesis into a book. In particular, I would like to thank Stephen Garton—then dean, now provost—for taking the gamble of employing me. I also thank Duncan Ivison—then head of school, now dean—for continuing the gamble. I hope they feel this publication is enough payoff to move on to new risks. For some early readings and advice, I am grateful to Clare Corbould, Peter Denney, Chris

Hilliard, Kirsten McKenzie, Dirk Moses, and Stephen Robertson. Shane White and Glenda Sluga are responsible for getting me to undertake the task in the first place: I accept now their superior judgment in this matter but would like to point out that they were still horribly wrong to believe I could do it in "a mere six months!" My debt to Michael McDonnell—my official mentor at Sydney—seems too sprawling to catalog properly here. If his sage advice and visionary critiques have not been fully reflected in this book, I hope he knows they have yet lodged in my mind for later, better work.

My new colleagues at Macquarie University have been more welcoming than I could have hoped, and collectively helped to resolve the problem of the book's title. Mary Spongberg and Leigh Boucher have been particularly helpful to me and this project. Meeting the Bennelong scholars, Keith Smith and Emma Dortins, proved a timely boon. Likewise, the old student friendships of Alex Cook, Ariana Killoran, David Moshfegh, Priya Satia, Daniel Ussishkin, and especially Marina Bollinger were crucial. I am humbled to acknowledge the personal and intellectual support of Nick Thomas for nearly fifteen years: his research and approach ever encourages. I am also grateful to my editor, Nathan MacBrien, and all at the publishers who sustained this book.

Finally, I thank my beloved extended family for their moral countenance—most of all my husband, Iain McCalman, who was and remains my original inspiration, my keenest editor, my loyalest fan, and always my loftiest example of a historian and a teacher. Our four-year-old son, Rohan, did absolutely nothing to aid the production of this book—and in fact hindered it most of the way—but his existence makes its completion feel all the sweeter.

Sydney, 2011

A Note on Names

Several of the names and terms used in this book involve exceptionally fraught and as-yet unresolved histories, not the least of which are the two main collectives under investigation. "Native American" and "Oceanian" have been favored for their proximity to best current practice, though I am aware that they still carry some problems.

"Native American" here refers to indigenous peoples of all the Americas—though mostly of the northern continent—including those of the Far North, who are often excluded, but excluding those of Hawaii, who today seem to exist both in and out of the category. "Oceanian" refers to the indigenous peoples of what are today and somewhat controversially called Micronesia, Melanesia, and Polynesia (and hence here we situate Hawaii). In keeping with eighteenth-century European conceptions—the chief focus of this book—it *also* includes the indigenous peoples of Australasia but excludes those of Asia.

Of course, few peoples indicated by my terms "Native American" and "Oceanian" ever used such encompassing names in the period under discussion. My maintenance of them registers the ultimately Eurocentric perspective of the tale told in this book. Such a perspective is even more profoundly registered by my frequent use of the term "New World." The "New World" here unites both America and Oceania and as such is uniquely a concept of the European eighteenth century. I employ it for convenience's sake but mostly to remind of the historical—that is, the contingent, partial, and temporary—nature of most global divisions.

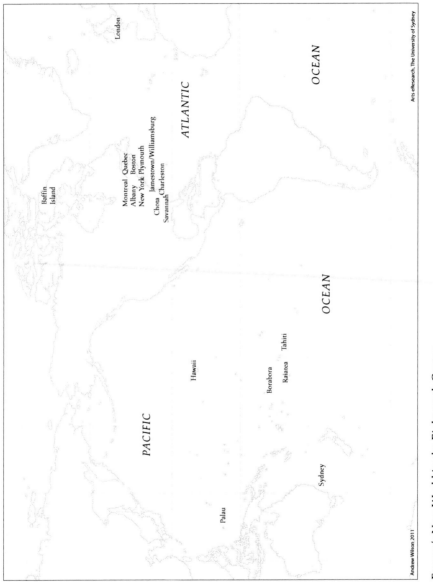

London

Baffin
Island

Montreal Quebec
Albany   Boston
New York Plymouth
Chota Jamestown/Williamsburg
Savannah Charleston

ATLANTIC

OCEAN

PACIFIC

Hawaii

Borabora
Raiatea   Tahiti

OCEAN

Palau

Sydney

Andrew Wilson 2011

Arts eResearch, The University of Sydney

Europe's New World in the Eighteenth Century

Introduction

This book originated in a question about the popularity of the first Pacific Islander to visit Britain. Mai of Raiatea arrived in 1774 with the return of James Cook's second voyage to the Pacific and stayed for two years.[1] As many writers have shown, the Islander proved a sensation while in Britain: he impressed the king, charmed the *bon ton*, intrigued provincial grandees, delighted the writers of Grub Street, inspired artists, and drew crowds of onlookers wherever he went in villages, towns, and city streets, respectively.[2] He occasioned an eight-foot portrait by Joshua Reynolds, a blockbuster pantomime by John O'Keeffe, meditations by Frances Burney, poetry by William Cowper, and scores of broadside articles, cheap woodcuts, penny ballads, and other ephemeral printed matter. But why was he so popular? The existing literature on Mai, though much of it erudite and intriguing, has surprisingly little to say about this seemingly basic question. Most commentators have offered one or a combination of two brief explanations: Mai answered perfectly the current vogue for "natural man" or "noble savagery" and/or he had a special individual and cultural ability to create his own celebrity.

While both explanations are reasonable, each raises immediate counter-questions. Why didn't other "natural men" visiting in the same period—say, the Inuit who arrived just one year before Mai—generate the same fascination? Why didn't other "noble savages" who were also deemed "knowing and strategic" attain equal fame?[3] Bennelong from the Port Jackson colony, for example, was often said to be both amiable and unnervingly politic, but his reception in Britain in the 1790s was negligible. Clearly, to address these objections we need to know more about the appeal of whatever it was that Mai embodied for Britons in the eighteenth century (if not also the mysterious quality of early-modern charisma). We need, in other words, to situate the sensation of Mai within a larger historical tradition. Previous histories have tended not to do this because they have been so captive to the notion of Mai as *the first*. The "first Pacific Islander to visit Britain" is a description that we easily accept, but what did such a label mean in Mai's period?

The category "Pacific Islander" turns out to have been far less interesting, or even coherent, than "New World person" to Britons of the 1770s. During his stay, Mai was seen less as Britain's first Pacific Islander visitor and more as the latest version of visitor from the New World. In the eighteenth-century British imaginary, Mai's corner of the New World was connected to older-known parts through a variety of mechanisms—history, geography, genealogy—but mostly through the epithet of "savage" given all its inhabitants. New World people had been traveling to the British Isles from at least as early as 1501. They came in a range of guises—from fishermen to diplomats, trophies, slaves, interpreters, and sailors—but they were always received under the general category of "savage." As a savage visitor in the eighteenth century, Mai was indeed part of a long tradition.

As a *popular* savage visitor, however, Mai's pedigree was considerably shorter. It was not until the early 1700s that New World peoples started to attract serious attention in Britain. Only when four supposed Iroquois kings turned up in 1710 did Britons evince a deep and widespread fascination: from the court to the street, they now clamored to greet the arrivals and from every level of society generated a large corpus of writings and images about them. Once begun, the fascination became entrenched. The same pitch of excitement greeted every significant indigenous envoy from America for the next fifty years—including the seven Cherokee of 1730, the Creek Tomochichi in 1734, and the entourage surrounding Ostenaco in 1762, to name just the better known. From the 1760s, when Oceania began to replace America as the center of the New World in British minds, attention shifted accordingly to indigenous Oceanian visitors. Mai's visit was in many ways the greatest sensation of all, inspiring crowds and communications of a variety and volume never before approached.

Yet Mai's visit also proved to be the zenith of eighteenth-century fascination for New World savages. While Oceanians from places as far-flung as Palau and Hawaii continued to arrive in Britain at regular intervals after Mai, they did so each time to markedly lessening effect. By the time the first Aboriginal Australian disembarked in 1793—as the latest version again of a New World savage—the reaction was minuscule. No officials attended, no mobs materialized, no publications appeared. After nearly seventy years of sustained engagement, Britons seemed suddenly to have tired of the phenomenon of the savage visitor.

THE SAVAGE VISIT

From a question about the appeal of one particular arrival in the 1770s, then, my project quickly became an investigation into the broad rise and then relatively rapid decline in popularity of all New World visitors throughout the eighteenth century. Its chief focus is the nature of the attraction surrounding such people in Britain at this time. Why did ordinary Britons become so fascinated with so-called savages for most of the eighteenth century but then lose their interest from the 1780s? What, in other words, were the specifics of everyday appeal and neglect? Evidently, any gesture here to the perennial or universal appeal of savagery as a mirror to the supposedly "not-savage" will be inadequate. Although a dominant assumption, savagery did *not* always intrigue the self-appointed civilized; it did *not* always compel as a means of reflecting back the good or the ill of a society. Like any form of exotica, savagery has a history, functioning in different ways when figured in different places or in different periods.

The Savage Visit analyzes a selection of visits by different New World people to Britain, sketching in episodic fashion the main contours of the phenomenon during the eighteenth century. It finds that for the bulk of the period, savage visitors proved particularly popular because they were then particularly "good to think."[4] More than simple conduits for favorable or pejorative commentaries on contemporary British civilization, they served also to enable or enhance a specific debate about British civilization at this time. That debate centered on the question of expansion, and included a greater range and a fiercer heat of opinion than is often realized. Although this period witnessed the emergence of a "cult of commerce" and with it the consolidation of a "nascent imperial sensibility," it did not enjoy full consensus on these matters.[5] The classical case against trade, growth, militarization, and eventual empire was livelier, commoner, and fresher then usually credited by cultural, social, and economic historians. The visiting savage provided a rare forum in which Britons of all shades could discuss this issue. It appealed equally to various positions, and in equally diverse ways, as a powerful metaphor for what British expansion might or might not bring. That Britons became increasingly indifferent to so-called savages at century's end reflected not only a major shift in the understanding of "the problem of British civilization" but also a major shift in the relations between opposing discourses.

. . .

The historiography on New World travelers to early-modern Britain is patchy at best. Few scholars have focused especially on the question of impact and none have combined analysis of all those who fell under the rubric of "New World" at the time. Native American travelers have been secluded from Oceanian travelers because historians have tended to work within later notions of nationality rather than contemporary group definitions. Of the former, some excellent work now exists. Michael Oberg on the Croatan Manteo of 1584, Kathleen Brown on Pocahontas's sojourn in 1616, and Eric Hinderaker on the "Four Iroquois Kings" of 1710, for examples, have all advanced the micro-study of individual travelers, while Alden Vaughan in 2006 published what is certainly the best overview of Native Americans in Britain from first arrival to 1776.[6] Perhaps because of their lack of a larger context, however, none of these studies make any particularly exceptional claim about reception. Vaughan's otherwise meticulous book, *Transatlantic Encounters*, ends with the blanket statement that Native Americans were "endlessly fascinating" to Britons; as travelers they constituted a "semicontiguous and immensely popular parade that lasted nearly three centuries before 1776."[7]

The literature on Oceanian travelers is much thinner than its counterpart and suffers even more from an absence of grand context. Mai is the only figure to have generated a substantial scholarship, though as mentioned this corpus has rarely attended to the issue of appeal and has even less frequently considered the relationship between Mai and earlier envoys from the New World. Later Oceanian travelers have inspired negligible attention.[8]

This book owes a great deal to earlier work on its subject but places a determinedly new emphasis on discovering why, in effect, that subject came to exist in the first place. It reviews the subject of New World travelers in its eighteenth-century entirety, including peoples who are now properly studied apart but who nevertheless shared a significant common assignation at one time.

THE IDEA OF SAVAGERY
IN EIGHTEENTH-CENTURY BRITAIN

What exactly did this key unifying notion of savagery mean in the eighteenth century? Savagery is, of course, a well-traversed topic in intellectual history. Most formal accounts provide a long lineage, beginning with the idea's origins in ancient thought, tracing its survival in medieval theology, noting its increasing distinction by the Renaissance, and then ending with its status as chief synonym for the Enlightenment's potent category of "the state of nature."[9] It is generally conceded that savagery lost much of its historical texture into the nineteenth century, coming to indicate plain, negative qualities such as cruelty or ferocity.[10] Few of these histories, however, pay much heed to the relationship between the philosophical realm of most of their sources and the everyday life of their subject. Though hardly a simple task, its pervasive neglect means that the more generic sense of the idea of savagery is little iterated.

In order to get at the common notion of savagery in our period, it may be better to start at an alternate point in the foregoing sweep, when the term was first used with relative regularity in several European languages to describe humans.[11] The etymology of the word reveals that savagery was associated with humanity only from the fifteenth century.[12] Derived from the Latin *silvaticus* for forest, the word was previously employed with respect to the plants or animals of wooded environments. Since wooded environments were generally defined by their absence of human life, any connection made between the two now immediately registered an important dissonance. Like "Ishmaell the Sauage" from the fifteenth-century romance *Generydes*, who was *"oddely* wild in all his demeaning," savage people from early-modern times were first and foremost different because they lived in places that were not normally or familiarly occupied.[13]

The difference of savagery is no doubt its most central tenet. If the savage does cast back before the fifteenth century, it is usually to see himself in his cousin, the barbarian. Ancient and medieval barbarians were also primarily defined by their otherness. In Aristotelian thought, the *barbaros* was fundamentally different because he lacked the fundamental characteristic of reason. In medieval thought, the barbarian was he who failed to fulfill God's first article for men, which is to till the earth and subdue the animals (Gen 1: 26–28). The savage of the general early-modern era, then, contained within him traces of both the dissonance of unreason and that of unproductivity.[14]

The second key tenet of savagery as it came to be used by sixteenth-century Europeans was the way it asserted difference through dearth or simplicity. Mostly this was a dearth or simplicity of social practices, or of what Margaret Hodgen has called "cultural facts."[15] The godless and "gabbling" Caliban of Shakespeare's *Tempest*, for example, was savage because he lacked language and religion. Columbus called the Caribs savage because they lacked clothing, defenses, God, and a cooked diet.

Vespucci found the Brazilians savage because they lacked shame, government, laws, and a merchant class.[16]

In earlier times, the barbarian's lack was codified within varying versions of the *scala natura*. The Great Chain of Being, either ancient or medieval, placed the barbarian above the animals but below fully attained or fully acquitted humanity. Though each being in the chain was in a constant progress toward a purer nature or a purer salvation, it was also always stuck beneath or below or behind a higher state. This strangely mobile fixity is what survived into savagery. The general early-modern notion was marked by what it did not yet have, or did not yet have enough of.[17]

This is not to say that dearth or simplicity was necessarily reviled. The third major feature of savagery was its constant ambivalence in value. Before the nineteenth century, it is as easy to find positive accounts of savagery as it is to find negative ones (although, as many scholars have pointed out, the negative probably still outweighed the positive overall).[18] For every diatribe against "beastly," "horrible," "filthy," or "hideous" savages, that is, there were frequent praises for "gentle," "loving," "faithful," or "harmless" versions of the same.[19] Such dualism, of course, has a clear heritage in the primitivism and anti-primitivism that Arthur Lovejoy and others long ago identified throughout most Western thought. Beginning with the split in estimate between the loathsome, feral Cyclopes and the happy, sated Hyperboreans, this ambivalence about simple others continued through most classical literature, bowed before a greater tendency to see only ignobility in the Middle Ages, but then re-emerged by the Renaissance.[20]

A working definition of early-modern savagery, then, includes first a sense of radical otherness; second, a lack or simplicity of social practices; and third, an ambivalent valuation. Other attributes commonly added to definitions of savagery for this time, such as cannibalism, naturalism, and even nonhumanity, are not as ubiquitous as these three principles. Two contemporaneous events, however, were additionally important in shaping the early-modern understanding of savagery. The first was the discovery of the New World. Its coincidence with the rise of the use of savagery as a descriptor for humans formed the basis of an overriding association that held for at least three centuries. "From the sixteenth to the nineteenth centuries," writes Ter Ellingson, New World people "constituted the paradigmatic case for the 'savage,' and the term was most widely applied to them."[21] The second, vaguer event was the reinvention of barbarism. When the concept of the savage human emerged in the fifteenth century, the barbarian somehow simultaneously lost much of his millennia-old history to it. If savagery now incorporated the unreasonable and the unproductive, the barbarian became instead someone who exercised *poor* reason or had a *poor* impact upon the world—his impertinent will in these matters highlighted in contrast the savage's inherent innocence.[22] Far from an association with the most newly discovered peoples of the earth, barbarians became rather aligned with the "old new world"—those yet-shadowy regions of the vast Orient, which clearly could no longer be accused of lacking civilization but which apparently had still to acquit themselves on the question of quality.

This generic notion of savagery, formed through the sixteenth century with its strong ties to the New World and noted distinction from a reconfigured barbarism, was still mostly current by the Age of Enlightenment. The period's signature "meaning compendiums" attest most tidily to the continuation: most dictionaries and encyclopedias of the eighteenth century include the three basic tenets outlined above, as well as frequent references both to the New World and to a fundamental naïveté. Samuel Johnson's famous *Dictionary* from the middle of the era scattered synonyms for savagery throughout its pages, which can be roughly ordered into first those that indicated profound difference—"immane"; second, those that indicated social deficiency—"rude," "rustical," "nomadick," "uncivilised," "pagan," "not tamed"; and third, those that indicated a negative quality—"brutal," "cruel," "churlish," "fierce," "bloody," "rapacious," "outrageous," "truculent" (Johnson himself was never ambivalent about the value of savagery). Before Johnson's *Dictionary,* the best-known English arbiter on meanings was probably Ephraim Chambers' *Cyclopaedia* (1728). It defined savagery as a state of wildness "without any fix'd Habitation, Religion, Law, or Policy" and noted too that "A great Part of *America* is peopled with *Savages.*" Johnson's great rival, John Ash, brought out his *New and Complete Dictionary* in 1775, which mostly agreed with its predecessors but added an emphasis on the "untaught" essence of savagery.[23]

Broad claims by intellectual historians that savagery in the Enlightenment simply "equated" to the state of nature, or the "purely natural," thus overlook some of the nuances evident in everyday understandings of the word by our period (and in its broadness can as well imply limitless nuances under the umbrella of "nature").[24] They miss, that is, the way in which ordinary uses of the word at this time worked within set, if yet capacious, parameters. An anonymous squib entitled *The Savage* demonstrates how savagery in this era was both larger and more precise than usually retailed. Published to commemorate the discovery of a supposed "wild child" on the European continent in 1726, the piece described savages as "unform'd, untaught, / From solitary Desarts brought"; they are strangers to guile, envy, pride, and avarice but they are also lustful, lawless, and "slavish to . . . each imperious Passion's Sway."[25] The ditty writer in this instance outlined a certain type of otherness that lacked in a very certain way. He also incidentally evoked distinguished intellectual traditions about particular outsiders in his usage even if he himself did not have a "philosophical cast of mind."[26]

. . .

Recently some historians have questioned the extended study of savagery. Instead of giving more attention to a demeaning stereotype, they encourage investigations into how people so called were on occasion seen as real rather than idealized figures.[27] Along with some good evidence, such scholars have probably been inspired by two main prompts—a modern reluctance to add to the burden of a victim's past (which may also threaten to smother the story of hidden resistances) and pronouncements such as Hayden White's in 1976 that "there is nothing more to say" about the theme of savagery.[28]

The work of Troy Bickham and Stephanie Pratt, for example, has uncovered some compelling instances of a more realist approach to Native Americans in eighteenth-century Britain. But as I discuss later in this book, neither author demonstrates a waning of the *predominant* attachment of the stereotype of savagery. To the problem of studying oppressive epithets, I can only offer the well-worn though sincere opinion that analysis of how a stereotype germinated, thrived, and later hybridized in the past underscores its radical contingency and always the existence somewhere of trenchant refusers. As for White, his own later essays are examples of how pertinent discourse can continue even for the best-rehearsed topics, mainly because the wider scholarly fields around them constantly alter shape. For White on savagery in the 1970s, the key alteration was the introduction of psychoanalysis. For this book today, the critical shift is rather in the picture we have now of eighteenth-century Britain. In the light of a veritable boom in studies over the last three decades, eighteenth-century Britain looks a lot more divided, dependent, anxious, curious, and dynamic than it once did. Does the behavior or purchase of the supposedly overstudied notion of savagery also look different in this reconfigured terrain?

THE PECULIAR MODERNITY OF
EIGHTEENTH-CENTURY BRITAIN

Despite the revitalization of the field of eighteenth-century British history, few have ventured to offer a synthesis of the recent literature. Who, after all, wants to rationalize a corpus that delineates both a burgeoning consumer society and a predominantly agrarian economy? Both an empire of global reach and a culture of notable xenophobia? Both an expanding fiscal-military state and a persistent horror of debt and war? Both patronage and individualism? Commercialism and landed authority. Politeness and slavery. These are the key paradoxes retailed in current histories of the era and together they constitute what Paul Langford has called its "peculiar modernity".[29] For many, this amounts to a vision of eighteenth-century Britain as an *ancien régime* with an oddly familiar dynamism.[30]

As Norma Landau remarked near the beginning of the revisionist impetus, recent historians wish to "capture [the] seeming paradoxes [of] eighteenth-century society" rather than explain them away as awkward steps toward either progressive liberalism or the proletarian state.[31] But this does not mean that they always wish to account for contradiction—to analyze the extent to which "seeming paradoxes" actually threatened historical cohesion. Most scholars indeed paint pictures of a fairly functional society. Even those interested primarily in studying minorities, marginals, and otherwise resistant types still often point to the overall dominance, rather than failure, of hegemony in this era.[32]

Some historians, however, see a less stable entity. They argue, as one of the more idiosyncratic of their number has put it, that eighteenth-century Britain was marked most of all by a "fermenting and ungovernable debate over itself."[33] For more than three decades, J.G.A. Pocock has made the case for conflict in eighteenth-century Britain, though—granted—he has been less interested in conflict between social groups than between discursive positions.[34] Far from being an engagement in mere surfaces, however, his analyses of the antagonistic ways in which Britons discussed the paradoxes of their age suggest that it was precisely these disagreements that posed the greatest threat to overall unity.

Pocock's two chief "opposing paradigms" for eighteenth-century Britain have been referred to in shorthand as classical republicanism and modern commercialism, or in longhand as "the Old Whig, Tory, Commonwealth and Country reaction against the financial, oligarchic, and imperial regime that came into being after 1688" and the latter's apologists.[35] In our context, the main thrust of the republican case was less about a true adherence to neo-roman or even antimonarchical ideas of active citizenship and more about a critique of the perceived shift in the economic bases of political power. At the turn of the seventeenth century it was felt that the emergence of a commercial economy spelled a government newly reliant on the "monied interest" and thus newly exposed to the threat of corruption. Since monied men themselves were reliant on unpredictable relations of exchange—unlike their historic counterpart in real property owners, who maintained a glorious autonomy—this added to concerns about instability. Moreover, a government tied to commercial interests would necessarily have to institute two of the greatest bugbears of classical political theory—a standing army to protect new global trading posts and a massive national debt to pay for so much new warmongering. Since most observers agreed that it was the Revolution Settlement of 1688 which formalized these changes in Britain, republican critique in the eighteenth century was peculiarly characterized by negative interpretations of Revolutionary issues. It was marked, in other words, by an antipathy to parliament, a defense of monarchical right, a fear of the degradation of Anglican centrality, and a general hostility to the sociable and tolerant culture necessary for commercial practice— together with more typical anxieties about war and money.

What is most significant for Pocock in the identification of discursive division at this time is that it was the republican model that dictated initial terms. The case for commerce was "hammered out with difficulty in the face of [republican ideals]"; its proponents "had to fight [their] way to . . . recognition in the teeth of the [republican ideal]."[36] It followed, thus, that apologists for commerce were also preoccupied, to perhaps an otherwise baffling extent, with issues from 1688: the good governance of the court, the containment of the sovereign, the continued health of the Church, and the wonderment of an ever-elaborating social manner—as well as, of course, with war and money. Though commerce came later to command fresh terms—based on wealth over stability and politeness over virtue—Pocock reiterates that its ultimate vindication was not the result of a "unidirectional transformation of thought in favour of the acceptance of 'liberal' or 'market' man, but [rather of] a bitter, conscious and ambivalent dialogue."[37]

Unfortunately, Pocock has rarely ventured outside of the realm of the "unrepresentative elite" when investigating this conflict, and few of his readers have wandered where he has declined to go.[38] But in many ways, the popular reaction to New World visitors until the 1780s shows that this division over commercialization was a comprehensive fault line. The content of the myriad productions on the visitors revolved consistently around the changing roles of Britain's parliament, churchmen, armed forces, financiers, and the new "culture" peddlers. Significantly, too, these popular works were marked by intense discord rather than consensus. If the conflict manifested in the response to New World arrivals was not always articulated as one between classical republicanism and modern commercialism, it nonetheless shared similar groupings of concern as well as a similar whiff of incommensurability. In the fuzzy world of the general urban literate, this conflict is perhaps better defined as a fluid tussle over the question of expansion.[39]

Expansion is of course both the motor and reason for all commercial enterprise, but in our context it also captures the sense of endless proliferation that commercialization was believed to wreak on contemporary society—new forms of governance, new needs for guns and credit, new insistences on sociable behavior, and so on. Moreover, expansion invokes, or brings to the fore, the literal move into new worlds that contemporaries commonly noted as the means by which such newness was afforded. Expansion highlights the imperialistic thrust of eighteenth-century British commerce. The everyday debate over expansionism was fluid because its spokespeople rarely respected formal ideological boundaries. The same Grub Street journal could satirize the megalomania of expansionist ministers one day but congratulate the government on a victory in battle the next. The same balladeer could denounce the influx of expansion's luxury goods into London in one verse but celebrate the spread of British trade in the following. Though ideology on the ground in eighteenth-century Britain came packaged in bits, it was for all its messiness no less a coherent position in discourse.

Expansion, then, lay at the heart of the reaction to New World visitors. The great *appeal* of such people, however, depended not on their ability to create common ground on the issue but on their ability to provide a means of debating expansion from multiple positions. The key to this attribute was their unquestioned status as savages. It was specifically as agreed embodiments of radically distinct simplicity, with a long history of ambivalent valuation, that New World visitors in eighteenth-century Britain became "good to think." Their radically distinct simplicity stood in eloquent relation to all that expansion was imagined to effect. And their ambivalent valuation meant that any discursive articulation of that relation was possible. For instance, visiting savages could be held up as emblems of the retrograde backwardness that awaited those who failed to expand, or they could be made into avatars of the pure orderliness that would come from expansion's full pursuit. Conversely, savages in Britain could be seen as *memento mori* of the innocence lost in the move away from classical political economy, or they could be demonized as specters of the dependent brutishness entailed in embracing an exchange culture. Savagery did not foster consensus on expansion but its innate distinction and rich flexibility made the concept comprehensively attractive.[40]

The waning of interest in New World visitors from the 1780s was not merely an instance of overfamiliarity. After all, such folk had been arriving on British shores for nearly three hundred years—they had seemingly acquired fresh luster after two hundred and then suddenly lost their appeal within eighty. The rise and fall of fashions usually have histories independent of modern estimates for mass fatigue. Likewise, the turn away from New World visitors was not a sign of a change in the definition of savagery—the term continued to indicate radically distinct simplicity into the late 1700s, even if it now tended to be judged with increasing reprove. Rather, the shift took the form of a change in the *purchase* of savagery on the debate about expansionism, which in turn indicated a change in the terms of the debate itself. Savagery proved less and less useful to the articulation of opinions about Britain's commercial future because, bluntly, that future had already arrived. By the 1790s, the "bitter dialogue" over expansionism had mostly resolved in favor of the advocates. This is not to say that agreement about Britain's destiny now reigned but it does suggest that symbols of fundamental difference were no longer as potent in the more reform-minded debates that followed.

The conflict over expansion had been one of first principles: it had focused on the probity of whether Britain should become an expansionist state at all. Later conflicts about the empire created by that expansion centered more on secondary concerns: they were less interested in questions of *ought* than in questions of *how*. The diversity of the reaction to New World visitors, which in itself explains their appeal, shows that Britons for much of the eighteenth century were not at all unanimous about their national trajectory. Imperial identity can be no more assumed a dominant trait in this era than the unfolding of empire was a certainty. Both were deeply contingent because both were deeply controversial.

. . .

The Savage Visit takes a simple, chronological structure. Chapter 1 narrates the history of New World travelers to the British Isles before the eighteenth century, establishing the disparate and essentially casual nature of their reception. Chapters 2 to 4 draw the rising arc of eighteenth-century interest in New World envoys, detailing particular visits from 1710 to the 1760s. Chapter 5 analyzes the critical shift regarding ideal savagery from America to Oceania in the 1760s and 1770s, while chapter 6, on Mai, chronicles the visit that witnessed the height of fascination for people of his kind. Chapters 7 and 8 delineate the downward curve of British interest in New World folk, concluding with a recent controversy that links the phenomenon of the eighteenth-century savage visitor to our day.

It remains only to make clear that, given my concern to understand the "everyday appeal and neglect" of a phenomenon in the British past, this book has a necessarily metropolitan emphasis. The work does, however, also include many micro-histories of the individuals who constituted that phenomenon—each chapter contains short, interlinked narratives of the travelers' backgrounds, ambitions, interpretations, and returns. But unlike the analysis of metropolitan engagement, these micro-histories do not pretend to amount to one overarching thesis—least of all about the nature of the eighteenth-century indigenous travel experience. To do so would be to perpetuate contemporary British assumptions about the sameness of peoples we now believe to be vastly different. Alden Vaughan has recently reminded us of the difficulty in constructing these micro-histories at all. As with any folk who leave little or no records of their personal existence, the men and women who traveled from the New World to Britain in our era are mostly glimpsed between lines written by others, among shades painted in portraits, and behind rumors spread after they left. Although dispiriting at some level, Vaughan also reminds that this paucity of evidence is still richer than what we know about "many thousands of Europeans and Africans who went in the opposite direction."[41]

1. The New World in England before the Eighteenth Century

The earliest known visit by New World peoples to England was that of three Newfoundlanders—probably Beothuks—brought over with some returning Bristol-based fishermen in 1501.[1] These fishermen were actually Portuguese merchants operating under English patents. They brought the Beothuks to the court of Henry VII, the granter of their patent, no doubt as a means of proving their endeavors to their patron. There is little data as to the motive of the Beothuks in submitting to the journey—if submit they did—although it bears remembering that such folk were primarily fishermen themselves who may have considered it beneficial to form alliances with newcomers to their waters.

A contemporary English chronicle by one Richard Fabyan claimed that "this year were browght unto the kyng iii men takyn in the Newe Found Ile land . . . These were clothed in bestys skinnys and ete Rawe Flesh and spake such spech that noo man cowde undyrstand theym."[2] Two years later Fabyan reported that he saw two of the Indians still alive in Westminster, "apparaylyd afftyr Inglysh men [so that I] cowde not dyscern From Inglysh men . . . But as for spech I hard noon of theym uttyr oon word."[3] Although Fabyan did not call these men savage nor offer much opinion on the merits of their features either way, the chronicler did stress their unusual dress, diet, and language. What caught his eye was the simplicity, baseness, or downright opacity of three key personal practices. Such alignment of lack with what we would call social or cultural characteristics would become one of the abiding features of the early-modern understanding of savagery in England. Possibly Fabyan was the first writer in English to make the connection between this particular lack and New World people.

The Beothuks' presence in England also inaugurated another tradi-

14

tion associated with English commentary on New World people—at least for the first two hundred years of English consideration of the problem. This was the relative *inattention* paid to such folk when they arrived in England during the sixteenth or seventeenth centuries, compared to the fanfare they received in the eighteenth century. Fabyan's is, as far as we know, the only commentary to survive on the Beothuks. When placed in the context of later, similarly sparse documentation left of New World people in England, however, it would seem that it was perhaps one of only a few to exist in the first place. Admittedly, the paucity of evidence of interest in traveling New World peoples in early-modern England may tell more of the restricted circumstances of the travelers than the limited fascination of the English—many knew simply their escorts, the people they met at port, and for some the courts to which they were brought, so they did not truly have the opportunity of impressing large numbers of English folk. Yet the minimal sources also fit with the more subdued reaction that many historians now claim was the case in England toward the New World in general.

Following the historian John Elliott's "blunted impact" thesis of the 1970s, numerous scholars have shown how newness was absorbed into European knowledge—and especially English knowledge—far more gradually and quietly than once assumed.[4] For the English sixteenth century, for example, Peter Burke has studied histories, bibliographies, chronologies, and encyclopedias and found that the discovery of America was often "treated as a second-rate event, or even ignored altogether," compared to the volume and manner in which readers and writers consumed publications on other places.[5] David Armitage, indeed, has argued that most of the significant publications on the New World appeared after 1700, as part of England's "belated receptiveness" to discovery.[6]

This initial chapter is chiefly a narrative of some of the visits by New World people to England during the sixteenth and seventeenth centuries. It argues that while the earliest commentators on these arrivals mostly associated them with the concept of savagery—either by the word itself or by description of an alterity based on extreme simplicities of habit—they did not consider them to be of momentous or widespread significance.

THE SIXTEENTH CENTURY: KINGS, CAPTIVES, AND CULTURAL BROKERS

The next known appearance of a Native American in England occurred in 1530 or 1531, described by Richard Hakluyt some sixty years after the event. This arrival comprised a party of just one—apparently a king from Brazil—escorted by the English slaver-captain William Hawkins. Hakluyt records that Hawkins, during one of his forays from Africa to Portuguese Brazil, became known to "one of the savage kings of the countrey."[7] Hakluyt claims that the Brazilian king was "contented to take ship with him," perhaps answering a curiosity or entrepreneurial spirit in himself at the same time as he answered Hawkins's desire to show off an exotic contact to his own sovereign, Henry VIII. The Brazilian made a pact with the slaver that he should leave one of his men behind as a guaranty of the king's safe return. As it turned out, this pact caused some controversy. Hakluyt relates that "having remained here the space almost of a whole yeere . . . M. Hawkins purposed to convey [the Brazilian] againe into his countrey: but it fell out in the way, that . . . the said Savage king died at sea." Hawkins's men naturally feared for the life of the English guaranty waiting in Brazil, but fortunately "the Savages being fully perswaded of the honest dealing of our men with their prince, restored again the said pledge."[8]

While in England, "the Brasilian king . . . was brought up to London and presented to K. Henry the 8 . . . at the sight of whom the King and all the Nobilitie did not a little marvaile, and not without cause . . . in his cheeks were holes made according to their Savage manner, and therein small bones were planted, standing an inche out from the said holes . . . All his apparel, behaviour, and gesture, were very strange to the beholders."[9] Hakluyt was all too ready to give the label of savagery to this visitor; indeed, in his *Navigations*, Hakluyt had declared that all inhabitants of the New World "may very well and truly be called savage."[10] It is not clear whether the eyewitness observers of the Brazilian king in the 1530s also used the term, since Hakluyt's words are all that remain for this arrival. But it is noteworthy that the features which Hakluyt's record claimed to be most salient—the king's apparel and his manner—were of the same order as those remarked for the Beothuks. Once again, it was the strange "behaviour and gesture"—including an animality, and thus baseness, of adornment—that commentators seemed most to focus on in their apprehension of the New World man.

Hakluyt was not himself an eyewitness to the Brazilian king in England, as I have mentioned, and there are no surviving contemporary records. Hakluyt's account suggests that the Brazilian's greatest impact was at the royal court. However, since no official chronicle exists, one might assume that it was not a deeply or long-sustained wonder even there. That no commoner record exists reflects either the Brazilian's minimal impact on ordinary Londoners or, more probably, his lack of exposure to commoners at all. Although compelling for the latter-day historian, it seems that the event of a New World person in an Old World land during the sixteenth century did not prove a tremendous sensation.

While the Brazilian king appeared to journey to England voluntarily, the same cannot be said of the next two arriving parties of Native Americans. The explorer Martin Frobisher, in his first two voyages in search of the El Doradic northwest passage, brought over a total of four Inuit people from Baffin Island, all captured and transported against their will. Ironically, Queen Elizabeth, Frobisher's patron, had beforehand given explicit instructions against forceful kidnapping: "you shall not bring above three or four persons of that country, the which shall be of divers ages, and shall be taken in such sort as you may best avoid offence of that people."[11] The Queen's remarks attest to an implicit point about the understanding of New World people: they were clearly not considered by all to be of a state so lacking that it fell short of usual official standards for interaction. The Queen held New World peoples to be deserving of typical diplomacy, whether or not she also thought them savage. Frobisher ended up meeting her strictures about number and age, but hardly her injunctions against offence. The main chronicler of the Frobisher voyages, George Best, describes how the captain on his first voyage of 1576 lured some Inuit to his ship with a bell. When one reached out his hand for the attraction, "he was thereby taken himself . . . the Captain let the bell fal, & cought the man fast, and plucked him with maine force boate and al into his bark."[12] Frobisher maintained that the kidnapping was in retaliation for an earlier capture of five of his own men, though their disappearance was never confirmed to have been due to the Inuit. During his second voyage of 1577, Frobisher's men wrestled one man into captivity and also "brought away" a woman and child, reputedly to continue the punishment for his missing five men but in addition to begin forging a means of communication with the Baffin Islanders.[13]

All four Frobisher captives died while in England. The Inuit man who arrived in 1576 survived less than a month. During his few weeks in England he must have been bedridden for the majority, since he was suffering from both a self-inflicted wound in his mouth and what Best recorded as a "colde . . . taken at Sea."[14] Since Best believed he subsequently died from this cold, it was probably rather serious. The self-inflicted wound had been caused on board ship by the Inuit biting his "tong in twayne," to show both his "disdain" for his captors and no doubt also his despair.[15] The archives of Frobisher's employer, the Cathay Company, which took financial responsibility for the captive, show that he cost them payments for nurses, bedding, and a surgeon.[16] Here was hardly a man fit to be parading the streets as a wonder.

Yet some historians have since claimed that this Inuit became the "talk of the realm," a major curiosity to Londoners and all who heard of him.[17] Such a conclusion derives from a single source, written by one of the primary financiers of Frobisher's voyage, Michael Lok. Lok had claimed in his *Account of the First Voyage* that the Inuit was "such a wonder unto the whole city and to the rest of the realm that heard of it as seemed never to have happened the like great matter to any man's knowledge."[18] Best concurred that "the like of this strange infidel was never seen, red, nor harde of before," though he did not make large claims for the Inuit's won-drousness on account of this strangeness.[19] Lok had a great deal invested in promoting the pioneering quality of the Frobisher voyage: he may well have exaggerated the appeal of the captured man to further his general push for recognition of the enterprise as a whole.

As with the Beothuks and the Brazilian king, the Inuit man of 1576 inspired few surviving documents. No popular pamphlets or squibs exist to corroborate the official accounts of Best and Lok. There were apparently some images made of the traveler, though unfortunately none survive. The Cathay Company commissioned a well-respected artist, Cornelius Ketel, to paint several of the Inuit's portrait, as well as, later, a wax artist, William Cure, to make his death mask. These images were surely created as gifts to patrons or as proud testaments of adventure on the part of the company—one was explicitly destined for the queen. Unlike many eighteenth-century images of New World travelers, however, they were not produced to provoke or satisfy a popular curiosity. It is true that at least two European artists made copies of Ketel's work, which survive to this day, but these circulated chiefly within a learned continental crowd who had always evinced a slightly greater fascination than the English for things of the New World.[20]

What Best and Lok said in description of the Inuit is surprisingly min-imal: Best confined himself to remarks about his lack of comprehensible language; Lok, rather unusually when compared with similar documents, concentrated mostly on the traveler's physical appearance, detailing his full body, squat proportions, and "dark Sallow" coloring.[21] Lok also com-mented on the Inuit's "sullen," "churlish," and "sharp" countenance, which as Alden Vaughan quips was perhaps not undue "for a fatally ill captive a thousand miles from home."[22] The derivative images in some ways offer more insight into typical English preoccupations, despite their problematic remove: they show a man wrapped in skins and bearing a bow and a paddle. Such attention to dress and accoutrement fitted with the majority of texts about New World people at this time, suggesting the simplicity of the Inuit's modes of covering, hunting and transport, and thus underscoring the basic society assumed of all early-modern savages.[23]

Compared to the 1576 Inuit, the three Native Americans whom Frobisher brought over with the return of his second Arctic voyage in 1577 did arouse some general interest. These three were also probably Inuit: they comprised a man captured on one day in Baffin Island and a woman and her infant captured on another day. Although to their English audience they appeared a conventional family group, it is doubtful that the adults even knew each other. As trophies and as reparations, these adults were also reckoned by Frobisher to promise a gateway into understanding the language of the new lands.[24] As such, they are among the first New World travelers to be explicitly acknowledged as potential "native informants," or, as is more commonly preferred today, "cultural brokers"—a role that many later successors were expected to fulfill as their chief purpose.[25]

The three Inuit disembarked in Bristol in October 1577, and were soon presented to an admiring mayor. Whether staged by Frobisher's men or by the mayor himself, the male Inuit, known as Kalicho, was directed on 9 October to demonstrate some of his skills before a crowd on Avon River. According to a local chronicle written over fifty years later, Kalicho paddled in his skin kayak and killed two ducks with a dart.[26] The chronicle also reported the Inuit's raw-meat diet and, in one edition, his propensity to eat a fowl's entire entrails, "including the dung."[27] This mayoral viewing would indeed have been a public occasion, although it is a shame that once again we have no firsthand account. Frobisher intended to transport the group to London to meet Queen Elizabeth, where they may well have gained the significant popularity that their Bristol outing foreshadowed. But before he could do so, all three died in quick succession. Kalicho died on 7 November, probably from injuries sustained during his capture, but also perhaps from some manifestation of the "anglophobia" attributed to him in his official postmortem.[28] The woman, known as Arnaq, died four days later, probably from an infectious disease, while her infant son, known as Nutaaq and still nursing, followed within the fortnight.

A Dr. Edward Dodding examined Kalicho just before his death and performed an autopsy on him afterward. His report detailed broken ribs and a cerebral injury, though his causes for death included also what he considered a "too liberal diet." His enormous stomach, Dodding wrote, seemed "much larger than is the case with our people; a consequence, I think, of his unhealthy voraciousness." Dodding's reprimand stretched to Kalicho's medical manners as well: "in the early onset of [his] illness . . . I recommended bloodletting . . . But the foolish, and only too uncivilized, timidity of this uncivilized man forbade it."[29] Clearly Dodding had little patience for the ill-fated traveler; indeed, he concluded that his demise was to be lamented "not so much [for] the man himself as because the great hope of seeing him which our most gracious Queen had entertained had now slipped through her fingers."[30]

What Dodding took to be a lack of civilization was more explicitly depicted as savagery by the graphic images made of the three Inuit.[31] Unlike the anonymous traveler of the previous year, these Inuit had images made of them which survive today. Once again Ketel was commissioned to portray the captives for the Cathay Company, but once again these have been lost. However, some sketches made by the later colonist John White remain (see, for example, figure 1.1), and what is more they were known to have circulated at least around the learned publishing circles of Europe, since versions appear in various European editions of books about New World exploration. Again, though, despite claims that the different images of these Inuit testify to a burgeoning popularity, most scholars concede that their reproduction was confined mainly to the continent. Notably, even the comments that prove the existence of some images in England, now lost, were made by visiting Europeans. A German visitor to Hampton Court reported seeing "life-like portraits of the wild man and woman . . . brought alive to England," while a Swiss visitor, almost certainly viewing White's pictures, claimed that the subjects "looked like savages, wore skins, and the woman carried a child . . . upon her shoulder."[32] At this stage in the Old World's contemplation of the New World it seemed that only continental observers were stirred with any notable intrigue.

The German and the Swiss were under no illusions about what these captives represented—they signified "wildness," or its Latinate cognate, "savagery." White's images suggest that he also saw them in this light, at least in so far as he included deliberate indicators to crude existence—the animal skins of primitive dress and the bow of primitive provisioning. Importantly, the signs of savagery in this era were those that lay on the body or with the body; they were rarely understood to be evident by the body itself.

The last key group of Native Americans to arrive in England in the sixteenth century were the various cultural brokers whom Walter Raleigh

FIGURE I.I.   John White, drawing of Arnaq and Nutaaq, pen and
ink and watercolor, c. 1577. © The Trustees of the British Museum.

helped to bring over in the hopes of securing his vision of New World colonization. These travelers—numbering around a dozen between 1584 and
1618—have been most cogently discussed by Alden Vaughan.[33] Vaughan
shows how Raleigh's chosen guides—ranging from Algonquians to Guianans to Trinidadians—"drastically expanded" the role of Native Americans in England, establishing them as critical linguistic, diplomatic, and
geographic sources for later "transatlantic culture exchange."[34]

The first "Raleigh exports" were the now relatively well-known Manteo
and Wanchese from Croatan and Roanoke Islands, respectively. These

Americans were not escorted to England by Raleigh himself, but came with the first expedition to the New World conducted under the aegis of Raleigh's exclusive royal grant. The 1584 expedition was led by Captains Philip Amadas and Arthur Barlowe, the latter of whom appeared to be the one responsible for persuading "two savage men" to commit to a journey to meet his commander.[35] The method of persuasion is not retailed, and considering the later loyalty of Manteo but later opposition of Wanchese it is hard to speculate about its violence or lack thereof from this historical distance. Once in England, Raleigh immediately organized the Americans' tuition in English under the scholar, Thomas Harriot.[36] In Raleigh's borrowed estate on the Thames, Manteo and Wanchese apparently learnt a great deal of their would-be colonizer's language, but more importantly they seem to have taught Harriot and others about their own language, about various rivalries in their home region, about Algonquian ranks and codes and propensities, and about the geography and natural resources of their coastal plain.

Manteo and Wanchese, who cannot be assumed to have known each other before or even to have liked each other, stayed at Raleigh's house for eight months. In that time, we have record of a German tourist commenting on "their usual habit [of] rudely tanned skins . . . and a pelt before their privy parts," although he notes that in England they wore brown taffeta suits.[37] And we have a Hansard report mentioning "some of the people borne in those pties brought home . . . by whose meanes & direction . . . singular great commodities of that Lande are revealed & made knowen unto us."[38] Otherwise there is little note of Manteo and Wanchese in London. Probably they were much occupied in scholarly and political pursuits, yet it still seems that their presence held notably little popular fascination. Vaughan's comment that they "surely . . . enthralled larger crowds [than did Kalicho] during their far longer residence" is possibly overstated.[39]

What is plain is the understanding of these two men as savages. While some English people, and particularly the colonizers of the following generation, undoubtedly saw this condition as like "naked slavery [to the] divell," many also, like Barlowe himself when first encountering the Croatans and Roanokes, thought it rather more about the absence of "guile and treason," and consequently about having a "gentle, loving, and faithful" manner.[40] It is worth repeating that the central lack attributed to savagery in this era could be as positive as it could be negative, depending on the viewer.

Both Manteo and Wanchese returned to the Roanoke area in April

1585, accompanying the six-hundred-odd first prospective English colonizers of the New World. Wanchese soon abandoned the group, returning to Roanoke Island and explicitly aiding the opposition to English settlement. His rejection of the learning extended him may have signified his displeasure at having been made a cultural broker in the first place, or it may have indicated that while he had originally opted for the role he later came to regret it—perhaps through disgust with English practices or perhaps through a rivalry with Croatan Manteo. Manteo, on the other hand, remained firmly ensconced as a go-between for the rest of his life. He played a vital role in helping the first English colony survive for as long as it did. And he was among the party who managed to return to England when it folded in 1586.[41]

By the time Manteo arrived back in England a second time, Vaughan has discovered that there were also two other of his countrymen living in London, both sent out to Raleigh to be cultural brokers. One, a "Rawly," was a hostage who spent the next (and last) two years of his life with a Raleigh associate in Devonshire. The other, a "Towaye," lodged with Manteo at Raleigh's Thames abode, no doubt with the English expectation of becoming his successor. Rawly died in Bideford, but Towaye survived to join Manteo on his subsequent and final trip home to America. After this date, a veritable host of Native Americans traveled to England under the auspices of Raleigh's various New World quests—most, like their forerunners and with similarly hazy degrees of volition, were destined to become informative players on the transatlantic scene. Four Guianans arrived with Capt. Jacob Whiddon in 1594; at least four indigenes from the Arromaia and surrounding nations arrived with Raleigh himself in 1595; at least one Trinidadian came with Lawrence Keymis in 1596 (known as Indian John and probably resident in England for thirteen years); and one man from Spanish-held Guiana, soon called Christopher, landed with a now-disgraced Raleigh in 1618. This last, whose name was more likely Guayacunda, lived with Raleigh while incarcerated in the Tower of London, acting as a kind of servant, and witnessed the former adventurer's beheading on 29 October.[42]

Although most of these intercontinental interlocutors proved significant in later dealings with the New World, there is little evidence to say that they made much impression on civilian folk while in England. The evidence in general is so sparse that even Vaughan cannot say for sure where they all lodged or what they all did, though he suspects that some "must have lived in [Raleigh's] Durham House" and most "must have provided the imperialists with a vast array of . . . knowledge." Given their later great utility, such speculations seem well-founded, but less so is Vaughan's comment that they also "likely . . . fascinated London crowds."[43] The time for metropolitan clamor about New World exotica was still decidedly in the future.

Other than a subdued level of fascination, what these visits share is precisely a lack of commonality. That is, they attest to a range of levels of volition on the part of the traveler, from consensual to outright forced. They indicate a range of purpose on the part of the English "escort," from proving a feat to acquiring a potential informant. And they point to a range of interests among the English for exploring in the New World at all, from trade to adventure to prospective possession. This lack of cohesion echoes in essence the ad hoc quality of the English experience in America at this time. Such disparities probably explain the subdued reaction of English people to visiting Native Americans more than anything else.

English range in the New World is perhaps best exemplified through contrast. The biggest European players in America in the sixteenth century, unquestionably the Spanish, were not disparate in their objectives and methods. Almost immediately upon the return in 1493 of Columbus's initial voyage, the Spanish story of being in the New World became filtered through the meta-issue of conquest. Self-styled as *conquistadores*, determined for gold and silver acquisition, and facing huge and well-organized indigenous populations, the Spanish believed that nothing less than total ownership was appropriate or even feasible. To match their grandiose ambition, the Spanish similarly required an all-encompassing, or total, theory of justification, which in practice entailed a mixture of papal concession and certain interpretations of natural law, but which, in turn, had the wholesale effect of legitimizing indigenous enslavement.[44] Slavery became linked to conquest as the broad means to the broad end.

Examples of New World people in Spain during the sixteenth century show that Native Americans were almost always brought over and received in terms of this understanding about slavery. Columbus brought over the first party of Americans to Spain—and indeed to Europe—in 1493: they had been "taken by force," as Columbus himself readily admitted, to serve as slaves in the Castilian court.[45] So appropriate, even laudatory, did this move seem that Columbus endeavored to bring over 600 more American slaves in 1494. Soon Vespucci was in on the act, importing nearly 300 American slaves in 1500. After just seven years of contact, the scholar Harald Prins estimates that about 1,000 New World people had been enslaved and transported to the Iberian peninsula.[46]

The rate of enslaved transportation slowed into the sixteenth century, due to increased moral opposition at home. Still, at least another 1,000 New World slaves arrived in Spain before 1600, when it was eventually forbidden as a practice.[47] The vast majority of the substantial number of Native Americans arriving in Spain during this period, therefore, came as slaves. Given the figures, it would seem that even those who did not come as slaves were yet understood through the "lens" of slavery: they were defined as the exceptions to the rule. Of course, not all Spaniards approved of American enslavement, but those who opposed the official justification—such as Francisco de Vitoria and others at the University of Salamanca—did so, again, within the terms of this dominant concept.[48]

In contrast, the first English forays into America, which encountered far more scattered and seemingly unfathomable indigenes and which could not hope for the same plunder of precious metals, were less likely, because less able, to entertain a vision as comprehensive as Spain's.[49] Correspondingly, the English narrative of justification remained disjointed and piecemeal until at least the last third of the seventeenth century: England's more opportunistic and mixed approach to New World challenges meant that no "metafilter" emerged to match the Spanish preoccupation with conquest and thus with slavery. With no dominating context to overwrite them, New World people in sixteenth-century England were received in the same ad hoc manner that led them there in the first place.

Possibly, the mixed contexts of their arrivals contributed to the minimal impact that New World travelers had in early-modern England. Without a clear storyline about English activity in the New World in this era, the random examples of New World life in England may have been misunderstood or simply overlooked. This situation hardly changed into the seventeenth century.

THE SEVENTEENTH CENTURY:
PRINCESSES, PERFORMERS, AND PLEBEIANS

From around 1600 the record of New World arrival in England gets messier, due to both the increased traffic across the Atlantic and to the rising number of "repeat" voyagers. A categorical approach, therefore, may better reveal these journeys than chronology. Some of the categories in which New World people came to England in the seventeenth century extended earlier ones while others were newly forged. One established category, of course, was that of the cultural broker, which continued to thrive through at least the early decades of the 1600s, and especially as an aspect of relations between the English and the Powhatans around today's Virginia. Chief Powhatan saw early on a need for insider information about his latest rivals, the Virginian Company of London. Less than a year after the company's establishment in Jamestown, Powhatan was negotiating with colonists for a personal trade. In exchange for a young English boy, the chief agreed to send one of his own underlings, called Namontuck, to meet King James I and "to returne me the true report thereof."[50] Although commented on, tellingly, by the Venetian and the Spanish ambassadors in London at the time, Namontuck's presence in England in 1608 remains poorly recorded. It's not known if he did ever meet the king, though he is mentioned in Ben Jonson's play *Epicoene* (1609) as a figure residing for a short while in England.[51]

After a few months abroad, Namontuck was "redelivered" to Powhatan by John Smith, who also safely collected the English boy. The Native American traveler apparently proved a useful aid to the English later that year, helping to persuade his chief to accept—at least in ceremony—King James's political superiority. Thereafter, the scant records start to conflict: Smith insists that he tried to take Namontuck back to England a second time but that the man died at the hands of a "fellow . . . Savage" en route.[52] As Vaughan points out, no corroboration exists among the many accounts of this 1609 voyage, thus casting some suspicion on Smith's accuracy.[53] What is clear is that Powhatan kept on sending envoys to England for a few years after Namontuck's first return. The Virginian Company, for its part, facilitated these ventures not simply to acquire their own information, but now also to pursue what they estimated a civilizing mission. The company's charter of 1606 had included a will to "bring the . . . savages . . . to humane civilitie"; with Powhatan's unwitting assistance, it now launched its ambition to educate younger Native Americans out of their savagery, through English language training and Christian conversion conducted back in metropolitan territories.[54]

Unfortunately, none of these ill-known envoys are described well in the sources: while most commentators referred to them as savage, few elaborated on what that meant at the time. An exception is an engraving of two Powhatans called Eiakintomino and Matahan, who were presumed to be in England around 1615–16. They had been brought over by the Virginia Company, ostensibly for strategic, educational, and conversionary purposes, but here also used for explicit advertisement. In a broadside to help raise funds for its continuation, the company depicted their two charges flanking verse that implied its success in civilizing savages: "Deere Britaines," the Americans are presumed to say, "now, be You as kinde; / Bring Light, and Sight, to Us yet blinde: / Leade Us, by Doctrine and Behaviour, / Into one Sion, to one SAVIOUR." The Americans are figured with feathers in their hair, wearing skins, holding bows and arrows, and standing over tribal totems. Their crudity of apparel and lifestyle could not be more plainly represented. The foremost scholar on this image, Christian Feest, has turned up a Dutch watercolor, also dated 1615–16, that copied the Eiakintomino figure, though it strangely surrounded the man with European rather than American fauna. Other than this rather odd continental borrowing, the single copy of the broadside, now archived in London, speaks of a very minimal impact.[55]

Supposed cultural brokers also arrived from other Native American nations. Once again, the degree of consent varied. In 1605 Captain George Weymouth, exploring the coast of today's Maine for the English entrepreneur Sir Ferdinando Gorges, captured five Abenaki men and brought them to England. An eyewitness to the kidnapping, James Rosier, described how the English expedition enticed the Abenakis to their camp and then "suddenly laid hands upon them. And it was as much as five or six of us could doe to get them into the light horseman. For they were strong and so naked as our best hold was by their long haire."[56] Though Rosier admired the Abenakis for their "exceeding good invention, quicke understanding and readie capacitie," they were yet surely "salvages"—like all native people of America in Rosier's eyes: not entirely reliable and definitionally associated with their canoes, bows, and arrows.[57]

Upon arrival in Plymouth, Gorges took charge of three of the Abenakis, sending the other two to fellow entrepreneurs in London. Gorges was delighted with his captives, from whom he learnt after three years of "cohabitation" much about their country's rivers, "what Men of note were seated upon them, what power they were of, how allyed, what enemies they had, and the like."[58] Later, Gorges credited his unfortunate informants as being "the meanes under God of putting on foote and giving life to all our [New England] plantations."[59] Another English colonist, John Smith, when later exploring north of Jamestown in 1614, also acknowledged the invaluable help of one of the "Weymouth Five." Taking Tahanedo (or Dehanada or Dohannida) with him on his cartographic voyage, Smith claimed that "my main assistance next [to] God . . . was my acquaintance among the savages, especially with Dohannida . . . who had lived long in England."[60] Although these Native American go-betweens, like their predecessors, were undoubtedly crucial for English activity in the New World, they always remained "savages" in the terminology of their patrons. Whether ordinary English people who met them considered them to be as interesting as their patrons found them useful is debatable. Historian Carolyn Foreman asserted that "enormous crowds followed the [Weymouth] Indians about the streets of London, curious about their every move" but again there is no good evidence to prove this claim.[61]

The final Native American broker of significance to travel to seventeenth-century England was the relatively well-known Squanto, of the Patuxet tribe within the Wampanoag confederation around later (New) Plymouth. Like Weymouth's Abenakis, Squanto had originally been kidnapped by a ruthless Englishman—this time an associate of Smith's, Thomas Hunt, in 1614. Along with nearly thirty other Native Americans, Squanto was sold by Hunt into slavery at Malaga. How Squanto managed to travel from Spain to England is unclear, but he ended up a kind of informant-servant to a Gorges associate, John Slany, of the Newfoundland Company.[62] The relationship with Slany—perhaps interpreted by Squanto as salvation from a fate worse than death—seemed to endear him to at least one strand of the English overseas project: after Slany secured his journey back to Patuxet, Squanto volunteered his services to the Newfoundland Company, making a free return trip to England sometime in 1618–19. Squanto was of course later heralded as a "special instrument" to the Mayflower pilgrims from 1620 to 1622.[63]

Evidently, Squanto was an example of how to turn English desire for native information to best possible individual use. Despite acknowledgment of his help, however, Squanto was again always said to be a savage. When they heard of Hunt's shameful actions, Smith cried out for the "poore Salvages" and Gorges accused the captain of being "even more savage-like" than his cargo. What London passers-by thought of their latest New World arrival is not recorded for posterity.[64]

Another category of traveling Native American in the seventeenth century, which in part continued older patterns but which found new eminence in this era, was that of the royal emissary. Although many eighteenth-century envoys were said to be of royal blood, their predecessors were mostly persons in the service of higher leaders. Exceptions were the Brazilian King of 1531, and a very-little-known Miskito prince who came over from Central America in 1634. Sir Hans Sloane, when encountering Miskitos in their own country two generations later, learnt that this prince had journeyed with the Earl of Warwick, who had, in the name of Charles I, claimed "several islands in the West-Indies." Keen to establish a "correspondence" with the native peoples, this Earl persuaded the Miskito King to allow his son to travel home with him, leaving one of his own colonels behind—in now seemingly royal New World fashion—as a guaranty of good faith. Sloane recounts that "the Indian Prince . . . staid in England three years, in which time the Indian King [his father] died."[65] The prince survived his repatriation and assumed the Miskito kingship. Once again, there are modern accounts of this prince becoming a favorite of Charles I while in England, but there are no documents to testify to this or any other form of popularity.[66] Even royal New World people were taken well within English stride before the eighteenth century.

The most famous royal American traveler was undoubtedly Pocahontas, the "princess" daughter of Powhatan himself, who journeyed to England in 1616. On this occasion, the fame was genuine.[67] However, whether or not she was understood to be a representative of New World savagery—as all the Native Americans in England before her were—is another story. It is possible that Pocahontas's fame drew more from being the first example of full conversion, of the sameness that the New World could produce rather than of the difference that it represented upon first encounter. Despite their often go-between status, no previous New World visitors had ever been considered fully converted, or fully rid of their so-called primary or original savagery.

True, the early Virginia colonists had first met Pocahontas as a well-stationed "savage girl," then only about ten years of age and precocious with the newcomers. The colony's president, John Smith, infamously claimed that the girl-princess once saved his life before her irate father, and she was heralded as an important cultural broker from as early as 1609. After relations between colonists and Powhatans broke down around 1610, Pocahontas retreated to her father's camp. In 1613 she was taken hostage by the colonists in an effort to force a peace, but before her release many months later she had reputedly fallen in love with a Virginian planter called John Rolfe. With Powhatan's consent she married Rolfe in April 1614: the marriage proved to be the real pacifier between the tribes, one colonist reporting that "ever since . . . we have had friendly commerce and trade . . . with [all Powhatan's] subjects."[68]

Upon marriage, however, Pocahontas arguably completed her transition from savage to go-between to Englishwoman. After "careful instruction in Christian Religion," the princess was said to have "renounced her country idolatry, confessed the faith of Jesus Christ, and was baptized" with the name of Rebecca.[69] When she gave birth to a son, he was christened Thomas, after the Virginia governor, and always thought of as English. By the time she disembarked at (Old) Plymouth in June 1616, she had acquired a good grasp of the English language and of "our English manner."[70]

The voyage—complete with Rolfe, the Governor Thomas Dale, and an entourage of about ten Powhatans—was underwritten by the Virginia Company, with the aim of promoting its conversionary (and commercial) success. The party was a hit as soon as it arrived. No doubt the "still savage" brother-in-law, Tomocomo, and the other Powhatans were part of the novelty, but the fanfare accorded them was mostly due to the way Mrs. Rolfe was "respected" as a "Daughter of a King": in this instance, royalty seemed to refine converted Christianity and civility rather more than it did an earlier savagery.[71] Pocahontas did meet the English monarch, James I, and also separately his Queen, Anne. They entertained her at a court masque. She also met with the Bishop of London at Lambeth Palace, and several notable colonial entrepreneurs, including Raleigh and Harriot. John Smith caught up with her in London, and wrote that Pocahontas met "with divers other persons of good qualities, both publikely at the masks and otherwise, to her great satisfaction and content."[72] Her portrait was painted by the Dutch artist Simon van de Passe, from which many images were copied and circulated. They all presented a woman in full English finery, named both Rebecca and the daughter of the royal Powhatan, but carefully also noted to be Rolfe's wife, "converted and baptized in the Christian faith."[73]

What is most remarkable about Pocahontas's fame was how *little* of it consisted in comments about any strange diet, apparel, habits, gestures, or preferences. These were all topics that had attracted note from English people at the first instance with other Native American envoys. The unprecedented degree of Pocahontas's conversion out of savagery is perhaps best expressed in the snide remark of a Virginian Company stockholder, John Chamberlain, who was one of the few to continue to see her as a New World go-between and who consequently scorned the English adulation of her: "here is a fine picture of no fayre lady," he wrote to a colleague with an engraving of her portrait, "with all her tricking up and high stile and titles you might thincke her . . . to be somebody."[74]

Sadly, like the only other recorded female Native American to reside in England, Pocahontas succumbed to her own version of Anglophobia. She was ill by January 1617 and, though now on her way home, died at Gravesend in March. She was remembered at St. George's Church as "Rebecca Wrothe" and by the cleric Samuel Purchas as "the first fruit of Virginian conversion."[75] Most of the surviving Powhatan party either died as well or returned to a life of displacement.[76]

Other seventeenth-century categories of traveling Native American are more sinister. An important one, suggested in the sixteenth century but only truly flourishing in the seventeenth, was that of performer, or "wonder" in contemporary parlance. Of course, in some sense all New World people in England were spectacles, but a few were explicitly and directly displayed for profit. These generally have left scant or no traces, suggested now only in advertisements such as the one in a London broadside of 1670 for "the tall Black, called the Indian King . . . to be seen at the Golden Lion in Smithfield for twopence."[77] One better known Native American to have been publicly displayed was Epenew, a "savage" from "Capawuck" (Martha's Vineyard) who had been kidnapped by a Captain Edward Harlow in 1611. Upon arrival in England, Harlow "shewed him up and down London for money as a wonder" before the old New England hand, Ferdinando Gorges, took him over and housed him for three years for his own strategic purposes in Plymouth.[78] Epenew's name has passed down to us because many modern literary scholars have claimed him as the inspiration behind certain Shakespearean lines. Both Carolyn Foreman and Ronald Takaki remark that Epenew (although alive) triggered Trinculo in *The Tempest* to observe that in England people "will not give a doit to relieve a lame beggar, but they will give ten to see a dead Indian."[79] Sidney Lee, however, declares that Epenew was "no doubt the 'strange Indian' of large proportions who is mentioned in the play *Henry VIII* as fascinating a mob of London women."[80] The "strange Indian" of *Henry VIII* (1613), or rather of the play now known as *All Is True*, was said by Shakespeare to own "a great tool," but he entertained at court, not in the street, so the excited women were unlikely to have been mobbish.

The example of Epenew and of the more ghostly arrivals who endured public gawking admittedly indicate some kind of popular fascination for such folk. Certainly past scholars have believed this: Richard Altick declared that "from 1584 onward" there was a thriving "exhibition trade" in Native Americans from Virginia and New England, while Frank Kermode stated that "such exhibitions were profitable investments, and were a regular feature of colonial policy under James I."[81] Neither Altick nor Kermode, however, go on to offer evidence. True, Native Americans became caught up in the exhibition of "freak" peoples that bloomed in early-modern England. Yet the numbers do not in themselves demonstrate an overt preoccupation: suggestions of "Indians" or "Blacks" number roughly one handful in every 300 or so advertisements for the exhibition of other types of human.[82] The categories that much more commonly appealed at this time were the medically deformed or the medically miraculous (part rabbit or part goat, for examples).[83] Native Americans appeared to form one small part of the general category of "exotica," which in itself was not as popular as some others. What remains pertinent is how the savagery of New World people—their apparently defining feature—did not play an overwhelming part in the freakery industry of seventeenth-century England.

The final key category of traveling Native American is covered by a broad sense of "working plebeian"—those toilers who rarely make it onto the radar of early-modern history. Chiefly, these New World travelers seem to have ended up as sea hands, soldiers, or servants. Definitive records of Native American mariners are slim—suggested in the stories of "Jack Strawe" the Algonquian who worked on a cattle ship in 1626 or of John Wampas the Nipmuck who earned his own passage in 1675—but they may be guessed at simply from the increase in migrant workers in English ports during the seventeenth century.[84] Ports such as Plymouth were renowned at this time for harboring the greatest variety of migrant worker in the nation. With the escalating growth of maritime commerce, as well as continued journeys of exploration to New Worlds, shipping provided an easy, though notoriously ephemeral, industry of employment for transients.[85] Historians have claimed that the largest groups of migrant dock workers at this time were Irish, Chinese, and East Indian.[86] Certainly Native Americans would not have competed in numerical terms with such peoples in the 1600s, but they may well have mingled with these marginals, visiting English shores, and other lands, relatively unseen and unremembered.

A second type of hidden, and peripatetic, plebeian in early-modern England was the soldier. As the historian John Childs has written, "the British Isles were a veritable reservoir of mercenaries in the seventeenth century," attracting the vagrant and the adrift as well as some better-heeled noblemen seeking military kudos.[87] When John Smith wrote of another Harlow captive serving as a mercenary—this time a "Saluage" from Nohono called "Sakaweston"—he knew what he was talking about: Smith had also worked as a mercenary on the continent in many wars before becoming a colonial adventurer. Whether he was the one who arranged for Sakaweston to go "as a Souldier to the warres of Bohemia" in 1618, however, "after he had liued many yeeres in England," is not known.[88]

Third, many Native Americans in England at this time fell into the vague and capacious plebian category of "servant," a subgroup that Vaughan has called "the most heinous category of transatlantic encounters."[89] Whether brought over originally as potential brokers, or as trophies, or indeed as bonded labor, untold numbers of New World people—

possibly stranded after a change in circumstances—ended up in the service of Englishmen. Again, such folk flit through the records with barely a murmur. A former treasurer of the Virginia Company, Nicholas Ferrar, records that he expended one pound in maintenance of "my Indian" in one month in 1636; a London parish register records that "an India servant of Mr Robert Andrews" died as a youth of sixteen in 1675; and several advertisements in the *London Gazette* during the 1680s called for the return of runaway "Indians," such as "a Spanish Indian man called Diego or James," an "Indian woman about 40" called Sarah, and—most remarkably—a man called John Newmoose, "an Indian of an unusual shape, having a child growing out of his side."[90] Needless to mention, these near-forgotten travelers made negligible impression on English observers, their subordinate position overwhelming any mark of exoticism, savage or otherwise.

Just as the Spanish story of New World discovery provided an illustrative contrast to the English case in the sixteenth century, the French story of the same reveals something about the English case in the seventeenth century. The French approach to the New World had been very similar to England's in the 1500s: both France and England had entered the sphere of American engagement relatively late, and both countries first experienced that engagement via a series of haphazard and uncoordinated expeditions—some by patented explorers, some by prospective colonists, some by independent fishermen, and so on. Although both had started with the ambition of finding precious metals to match the loot found by Spain and Portugal, both in the end had to settle for—and later make a virtue out of—a trading relationship with America. That trading paradigm, however, had been scattered enough to develop without a grand theory of either occupation or subjection.[91]

In consequence, New World travelers had arrived in France in much the same way as they had arrived in England—on the basis of a range of contexts, received by a people with a range of attitudes toward them. The first recorded arrival was by a Tupinamba from Brazil called Essomericq in 1505. He had come via a trader who claimed a friendly partnership with the Tupi's family: although intended to last for only two years, the visit spanned more than twenty—Essomericq finally returned in the 1530s a converted Frenchman. Regularly spaced arrivals followed: many Native Americans came as potential go-betweens for potential traders—some voluntarily, some involuntarily; a few came as trophies to be shown off in front of important patrons; one little girl was brought over to become the companion of Jacques Cartier's wife.[92]

One key difference between the French and English cases during the sixteenth century was the greater frequency of arrival in France: Native Americans turned up in France nearly three times more often than they did in England.[93] The foremost authority on this subject, Olive Dickason, offers a convincing explanation for these larger numbers based on supply: she shows that both Native Americans and the Frenchmen they encountered in New France had much at stake in making such journeys work.[94] The demand-driven thesis, however, is not entirely implausible. It is possible to conjecture that metropolitan French culture evinced a somewhat deeper interest than metropolitan English culture in what the New World had to say about the Old World: Montaigne's reflective essays on savagery, for example, have no real equivalent in England—their closest comparison would be Hakluyt's polemical compilations about America's promise.[95] There is also evidence that French noblemen at least—if not the general populace—were particularly taken with the idea of savagery in their midst: when the aldermen of Rouen held a festival for Henri II in 1550 they included upward of fifty Tupinamba in a recreation of a South American village designed to suggest the king's exciting future.[96] If the French did display a higher degree of fascination than the English in New World arrivals, however, the manner in which they received them was just as disparate as that shown across the channel. Clearly, in such a case, interest was not linked to any sense of a metanarrative regarding the New World. Here, interest was probably rather due to the greater cosmopolitanism of French court culture during the early modern era.

Into the seventeenth century, however, the similarity in reception to New World travelers between France and England broke down—at least temporarily. The early English colonies grew in such a way that preserved the "eclectic" approach to appropriation.[97] The early French colonies, however, were not large or cohesive or confident enough after about 1620 to do anything but attempt assimilationist or integrationist policies.[98] For the French at this time, colonies not only allowed for the introduction of Catholic missions, as James Axtell notes; they demanded it.[99] The conversionary will inherent in missionary activity—and especially in that of the most successful French missionaries in the New World, the Jesuits—fed into colonial integrationism. For a finite period, then, until around 1680, the French story in the New World, like the Spanish story of the previous century, became mostly contained within a single narrative.

Exactly coincident with the establishment of messianic French colonies, the story of Native American presence in France also began to cohere. Conversion as a means of assimilation—and especially juvenile conversion—became the linking theme. Dickason notes that most New

World arrivals from this time were children, sent over by the Recollets and Jesuits to "become accustomed to our ways."[100] With such early indoctrination, together with an easier acquisition of French language, it was assumed that children would be less likely "ever to leave us," and would thus help to "retain [their] countrymen" more successfully. It was with great relief in 1636, for example, that the missionary Paul Le Jeune noted how "the savages are beginning to open their eyes and to recognize that children who are with us are well taught"—their full future attachment, after all, "the point to be aimed at."[101]

During this same period in the middle seventeenth century, English colonies also introduced missionaries, but these Protestants were never as numerous or as revolutionary as their Catholic counterparts. Conversion never became a dominant preoccupation among English colonists for the simple reason that assimilation never emerged as a *primary* goal for the overall English overseas project (although it was certainly an important goal for some). In parallel, conversion never either became a key theme of the history of New World travel to England. Certainly, juveniles never constituted a noteworthy proportion of the phenomenon across the channel.[102]

Whether the French cohesiveness of narrative in the seventeenth century came to account for a greater interest in New World people in France remains conjecturable. What is evident is that French and English experience in the New World in toto started to move nearer to one another again by the end of the 1600s. Into the eighteenth century, the two nations rediscovered common ground in their relations with the Americas as both became entangled in newly insatiable ideological imperatives.

INTO THE EIGHTEENTH CENTURY

As both Colbertist France and Restoration England moved toward more explicitly commercial economies, the trading relationship that had been left to the two latecomers on the American scene started to take on new gloss. It was gradually claimed in both countries that *commerce* promised far greater wealth and power than plunder ever would: Spain's dramatic decline through the seventeenth century appeared testament to this increasingly cherished belief.[103] With its unique insatiability, too, commerce had the effect of promoting the economic field above all others, such that even religious mission in Catholic France became subordinated to its concerns.

Most significantly, a commercializing state required new attendance to the efficiency of its trade. Under Colbert and his immediate successors in the ministries of finance and the navy, France began to institutionalize much of its activities in the Americas.[104] Likewise, increasingly powerful Councils of Trade and increasingly ambitious Navigation Acts in England effected greater governmental control over England's overseas interests (and in doing so finally brought them into some narrative coherence).[105] Together, these processes changed the older rivalry between France and England in the New World from an irregular tussle over territory to a "cutthroat race for Atlantic trade."[106] In this race, Native Americans came to be seen in a freshly uniform way by both parties. As a crucial third party, their loyalty could now be the deciding factor in determining superiority in any one region. No longer potential slaves or potential converts, as they had been to certain colonists of different ages, Native Americans were now seen overwhelmingly by the two major foreign powers as potential allies. For both France and England, alliance-building with indigenous populations became the new dominant mode for life in the New World; negotiation, or diplomacy, the new name of the game.

In 1696 a relatively obscure English merchant called John Nelson recognized that the French were deploying one tactic in this game that his people so far lacked:

> They have from time to time transported into France some of the
> most eminent and enterprizing Indians (not only of their own,
> but of ours . . .) for no other intent, than to amaze and dazzle them
> with the greatness and splendour of the French Court and Armie
> where the King hath so thought it worth his countenancing as to send
> them into Flanders, where the Armies have been expressly mustered
> before them, to show their greatness.

For Nelson, it was time to meet fire with fire. "No better method can be taken than by imitating the French . . . to have some chiefs of the diverse nations of the Indians to be sent into England whereby to give a counterpoise unto the French reputation.[107]

2. Four from Iroquoia

The Appeal of Savagery

The merchant John Nelson turned out to have more than just the fate of English commerce in mind when he recommended sending Native Americans to London so as to undermine the French. In 1696, when he advised such a course, Nelson had only recently been released from the Bastille, to which French colonists had sent him as punishment for espionage against New France. In a vengeful mood, Nelson also recommended in the same memorial that England consider a renewal of what would become known as the "Glorious Enterprise"—a simultaneous attack on Montreal and Quebec by the combined forces of colonists, natives, and the British navy in order to quash New France forever.[1] Coincidentally, it was in a later effort to implement such a renewal—advocated by numerous colonists since 1690—that the first truly popular delegation of Native Americans arrived in Britain.

The delegation of 1710 was quickly dubbed and always remembered as the Four Iroquois Kings, though they were neither all Iroquois nor any of them kings. This misnaming of kin and title was just one of several themes that the 1710 "Iroquois" established as a recurring feature for every New World arrival until the end of the eighteenth century.[2] Some other themes included a purpose to negotiate an official agreement; a tour of key political, military, and cultural sites around London; a relatively hefty expenses bill, including an inventory of gifts for return; and, ironically, an exclamation on the part of British observers at all levels about the uniqueness, every time, of seeing "real" live savages in their midst.

The most important feature of the Four Iroquois Kings, however, in terms of their place in a tradition of other New World envoys, was their inauguration of a much deeper and broader level of fascination than had ever before presented. In addition to invitations from relevant dignitar-

ies, this delegation attracted clamoring crowds wherever they went, fill-
ing beer gardens, stopping theater performances, and delighting the poor,
who sometimes rushed to touch them. They also inspired written and
graphic outpourings from diarists, editors, hacks, poets, balladeers, pam-
phleteers, painters, and engravers. Such an escalation in interest was due
to a new alignment between what the visitors represented and some key
concerns of contemporary British public discourse. Specifically, the Four
Iroquois Kings stirred fresh levels of interest through the ways in which
their reputed savagery resonated with problems regarding war, governance, and social order, which together may be defined in this period as
the consequences of continued overseas expansion.

Few scholars have tried to explain the visitors' greater appeal—though
many have acknowledged that it was indeed apparent. Best known is
Eric Hinderaker, who implied that the Iroquois compelled through their
unsettling juxtaposition of "Indianness" and "kingliness."[3] Alternatively,
in the most complete account of the visit published in 1952, Richmond
Bond argued that they were welcomed because they provided metropolitan Britons with light relief during a particularly trying year.[4] Neither
view, however, bears much analytical prodding: proponents of the oxy-
moronic "noble savagery" thesis neglect to consider why earlier titled
Native Americans did not similarly capture the British imagination, while
proponents of the escapism model fail to recognize that the flurry of commentary surrounding the Iroquois often related directly to the anxieties
they were supposed to deflect. In 1710, the idea of noble savagery was not
new—it was rather newly salient to British concerns. Far from offering
escape from the burning issues of the day, the Four Iroquois Kings—as
clear embodiments of savagery (noble or otherwise)—promised a powerful, and rare, means of opening them up for discussion.[5]

Of course, popularity was only one aspect of the Iroquois' visit to Britain. They came for complex diplomatic reasons, managed variously their
interaction with officials, onlookers, and the structures of the city, and
returned back to Iroquoia with some mixed results and promises, all in
the space of a season. Their story of negotiation is woven here into my
account of their singular impact.

THE IROQUOIS AND EUROPEAN COMPETITION

In the late seventeenth century, the Iroquois League comprised a confed-
eracy of five nations based in what is now upstate New York. These five
nations were the Mohawks, the Oneidas, the Onondagas, the Cayugas,

and the Senecas. They had converged into a dominant political alliance against other Native American nations from around the 1630s.[6] Of the Europeans who later reckoned with them, only the French regularly called these peoples *Iroquois*. The English in America usually called them the Five Nations (or the Six Nations after the Tuscaroras joined in 1722).

Iroquois relations with Europeans took on new significance after the English secured Nieuw Nederlandt in 1674. For the English, the Iroquois were no longer just a scattered group of locals with whom to strike haphazard trading deals but now potential allies in a scheme to dominate whole trading systems through large swathes of North America. For the French, the Iroquois shifted from potential converts to being, as for England, the new keys to foreign control of the region's economic promise. Though newly sought as political associates, the Iroquois found it difficult to turn this changed dynamic to advantage. Local foreign superiority alternated numerously between English and French colonists during this period and mostly the vengeance on Iroquois members who had sided with the losing power was terrible—either directly through violence or indirectly through neglect in later treaties. Most Iroquois tried to steer a path of neutrality, never consenting en masse to be crown subjects of either newcomer—though this also infuriated the Europeans from time to time.[7]

By the late 1680s, nonetheless, much of Iroquoia tended to favor the English over the French. The evident failure at this stage of New France to live up to its formal 1667 promise to protect the Iroquois fur trade in the lakes region from other Native American nations proved to be one disappointment too many.[8] The informal alliance brokered with the English during this period was called the Covenant Chain—an absorption of English colonists into a pre-existing, loose agreement among different parties to look out for one another's interests.[9] The Covenant Chain meant that Iroquois loyalty was expected in 1689 when England formally declared war on France: Iroquois warriors found themselves implicated in the bloody North American theater of this conflict for eight long years.[10] It was during "King William's War," as the conflict was known in the New World, that the first stab at the Glorious Enterprise was made. The plan for a two-pronged attack on Quebec by sea and Montreal by land had Iroquois warriors down for most of the land-based fighting. Due to poor coordination of funds and troops in New York, however, the campaign quickly failed—but not before exposing Iroquois intentions to the enemy.[11]

The French had not forgotten or forgiven Iroquois leanings by the time the Treaty of Ryswick confirmed their defeat in 1697. They argued that the peace did not cover the Iroquois as English subjects and proceeded to bombard them—or rather have them bombarded by other, French-allied Native Americans—until the Iroquois brokered their own separate treaty three years later.[12] Massively reduced in numbers and in supplies, the Iroquois settled once again on neutrality.

In 1709, under the auspices of the next great war between England and France, the Glorious Enterprise reared a second time. "Queen Anne's War" was effectively a continuation of the previous conflict: the next round in England's desire to aid Europe's Protestant Grand Alliance against the threat of Bourbon Catholic supremacy on the continent. Like earlier wars, it too traveled to North America, raging from 1702 to 1713. The plan to "reduce" New France once and for all during this war came not from a colonial office but from an independent British entrepreneur named Samuel Vetch. Vetch had long been involved in British ventures in the New World, including the ill-fated Darien scheme in Panama in the late 1690s. Passingly like John Nelson before him, Vetch was known for his wily energy and overweening self-interest.[13] In June 1708, he had submitted to Lord Sunderland, then the secretary of state in Whitehall, his detailed proposal. The memorandum, *Canada Survey'd*, discussed the advantages that France enjoyed in the north—a rich fur and fish trade, an increasing population, several strategic strongholds, and a powerful if uneven influence over the indigenes—together with an "easy method" of destroying them. The method required merely two naval battalions from the crown to assist a contingent of some 2,500 men from the surrounding colonies and as many of the "five Nation savages" as could be persuaded back from neutrality. Vetch ended by stating that the success of such a mission would make Her Majesty "sole Sovereign . . . over hundreds of nations of new subjects, who will become intirely obedient to her laws, when they have no priests to poyson them, nor no rivall Monarch to debauch them from her interest."[14]

In warmongering mode, Anne's Privy Council accepted the plan, pledging the Admiralty's support and commanding the governors of the relevant colonies to fall in accordingly. By the summer of 1709, the governors of New York, New Jersey, Connecticut, Pennsylvania, Massachusetts, New Haven, and Rhode Island had collectively promised around 4,000 men and adequate provisions for a three-month campaign. It fell to New York Lieutenant Governor Richard Ingoldsby to undertake the remaining task of approaching the Iroquois. In July, Ingoldsby laid on a grand feast at Albany, inviting hundreds of members of all the five

nations to enjoy British largesse while he enumerated the "many Per-
fidious and base actions" that the French had taken against them in the
past. By reminding them of all the times that the French had "set the far
Indians upon you and furnished them with arms and ammunition," as
well as "encroach" upon your hunting grounds until they are downright
"dangerous," Ingoldsby was not telling Iroquois leaders anything new.[15]
In any situation of direct conflict between British and French, the League
knew they would have to negotiate between two sides. After two days
of consideration, most of the Mohawks and the majority of the Oneidas
and Cayugas decided to side with Britain. The remaining Onondagas and
Senecas were eventually won over by the promise of additional colonial
backup. The historian Richard Aquila has underscored the risk such a
move entailed for the Iroquois: even a successful campaign might entail
unsupportable losses, while defeat would incur almost unimaginable devastation from the enemy.[16]

With their end of the bargain achieved, colonial and native troops
stood assembled at Wood Creek and in Boston Harbor for the rest of the
summer. Waiting for the promised fleet to show up, most went through
all their provisions. No dispatch arrived to explain the ships' delay. Vetch,
stationed in Boston, was mindful of keeping the Iroquois' faith alive, and
arranged for "four or five of the most Credible of the five Nations" to come
to Boston "to see the Fleet and Army." New Yorkers based in Wood Creek
duly sent five selected representatives to the city—of whom we know the
identity of only one—whereupon they were soothed and gifted by the
governor, despite his embarrassing inability still to show them any battalion. Finally, in September, Vetch conceded that Whitehall had betrayed
them and no fleet was ever going to show.[17] Unbeknownst to the colonists
until much later, Anne had long before diverted the force to a new hotspot
on the Iberian Peninsula. Vetch wrote angrily to Sunderland about his
"vast disappointment of the non arrivall of the ffleet" and described the
crushed feelings of colonists and Iroquois alike, "supposing themselves
intirely forgot or neglected by the court."[18]

Still, Vetch was not dissuaded from the inherent soundness of his plan.
Along with some of his fellow campaigners from Wood Creek, he believed
that Whitehall could be reconvinced to support it. Moreover, they also
thought that the idea of involving Iroquois representatives, as had been
enacted in Boston, was worth keeping. Together they proposed that "some
suitable persons be sent home from the severall Governments . . . truly
to represent the case to the Queen . . . that wee may yet be enabled to
put In Execution what she has with so much Grace, Commanded us to

undertake. . . . Likewise [we propose] that two or three of the Sachims & Principall Captains belonging to Each of the five Nations be sent over with them [as] the most proper methods for securing the Indians In our interest."[19] A later congress of governors ratified the proposal on 14 October 1709, including a declaration that "a Sachim of each tribe of ye five Nations at their election be procured to attend [the] voyage."[20]

In reality, waiting for a now-thoroughly skeptical ally to enact formal electoral procedures was never going to pay off for the colonists. One of the key Wood Creek leaders and longtime associate of the Iroquois around Albany, Colonel Peter Schuyler, was probably the one who "elected" the four eventual travelers for them. He arrived in Boston in December 1709 with three Mohawks and a Mohegan (whose nation was not Iroquois, of course, though it was nominally under the League's thumb at the time). As Stephanie Pratt has commented, it is no coincidence that Schuyler found the Mohawks easiest to recruit.[21] With territory nearest to Albany and thus to the Canadian border, they were the Iroquois most likely to be familiar with English ways and most resentful of French threats. The Mohegans likewise hailed from the Albany region.

The four chosen delegates were all young, Christian men. The reputed leader was Hendrick Tejonihokarawa, extremely devout, and probably the only one of the four with true chiefly status. Second, Brant Saquainquaragton was an eminent though not chiefly Mohawk and had been a member of the earlier Boston touring party. Third, John Onigoheriago was also very devout and possibly Hendrick's brother. Finally, Etowaucum was the Mohegan leader, baptized with the name of Nicholas. Although all Native American nations around the New England region were by now well-seasoned communicators with newcomers of every shade, this was the first group to express strong interest in carrying their diplomacy overseas.[22]

Accompanying the delegation were three colonists: Schuyler himself, Schuyler's cousin Abraham, who had even greater experience with the Iroquois and thus acted as interpreter, and one Major David Pigeon, requested by Schuyler as an officer who had at least some firsthand knowledge of Whitehall protocol.[23] The seven set sail on Her Majesty's *Reserve* on 28 February 1710. Vetch remained in America but continued his association by correspondence. He wrote compulsively to Sunderland, urging him to prepare seriously for the envoy's arrival: "[T]his Affaire is not only of the last consequence to All the British Inhabitants upon this Continent, but even to the Natives . . . who are the Barrier betwixt them and the ffrench [and] are so highly sensible of the absolute necessity of extirpating the ffrench, that they have sent their Agents along . . . alleadging that if the ffrench are not removed they must either abandon their Countrey, or Joyne in with them, either of which would be of so fatall consequence to the British Continent here, as to render it almost uninhabitable."[24] Vetch added, "It will be requisite the Indians see as much of the Grandure and Magnificence of Brittan as possible, for the french endeavour to possess them all with their wonderful notions."[25]

THE IROQUOIS IN LONDON

The *Reserve* docked at Portsmouth on 2 April, and the delegation was in London one week later. London was an especially tumultuous place in 1710. Even aside from the particular politics of that year, the city was undergoing dramatic flux. Its population of half a million outstripped any other British town by a factor of nearly ten. What was most distinctive about the population, however, was its volubility. With a far greater mortality rate to birth rate, but a steady growth of around 3,000 new persons every year, the city was known for both its chronic health conditions as well as its massive attraction to migrants.[26] Cramped housing, profligate homelessness, open sewers and thick, polluted air characterized its everyday running while its great mix of peoples—including many Jews, Irish, Huguenots, and Africans—added to its sense of endless energy.

For critics of the city in the early eighteenth century, London was known as a "wen."[27] But this association with a frothing boil referred only secondarily to its filth and ferment. Primarily, the nickname referred to a sense that London symbolized a newly emergent political corruption. Specifically, critics held that London represented in solid form the moral failings of the nation's recent turn to expansionist policies. These critics could take the form of old-fashioned, hard-line Tories, who traced a straight line back from expansion to corruption to certain compromises made in the Revolution Settlement over monarchical rights and Church centrality. More typically, though, they were Britons of a fuzzy "country persuasion," who felt that their government had become too mixed up with the "monied interest," and thus now too ready to underwrite foreign wars, foreign debts, and indeed the toleration of foreigners themselves.[28]

Of course, not everyone agreed that London was so vile. The city had plenty of admirers, too. As with the critics, these folk thought London embodied the chief aspects of contemporary British change, though where the former saw depravity and social degeneration, the latter saw vitality and newborn opportunities. To them, the city's burgeoning coffeehouses, shops, theaters, clubs, taverns, and markets represented not only the increased wealth but also the greater sociability of a commercializing polity. Its rebuilt Royal Exchange stood for the might of British finance, its booming dockyards the vigor of British militancy. Splendid St. Paul's Cathedral, finally completed in 1710, reminded anyone who looked up at the London skyline that the glory of the Church of England was yet secure. The launch of the city's first daily newspaper in 1702, *The Daily Courant*, was seen only to add to the already lively and relatively free press of tri-weeklies, monthlies, and one-off broadsides that took as its main task the narration of all this progress.[29] Such admirers could likewise be party loyalists—in this case, the type of Whig for whom expansion lay at the very heart of their version of British power. Or, more commonly, they were everyday folk who suddenly found themselves benefiting from the nation's freshly expansive mode.

Loved or loathed, London was where the British eighteenth century happened most vividly. It was certainly where the political drama of 1710 was most obviously centered. Indeed, it was in the very month of the Four Iroquois' arrival that the mixed ministry at Whitehall that had served under Anne for nearly nine years began its purge of Whig sympathizers and its tendency toward a more High Tory leadership. Although the House of Commons and probably public opinion had favored a Tory-like skepticism of whiggish principles for most of the decade, the royal ministry had always acted in some ways above party.[30] Anne had preferred a mixture of moderates from both sides in her executive, even while she herself followed an "instinctive Toryism."[31] Her leading courtiers, Lord Godolphin and the Duke of Marlborough, called themselves Tory but were committed to what was increasingly seen as the Whig cause of continuing war against the Bourbons. After several embarrassing and costly defeats in 1707, their association with this war was proving fatal.

The reputation of the ministry suffered a further blow in 1709 when the sudden influx into London of over 10,000 German refugees from the war stirred up deep-lying xenophobic hostilities.[32] Together with an unusually harsh winter and exceptionally poor harvest, the year ended with an unexpected flurry around the rantings of a High Churchman called Dr. Henry Sacheverell. Sacheverell was a well-known extremist, having preached many times previously against what he saw as the "heresy" and "anarchy" of Britain's post-settlement government. This time, however, his fury reached a more disaffected audience, who were provoked still further in their angst by Godolphin's over-swift impeachment of the clergyman for "high crimes against the state."[33] By January 1710, over

100,000 copies of Sacheverell's sermon were circulating in the city.[34] The doctor's trial in February heralded unprecedented rioting, notably against London institutions of Dissent, war, and finance. To match Sacheverell's ravings against toleration, militarization, and the monied interest—the three worst features of the Revolution Settlement as he saw it—angry mobs attacked the meeting halls of Dissenting denominations, the homes of some well-known Whig warmongers, and the Bank of England itself.[35] By early 1710, the everyday "country" critique of contemporary power was mixing violently with High Tory dogmatism. No wonder Anne was keen to realign the image of her leadership.[36]

As charges of one of the most ardent Whigs in the ministry, Lord Sunderland, the Four Iroquois Kings were inevitably seen in the first instance as pawns of the now deeply hated, war-supporting sector of court. Sunderland knew his job was on the line, together with his party's military ambitions, so he took the gamble that the fulminating Vetch back in Boston was right about the envoy's potential significance. He undertook to house, clothe, entertain, and fund the delegates on the chance that they did indeed hold one of the keys to "extirpating the ffrench" in the frustrating contest between nations.

He arranged for the Iroquois to stay at a well-regarded establishment called the "Two Crowns and Cushions" on King Street, near Covent Garden. The proprietor's one-month-old son, Thomas Arne, the future composer of *Rule Britannia*, offers in retrospect a further uncanny early connection between the Iroquois and aggressive British expansionism.[37] Sunderland also arranged for their royal outfitting in waistcoats, breeches, and stockings.

On 19 April the Iroquois met with Queen Anne at St. James's Palace. A much-copied pamphlet at the time described their appearance in court that day as "awful and majestic . . . the Marks with which they disfigure their Faces, do not carry so much Terror as Regard."[38] They presented a speech to the assembled company, prepared by themselves—or so Abraham Schuyler claimed when he later sought payment for his "interpretive services."[39] It was the minor officer, David Pigeon, however, who read out the words:

> GREAT QUEEN! . . . we have undertaken a long and tedious Voyage, which none of our Predecessors could ever be prevail'd upon to undertake . . . We doubt not but our *Great Queen*, has been acquainted with our long and tedious War, in Conjunction with Her Children (meaning Subjects) against Her Enemies the French; and that we have been as a strong Wall for their Security, even to the loss of our best Men . . .

LIBRARY, UNIVERSITY OF CHESTER

> We were mightily rejoiced when we heard that our Great Queen
> had resolved to send an Army to reduce *Canada* . . . in Token of our
> Friendship, we hung up the *Kettle,* and took up the *Hatchet* . . . We
> waited long in Expectation of the Fleet from *England* . . . But at last
> we were told, that our *Great Queen,* by some important Affair, was
> prevented in her Design for that Season. This made us extream
> Sorrowful, lest the *French,* who hitherto had dreaded Us, should now
> think Us unable to make War against them. The Reduction of *Canada*
> is of such Weight, that after the effecting thereof, We should have
> *Free Hunting* and a great Trade with Our *Great Queen's* Children: and
> as a Token of [our] Sincerity, We do here . . . present Our *Great Queen*
> with these *BELTS* of *WAMPUM.*

The speech concluded with the suggestion that without a renewed promise of help the Iroquois must "forsake our Country and seek other Habita-
tions, or stand Neuter; either of which will be much against our Inclinations." The penultimate paragraph added a plea for British missionaries to
instruct them on the "Saviour of the World," to counter the "insinuations"
of French priests and presents.[40]

Perhaps surprisingly for the times, Anne consented to all the Iroquois'
requests. Sunderland had clearly done much preparatory work to make
the meeting run his way. He had wagered that the idea of total surrender
in 1710 was still too humiliating for any courtier to embrace, despite the
growing tide of antiwar feeling. Anne's ministry for now decided to pursue a moderate line of continuing naval defenses for overseas concerns
while stepping back from new offensives on the continent.[41] In this way,
the Iroquois became linked, after their initial association with ultra-
whiggism, to a more acceptable, more modest vision of British militancy.

The deal between crown and ally was sealed with appropriate exchanges on both sides. The Iroquois bestowed some shell necklaces and
bracelets as well as their usual wampum belts of agreement (sometimes
given, significantly, as reminders of past agreements). Anne in turn reci-
procated with one of her own most valued commodities, 200 guineas in
cash.[42]

Agreement entailed several meetings between the Iroquois and certain important figures at Whitehall and in the Church. Sunderland was
ordered to arrange these, as well as a tour for the visitors of "all that is
remarkable here"—the sites of power, strength, prosperity, and resolve
that would underscore once again Britain's more-than-ample ability to
follow through with its commitments.[43] Accordingly, over the next few
weeks, the delegates met with the Lords Commissioner for Trade and Plan-

tations, the Archbishop of Canterbury, the Bishop of London, officers of the Hudson's Bay Company, and the colonist William Penn.[44] In addition, they traveled on barges down the Thames to Greenwich Park, calling on the Astronomer Royal and on Christopher Wren's glorious residence for seamen. They were taken to the bustling docks at Woolwich and the huge arsenal at the Tower. They saw Exchange Alley, Gresham College, and Guildhall. They attended services at St. James's Chapel as well as St. Paul's Cathedral. They dined at the Houses of Parliament and at the magnificent homes of aristocrats such as the Duke of Montagu. And they strolled through thriving marketplaces, sipped coffee at Jonathan's and Will's, and relaxed in numerous highbrow taverns.[45]

Moreover, the Iroquois toured Bedlam asylum, Bishopsgate work-house, and Christ's Hospital school. As with the meaning of the venues, the connection between British might and responsible social orderliness was not left unemphasized.[46]

That Sunderland had the Iroquois transported to most of these sites in ornate open carriages, driven by the queen's master of ceremonies, Sir Charles Cottrell, in full dress regalia, was probably meant also to draw ordinary Londoners' attention to the message behind these symbolic venues, as much as it was to compliment the Iroquois.[47] But no one could have predicted the degree of public interest that did arise around the delegation. Myriad publications soon reported that "rabbles," "throngs," "crowds," and "mobs" were attending the Iroquois wherever they went in the city.[48] At one venue, among a "thronging" of "our people," a poor preg-nant woman was said to "Long to Kiss one of their Hands, with which his Indian Majesty being made acquainted, permitted the same, and afterward gave her a Half Guinea to Buy her some Blankets."[49] In Covent Garden, at least one tradesman changed his shop sign to the "Four Indian Kings" while some schoolchildren in Newgate laid on a dinner for them "in respect of their fame."[50]

With no co-residing chaperone, the Iroquois may well have enjoyed some unofficial tours of the city, too. Certainly the nearby drinking estab-lishments relied on it: they were soon advertising the Iroquois' presence at their alehouses, beer gardens, and cockfighting pits in order to profi-teer from the crush of patrons who were sure to appear.[51] The Iroquois were also said to attend a bear fight at Hockley-in-the-Hole, a "consort of vocal musick" at a popular choral assembly, a "Tryal of Skill" between two duelists (using at least six different weapons), and a puppet theater—with special appearance by a sword-dancing five-year-old girl.[52] One enter-tainment that definitely lured the visitors was a Haymarket production of *Macbeth* on 24 April: observers noted that a near-riot broke out when audience members protested their inability to view the Iroquois properly. "The Mobocracy . . . declared that they had come to see the Kings," went one commentary, "and 'since we have paid our money [the Mob was said to yell] the Kings we will have.'" The theater manager (also acting the title role at the time) was obliged to stop the proceedings and rearrange the seating so that the Iroquois spent the rest of the play on stage with him and the other players.[53] Considering this uproar over a matter of mere visibility, it is probable that the visitors did indeed call in on most of the other performances at which they were promised, or else the patrons' disappointment would have hit the headlines.

What the Iroquois made of all these sites and invitations, as many previous historians have found, is more than usually obscure—barely any record of the visitors' words, gestures, or expressions remain for analysis.[54] The remarks that do come down—mostly about their awe and approbation—are wrought entirely from polemical, secondhand commentaries. An observation that can be made is that they rarely protested their arrangements; apart from one—probably Saquainquaragton—who sometimes stayed in his lodgings due to illness, the Iroquois attended or acquiesced to most functions laid on for them.[55] Their own strict diplomatic protocol, together with their apparently pre-established Anglophilia, no doubt fueled this propriety. It is worth noting, too, that they may have been rendered fairly mute even at the time, since their colonial escorts and interpreters were often separated from them.

Though themselves difficult to read, it is plain to see that the Four Iroquois Kings constituted a popularity distinct from that generated by any previous visiting Native American contingent. No earlier envoy had come close to inspiring the breadth or depth of interest shown them. Popularity, however, did not necessarily entail understanding. If all Britons now viewed Native Americans as potential determinants in overseas enterprises, only those directly connected to official doings probably endowed that role with much sense of autonomy or individual agency. Most ordinary folk appeared still to consider New World people as savage archetypes, even as they appreciated their increasingly political position among foreign powers. The resounding silence surrounding the Iroquois' reaction to all they witnessed in London stands as the most eloquent testament to this idealization. It is also neatly evident in graphic form in a playbill promoting the Iroquois' presence at Punch's puppet theater: in this broadside, the visitors are drawn in crude woodcut as swarthy caricatures, with one brandishing a primitive weapon.[56] Their potential confusion with the marionettes they were supposed to have attended seems hardly accidental.

This is not to say, however, that ordinary Britons were apolitical in the way they believed the Iroquois to be savages. It is to the strategic uses made of New World savagery that we now turn.

SAVAGES INTO DISCOURSE

As intimated, the first representations of the Iroquois were strongly partisan. Possibly the most lasting instance of the Whig or official representation of the Iroquois came in the form of paintings commissioned by Sunderland on behalf of the queen. These portraits were impressive oils, full-length in size, executed by the Dutch expatriate and frequent "face-painter" for the crown, Jan Verelst (figures 2.1–2.4).[57]

Following standard European portraiture conventions, Verelst's subjects stand before a background and with accoutrements indicative of their identity and promise.[58] The Iroquois are presented amid densely wooded landscapes, and behind each man is a totemic animal: Tejonihokarawa and Onigoheriago are before a wolf, Saquainquaragton is before a bear, and Etowaucum is before a tortoise. The alleged leader, Tejonihokarawa, holds aloft a wampum belt, while the others sport facial tattoos, feather earrings, leather moccasins, unfamiliar hairstyles, and plenty of flesh. The original *silvaticus* of savagery could not have been more explicitly proffered in these works, nor either the simplicity of social practices presumed of such forest-dwelling folk.

What is most distinctive about the portraits, however, is the arrestingly militant stance of the subjects. Each Iroquois appears upright and defiant, pulling attention in every case to the weapon that hovers nearby—the tomahawk at Tejonihokarawa's feet, the bow in Onigoheriago's hand, the gun held by Saquainquaragton, and the club held by Etowaucum. They look like supreme warriors, awesome and even beautiful, ever-prepared for battle because battle seems to have carved the essence of their existence. The simplicity of this kind of savagery would have unnerved any would-be enemy.

That these portraits had royal sanction, and soon hung in Kensington Palace next to portraits of various great British generals and admirals, effectively folded the Iroquois' presumed savagery into the government's cause.[59] If not directly compared to Britons, then at least Verelst's savages represented the best values of a British ally—might, resolve, and determination. With such friends, war becomes something that cannot go

FIGURE 2.1. Jan Verelst, *Tee Yee Neen Ho Ga Row,* 1710.
Library and Archives Canada, acc. no. 1977-35-4. Acquired
with a special grant from the Canadian government in 1977,
reproduction copy number c92415.

badly in the end. Perhaps more vaguely implied, too, is the circular point
that war brings with it friends that might not otherwise exist. Whiggish
interests not only in fighting the current wars but also in extending
Britain's sociable, transactional culture after and through the wars are all
subtly developed in these works.

Modern scholars have focused on less partisan readings of the Verelst
portraits. They have been chiefly concerned—in somewhat contradictory
fashion—to argue that the paintings reveal both a central slippage in representation and a gesture toward a more careful, ethnographic approach

FIGURE 2.2.   Jan Verelst, *Sa Ga Yeath Qua Pieth Tow*, 1710.
Library and Archives Canada, acc. no. 1977-35-2 Acquired
with a special grant from the Canadian government in
1977, reproduction copy number c92419.

to Native America. Eric Hinderaker claims that the images convey "the
essential paradox of the Four Indian Kings—the juxtaposition of royal
or noble figures with the primitive pursuits and wild landscapes associated with the New World."[60] He follows Bruce Robertson, who earlier
decided that this mixture of nobility and savagery produced a lingering
unease.[61] What each scholar has presupposed, however, is the incongruity of nobility with savagery. They are in good company, supported by
critics as diverse as Roxann Wheeler, who argues that nobility allowed
for the "selective acceptance" of New World people in Europe in spite of

FIGURE 2.3.   Jan Verelst, *How Nee Yeath Taw No Row*, 1710.
Library and Archives Canada, acc. no. 1977-35-3 Acquired
with a special grant from the Canadian government in
1977, reproduction copy number c92417

their savagery, and Hayden White, who argues from another direction
that the contrast between the two represented rather more an attack on
nobility than an embrace of savagery.[62]

But was nobility inherently opposed to savagery in eighteenth-century
Britain? A few scholars have questioned this assumption in relation to
visiting foreigners. Of the Four Iroquois Kings specifically, the visual
historian David Bindman has observed that "their pursuits as 'kings' are
not differentiated from those of their fellow 'savages.'" They are instead
portrayed as "being better" in degree, but crucially not in kind, than "the

FIGURE 2.4. Jan Verelst, *Etow Oh Koam,* 1710. Library and
Archives Canada, acc. no. 1977-35-1, Acquired with a special
grant from the Canadian government in 1977, reproduction
copy number c92421

rest of their people."[63] Of an earlier visiting African, Wylie Sypher has
noted how "gentility" worked to make his "savagery" shine "brighter."[64]
Sometimes nobility acted to emphasize savagery. Certainly one pamphleteer on the Four Iroquois Kings felt that their "awful and majestic" qualities added seamlessly to the "brown Complexions" and "austere Visages"
of their "savage Custom."[65] Verelst's portraits seem to agree with the
pamphleteer: the dignified stance of the subjects enhances rather than
mitigates their purported wild essence.

On the charge that the Verelst images signal a fresh attention to Native

American culture, critics are on even shakier ground. They have pointed
to the inclusion of accurate totems and apparel in the portraits, and add
that they join other instances of newly careful appreciation, such as the
Four Kings of Canada booklet of 1710, which listed scores of differences
between Iroquois and British customs, including burial rites, marriage
rites, and diet.[66] Such scholars, however, have not always distinguished
between detail and verisimilitude. In several ways, the exotic paraphernalia depicted by Verelst belies an underlying disregard: the girdles
around the Iroquois' waists were fashioned correctly after burden belts,
but they were meant to be worn over the shoulder; the upturned moccasins on the Iroquois' feet were surely authentic, but should really have
been downturned.[67] Historian J.C.H. King has established that Verelst
almost certainly drew these examples of difference from museum specimens rather than from the visitors' own articles.[68] Creating a *sense* of
otherness in the portraits overrode an interest in investigating the *nature*
of otherness. Furthermore, the mixing of European accoutrements with
Native American accoutrements hardly suggests a notable respect for
Iroquois cultural integrity.[69]

Gestures to cultural detail, then, worked very much like suggestions
of nobility in the Verelst paintings: both served to underscore a more
definitive savagery. Indeed, the inclusion of tattoos, feathers, leather craft-
ings and hand-made weaponry acted more likely as flags to the limited
lifestyles decreed of savages than as examples of acceptable or legitimate
difference. Far from splintering or challenging stereotypes, such features
mostly strengthened them.

The Verelst oils were copied by the well-known Huguenot engraver
John Simon—in engraved form as well as in cheaper mezzotinted form—
who then sold them widely throughout the city.[70] Such was the crush for
copies that Verelst had to print a protestation in the *London Gazette* on
18 May against the circulation of unauthorized versions.[71] The official
representation of the Four Iroquois clearly had a healthy following out of
court as well as within.

Other, competing partisan understandings of the Iroquois existed
alongside the government's. When the decorated but marginal Duke of
Ormonde put out a story in the popular monthly *Present State of Europe*
about the Iroquois' admiration of his royal Life Guards, it was to use
them as props for his more moderate Tory line.[72] Although he ended his
days an exiled Jacobite, Ormonde in 1710 was pursuing a gentler form of
opposition, the kind that was increasingly finding favor within Anne's
war-torn government: a commitment to smaller military operations, a

preference for naval rather than army campaigns, and a general reconsideration of some of the more obvious changes in monarchy and economy pursued since the Glorious Revolution.[73]

The Iroquois no doubt did view Ormonde's Life Guards at Hyde Park on 26 April, but whether they applauded the soldiers' humility and austerity as Ormonde suggested is less secured. "What then must be the commander," the Iroquois are said to have wondered, "if those under his Obedience, make so August . . . an Appearance?"[74] The Life Guards in the early eighteenth century represented throwbacks to a Restoration idea of monarchy. Existing purely to defend the monarch's absolute right to rule, they stood for a time when monarchs ideally dominated parliaments and withstood applications from external parties to consider special interests. That Ormonde advertised the Iroquois' sympathy with such a body was his attempt to wrest the positive image of savagery presented by Verelst away from the center toward a more critical, and traditional, position. In the same move, and not without relevance, savagery's admirable simplicity became more about ascetic loyalty than focused militancy.

First as determined warriors and then as ascetic loyalists, the visitors were beginning to show just how flexible was the idea of savagery thrust upon them in 1710. The flexibility of the ideology surrounding the Iroquois was also becoming evident. Soon after Ormonde's contrivance, the fiery pro-Whig annalist Abel Boyer spluttered that "the Speech which was said to have been made by [the Iroquois] . . . to the Duke of Ormonde, is Spurious."[75] Even more spurious, however, was the story that Thomas Hearne propagated about the visitors. Hearne was a far more stridently oppositional figure than Ormonde: a nonjuring antiquarian from Oxford, he held radical views against everything that the British government stood for after 1688.[76] Unlike Ormonde, Hearne never met the Iroquois but he claimed equal intimacy with their opinions. In his diary for 4 May, Hearne reported that they personally had been responsible for obtaining clemency for one of the convicted Sacheverell rioters. One hapless Daniel Demaree, sentenced to death on 25 April, now enjoyed freedom, according to Hearne, because of the "Intercesssion" of the "4 Indian Kings now in England."[77]

Such meddling was highly improbable, but it evidently presented Hearne with a meaningful way of explaining events.[78] It was neater for him to say that a foreign envoy—representing what seemed to him now-lost values in Britain—had ensured justice on the day rather than Anne herself, who was more complexly related to the changing role of monarchy at this time.[79] For Hearne, the Iroquois' savagery signified a simplicity of statehood that he aligned nostalgically with a pre-Revolution Britain, when faith and power were entwined and unquestioned, and when borders kept subjects within and outsiders firmly without. For this extreme political discontent, the idea of savagery meant more than just loyalty to the divine right of kings but also an inclination for isolationism, religiosity, and stasis.

The majority of Britons who clamored to see and record the Four Iroquois Kings were not, of course, party pundits. Most held far fuzzier views than the partisan stakeholders. Nonetheless, their reactions to the visitors demonstrated just as significant degrees of division and turned also mostly around the common issues of war, debt, and a commercializing society. Especially among the rising prose journeymen of the era, the Iroquois proved a lightning rod for discursive elaboration on their nation. They appeared in articles published by both apologist and oppositional periodicals. Even among like-minded writers, however, their savagery could be wrought in slightly different ways to further slightly different views.

Richard Steele was one of the first journalists to write about the visitors. In a late issue of his *Tatler* he had a few of his stock characters discuss the virtues of the "savages," comparing them tacitly with the best virtues of contemporary Britain. Though they were men who acted "according to the dictates of natural Justice," they were yet—or rather consequently—generous, polite, dignified, and honorable.[80] Most significantly, though, their demonstration of such qualities highlighted the equal merit of their hosts. To Steele, the British society that embraced the Iroquois was observant, solicitous, resourceful, civil, and strong. In *The Tatler*, the Four Iroquois Kings promoted the kind of equable, affable, progressive culture that was linked to apologist versions of commercial growth at this time. They did so by appearing as emblems of a kind of simplicity of manner that many claimed would follow in Britain after its liberation from the squabbling, inward mentality of the seventeenth century.[81]

Steele's fellow *philosophe* Joseph Addison took a somewhat alternative line in his *Spectator*.[82] One year after the Iroquois departed, Addison wrote a retrospective satire that pretended to have found one of the visitors' diaries. The alleged papers revealed astonishment at the magnificence of St. Paul's Cathedral, amazement at the excesses of London dress, wonder over the leisure time available to young people, and curiosity about the similarity of Whigs and Tories to elephants and rhinoceroses (Addison's zoogeography of the New World obviously not being a strong point). Although Addison's narrator concluded that "amidst these wild Remarks there now and then appears something very reasonable," the piece as a whole figured the Iroquois as naïve vessels rather than as equivalent partners. The sillier aspects of British wealth and sophistication were gently mocked in the satire, but when contrasted with the emptiness assumed of Iroquois culture they appeared a minor price to pay. For Addison, commercial culture was less about a simplicity of manner than an opportunity for national connection. Around about the same time, he famously remarked that commerce recommended itself because it "knit Mankind together in a mutual Intercourse of good Offices": the complexities it thrust on social relations were necessary to ensure a solid peace.[83]

Addison's *Spectator* article on the Iroquois was upheld by later eighteenth-century literary critics as a great example of the genre of ventriloquist satire.[84] To Addison's contemporary rival, Jonathan Swift, however, it signified only a kind of plagiarism. "It was made of a noble hint I gave him," Swift complained to a protégé: "I repent he ever had it. I intended to have written a book on the subject."[85] Although clearly attracted to the Iroquois as a means to some end, Swift never did write a sustained piece on them, perhaps put off by Addison's trumping. The increasingly disgruntled essayist did, though, write about Native Americans in general in a few subsequent articles.[86] For him, they embodied a charmless savagery—brutish, violent, and limited. What appealed about this condition to the oppositional polemicist in Swift was its capacity to offer devastating comparisons to Britain's own near-future. Like Steele, Swift used comparison as his rhetorical device, but unlike either journalist before him, he wielded it to lambaste the current state of Britain. With a government now dependent on unpredictable and definitionally insatiable moneymen, "I see nothing left for us," he opined, "but to truck and barter our Goods, like the *wild Indians*, with each other; or with our too powerful Neighbours."[87] Without land as its basis of power, Britain could no longer boast firm security, thought Swift, since a commercial state was for him intrinsically unstable, degrading, and thence a guarantor of war.[88] The Four Iroquois Kings did not feature explicitly, then, in Swift's writings, but they evidently appealed, and probably inspired some of Swift's later deployments of Native American savagery in ongoing vituperations against British commercialization.

Another oppositional voice in the period was Alexander Pope—half a generation younger than Swift but by the 1710s a fellow-member of the feisty Scriblerus Club and a rising literary star.[89] Pope referred to the Iroquois in his famous epic poem, *Windsor Forest*, published in 1713 after the Whigs' fall and during the Tories' brief four-year ascendancy.[90] The poem celebrated the Peace of Utrecht, which had just been pushed through, ending the controversial War of Spanish Succession (or "Queen Anne's War"). It remembered the Iroquois' short visit to Windsor before they headed back to Portsmouth, and imagined what such visitors would think of the country now. Instead of finding division and oppression, blood and worry, Pope believed, they would greet a free nation, one that brought people together rather than separated them, and which inspired courage and enterprise in all:

> The time shall come, when free as seas or wind
> Unbounded *Thames* shall flow for all mankind,
> Whole nations enter with each swelling tyde,
> And seas but join the regions they divide;
> Earth's distant ends our glory shall behold,
> And the new world launch forth to seek the old.
> (ll. 395–400)

Other than as vehicles for showing off British brilliance, however, Native American visitors had few virtues of their own for the poet:

> Then ships of uncouth form shall stem the tyde,
> And feather'd people croud my wealthy side,
> And naked youths and painted chiefs admire
> Our speech, our colour, and our strange attire!
> (ll. 401–4)

At least their simplicity seemed to protect them from developing the kind of vice that Pope thought had gripped Britain throughout the last several warmongering years.

More populist genres also followed the Iroquois. The *Four Indian Kings Garland*, a 183-line poem in two parts, became one of the most reprinted ballads of the eighteenth century. First appearing in mid-1710, it described the unhappy love affair between one of the Iroquois and a fair British maiden. After giving a "humble low submission"—in keeping with their "sad condition"—to "bold Britain's royal court," the visitors were said to entreat over matters of the heart. The problem was that as "wild Heathens" the Iroquois could never win the hand of "a Christian lady," since such "professions" were entirely incompatible with the advantages of a British "education." The ballad's view of savagery, thus, was not terribly complex, and, as Hinderaker points out, it relied heavily on a significant revision of the visitors' well-known conversions. But it worked neatly to promote a populist version of apologist nationalism. The ballad was reprinted over twenty times in varying ways and soon penetrated the outer provinces of Worcestershire, Gloucestershire, Yorkshire, and America itself.[91]

Other jingoistic tracts included the broadside *Epilogue*, which claimed to be a speech offered to the Iroquois before a performance at the Queen's Theatre, and the twenty-five-page *Pindaric Poem*, written by London's former poet laureate Elkanah Settle.[92] Both figured the visitors as lowly simpletons and the British nation as a model of altruism and security. The *Epilogue* claimed the Iroquois were "struck with Wonder at the Monarch's Sight" while Anne was said to be "so Good, so Gracious, and so Great a Queen" who offers assurance "against the threats of France and Rome." Settle's *Poem* (whose author later starred as one of the duncees in Pope's *The Dunciad*) likewise described the visitors as "so many kneeling petitioners before the Throne of . . . Benign Britannia . . . brought over in their naked simplicity and uncultivated innocence." The end of Britain's relationship with such savagery was, for Settle, purely philanthropic:

> Shades must retire, and Ignorance retreat,
> And Savage worship fly her Ancient Seat:
> When thro the *Indian* Clouds the Rays break forth
> (As the Sun forces thro the gloomy North,)
> And there to the Barbarian eyes display
> The Infant Beams of [our] Evangelic Day.[93]

Importantly, populist reactions could just as often be critical of the status quo—though few of any stripe seemed to endow the key explicating idea of savagery with much positive value. Another frequently reprinted ballad was *The Royal Strangers Ramble*—140 lines of satire about the emptiness of the civic culture shown to the visitors. While the Iroquois are unshod ignoramuses, barely human enough to understand the teaching of the Greatest Teacher of all, their hosts are far worse because they are needlessly mired in frivolity, distraction, licentiousness, and belligerence. The rhyme ends with a damning comparison of two hollow societies:

> Since no one brought less
> Of Wealth, Knowledge, or Dress
>   Than those who from *India* are come,
> And no one before
> Return'd from our Shore
>   With so little advantages Home.[94]

The pamphlet squib entitled *A True and Faithful Account of the Last Distemper and Death of Tom Whigg* was even more spiky. Its anonymous author accused a dying Tom Whigg of fomenting atheism in his clubs, juntos, and "other infernal cabals of this kind." The culprit was said to have hired a wit named Bickerstaff (Steele's chief persona in *The Tatler*) "to ridicule all Distinctions of . . . ancient Nobility." To this end, he brought "over hither four unknown Persons . . . under the notion of Kings . . . exposing 'em about Town all four in a Hackney-Coach, from Tavern to Tavern, and treating them, and lodging them I suppose four in a bed, with no other reasonable Design but that of lessening the Honour due to the Majesty of Kings, and rendering them little and contemptible in the Eyes of the Populace."[95] For this commentator, savagery truly was incongruous with nobility. His allegation of Whig machinations behind the Iroquois' visit was a virtual shot at the current government's supposedly low respect for monarchy. Here, it was the comparison suggested by the incumbents themselves between savagery and the British state that caused the offence, rather than any wily representation made of the relation by a critical author.

Other bits of ephemera on the visitors appeared throughout the rest of 1710—different versions of satires and ballads in chapbooks, broadsheets, and handbills, as well as further images in smaller oils, crude woodcuts, plagiarized engravings, and even some ivory miniatures by the miniaturist Bernard Lens.[96] By the time the Four Iroquois Kings arrived back in Boston on the *Dragon* merchant marine on 15 July, their fame had reached into most crevices of British metropolitan culture. Always, the visitors were designated savage, though sometimes this was a positive idealization and sometimes a negative archetyping. The variety of uses to which the Iroquois were put suggests that part of their popularity relied on the flexibility attributed to savagery in this era. Additionally, it relied on savagery's appeal to all contenders in the general argument about Britain's moral destiny raging through most levels of London society at the time. Savagery could be positive or negative, and also eloquent to progressives, conservatives, loyalists, or dissenters. Indeed, one of the most significant aspects of the Iroquois' representation was to underscore the depth of division current in the period. Their representation did not point *only* to the "possibilities of empire" and the "bounty and glory" of Britannia, as some historians claim, but *also* to the pitfalls, the hypocrisies, and the vices potential in expansion.[97] Visiting savagery in 1710 had proved a potent forum for airing strongly divergent views on the broad question of commerce in toto.

AFTERMATH

Along with the Iroquois and their colonial escorts, the *Dragon* carried home unusual gifts from the British queen: bolts of cloth, brass kettles, gilt mirrors, cutlery, harps, razors, jewelry, scissors, tobacco, firearms, and a magic picture lantern—among other things.[98] The range of booty in itself was a sort of inventory of the goods now becoming available from Britain's overseas outposts. What the four delegates did with all these goods is not always certain, though a large share would have been distributed to Five Nation members at the conference held by New York officials in Albany in early August 1710. This conference, cannily timed by Governor Robert Hunter and the colony's Commissioners for Indian Affairs, rode on the back of the envoy's apparent pleasure with Whitehall as well as their warmly welcomed return. League leaders pledged there and then to join the renewed push for New France. They even forgave the dubious make-up of the envoy, remarking that "altho' they were natives of the Mohogs nation yet we are well satisfyd as if there had been one from each of the five nations." The New York end of the Covenant Chain between Iroquois and British was repaired for the time being, sealed with the dispersal of medals, icons, and "other gifts."[99]

The post-envoy lives of the four returnees are traceable though sketchy. Hendrick Tejonihokarawa has sometimes been assumed to have had an exceptionally long career in colonial diplomacy, returning to Britain for another visit in 1740, fighting heroically against the French during the early 1750s, and dying a great friend of the superintendent of Indian Affairs, Sir William Johnson, in 1755. Recent scholarship, however—spearheaded by Barbara Sivertsen—has argued that this biography merges two different Hendricks. The later appearances were made by the better-known Hendrick Theyanoguin. The Hendrick who traveled to London in 1710 also become a respectable negotiator for the Iroquois, monitoring the land-lust of later British missionaries to New York and serving as an intermediary between colonists and non-Iroquois nations into the 1730s. But he probably died in his mid-sixties, around 1740, just as the next, unrelated Hendrick was becoming famous.[100]

The other three travelers fall into historical shadows more quickly. Brant Saquainquaragton died within months of return, though his later step-grandson, the Mohawk leader and British officer Joseph Brant, ensured that his name echoed through the century. John Onigoheriago survived longer, never attaining the high status once attributed to him but living to see his son, Joseph Sayoenwese, become a Mohawk sachem in his own right. Etowaucum the Mohegan, or Nicholas, remained for many years among his befriended Mohawks, though to little public distinction.[101]

Whether any of the four travelers participated directly in the military consequences of their trip is unknown. These consequences were two-fold, and both fairly limited. During the summer of 1710, colonists learnt that Anne had already reneged significantly on her promised support for another push on Canada. This was due chiefly to the convulsions that continued in her ministry after the Iroquois' departure. After Godolphin, Marlborough, and Sunderland were all sacked and replaced by Tories, the idea of aiding further colonial aggression fell somewhere between unsound and embarrassing.[102] Whitehall did eventually send one small fleet—to compensate for the lack of two full forces—and with that New Yorkers were able to secure Nova Scotia in October. But the dream of total conquest remained elusive.[103]

The following year, however, and somewhat out of the blue, the new Tory ministry decided to give the Glorious Enterprise one last chance. A year was reckoned long enough to erase the link between the colonial strategy and Whig leadership but not, apparently, so long as to discon-nect the memory of Whig leadership from a singular inability to resolve the problem of Canada. The first minister, Robert Harley, wagered that a win in the New World would further smear the reputation of his prede-cessors while appearing innovative in detail and execution.

In July, two large fleets arrived in Boston harbor. Three leaders of the Five Nations were present to confirm what had for so long been guar-anteed.[104] Conscious of their fragile reputation in military matters, the collective governors also arranged for League members to receive copies of Verelst's pictures of the 1710 travelers, to remind each nation of the happier moments in their relationship. Each of the five nations received a set, "and 4 in Frames with glasses over them [were given] to be hung up in the Onnondage Castle the center of the 5 nations where they always meet."[105] Nearly 1,000 Iroquois warriors ended up participating in the final 1711 attempt, but this effort eventually failed too. The landed assault collapsed when the naval force withdrew after ferocious storms around Egg Island.[106] The Glorious Enterprise had run its last try. Relations between Iroquois and British colonials never fully recovered.[107]

At least one of the 1710 travelers, however, is known to have partici-pated in the religious consequences of the trip: Hendrick Tejonihokarawa served as a lay preacher in the small mission that resulted from the envoy's official request for Christian instruction.[108] At the time, Anne had deferred this request to the Society for the Propagation of the Gospel in

Foreign Parts, which in turn had pledged two missionaries, an interpreter, a chapel, a house, a fort, and the plentiful dispersal of bibles.[109] When the Rev. William Andrews finally arrived in 1712, he apologized for the cut to one missionary as well as the abandonment of any interpretive service.[110] The mission survived for six years, but collapsed when Andrews quit the project, citing the intractability of the Iroquois and deciding that "there is no manner of pleasure to be proposed by being here . . . among these poor dark ignorant Creatures."[111] The Christian Iroquois of the area no doubt chalked up the closure to just one more betrayal by the British.[112]

The aftermath of the envoy back in London was not quite as dramatic as in America, though it had its moment. In March and April of 1712 the city experienced a rash of terrifying hooliganism, attributed to a mysterious gang called the Mohocks. This gang was said to roam the streets, assaulting innocent men, raping virginal women, slitting noses, destroying property, and rolling old people down hills in barrels.[113] The government issued an edict against its assembly, but no one was ever charged with being a Mohock and many doubted the gang's existence.[114] Commentators were, however, sure about the origins of the name: it was borrowed, said Daniel Defoe, from the *"Mohawks,* [who] are a small Nation of *Savages* in the Woods, on the back of our two Colonies of *New-England* and *New York*, the same from whence our four *Indian* Kings came lately of their own Fools Errand." Defoe himself had little time for the gang or their supposed mentors: the latter, he claimed, "were always esteem'd as the most Desperate, and most Cruel of the Natives of *North-America*."[115] Joseph Addison could not have agreed more, revealing his ever-declining opinion of the tribe as "Cannibals . . . who subsist by plundering and devouring all the Nations about them."[116]

Like the Iroquois visitors, the Mohocks proved useful to partisan polemic. Swift declared them to be "all Whigs . . . with malicious intent" while Hearne called them the "Whiggish gang . . . Indeed all Whigs are look'd upon as Mohocks, their principles and doctrines leading them to all manner of barbarity and inhumanity."[117] The Whiggish party paper, *Medley*, on the other hand, denounced the Mohock affair as a figment of an overwrought Tory imagination and the similarly inclined *Observator* suggested that the gang was really the vanguard of an underground Jacobite movement.[118] Beyond party politics, though, the Mohocks were less illuminating. Unlike the envoy before them, the gang did not appeal to broader debates within Britain. They did not speak to worries about the cost and benefits of war, the future of monarchy, the role of religion, or the creation of an exchange culture. In short, the Mohocks starred briefly as rather two-dimensional puppets in British party discourse before becoming absorbed into the prehistory of eighteenth-century Hell-Fire Clubs.[119] They were never as richly expressive of contemporary angst about commercial transformation as their real-life alleged forebears. And as such, they do not figure as interestingly in the record of British popular culture.

The four men who became known as the Iroquois Kings are still relatively hidden from history: though dismissed by some later commentators as pretenders, and hailed by others as "highly significant" statesmen, their own final reckoning of the trip of 1710 is unknown.[120] No doubt they were grateful to have survived a journey that had killed so many of their kind in earlier centuries, but what they really made of the mission and its outcomes probably hovered between madcap and momentous. For the British hosts, however, the visit had far-reaching effects. When the next major delegation of Native Americans showed up in Britain in 1730, it was largely organized, followed, and imagined in ways laid down by the Four Iroquois Kings' visit. The envoy of 1710 had burned a bright path: its inauguration of a new tradition of intense fascination for New World visitors established strong conventions for successors regarding protocol, itinerary, and mode of representation. Most of all, though, the envoy's popularity revealed the variety of division in British culture regarding expansive change.

3. Seven from the Cherokee, Nine from the Creeks

The next notable delegations to Britain from the New World occurred twenty years after the Iroquois' visit. Compared to the crises of 1710, Britain in 1730 seemed much more stable. The Whigs had gained back their ascendancy in 1714, which they then maintained for nearly fifty years. Anne had died the same year, finally ending the controversial Stuart dynasty and paving the way for the new, Whig-favored Hanoverian succession. A Riot Act had been introduced in 1715, following a recent Jacobite uprising but also ensuring against any repetition of the Sacheverell chaos of 1710. And, of course, most important, the country was no longer at war—it had, in fact, avoided any semblance of full-scale war since the Utrecht treaty of 1713.

The stability of the mid-Hanoverian age has attracted considerable scholarly attention. Ever since J. H. Plumb's classic *The Growth of Political Stability in England 1675–1725* (1967), historians have argued about its definition and existence.[1] Plumb defined stability as "the acceptance by society of its political institutions," which as Geoffrey Holmes states was certainly more "reality" than "pipe dream" by 1730.[2] But such a bold summary also invites questions about the era's ongoing fears of Jacobite rebellion, its ministerial fury over occasional disruptions to Hanoverian pageants, and its governmental crackdown on the freedom of the press through stamp acts and biased subsidization.[3] If society accepted its political institutions in this period, it did so unevenly and sometimes rather superficially. By the same token, the political institutions of the time knew their hold was precarious and ever-needful of vigilance.

Britain's interests in the New World around 1730 revealed a similar story. Between the 1720s and the 1750s, British North America enjoyed what Daniel Richter has called a "begrudging, mostly peaceful coexistence" between European rivals and indigenous populations.[4] In response, the colonial economy prospered, at least doubling its exports to the homeland in the same span.[5] Yet skirmishes still broke out sporadically, their containment often reflecting some limitation on the part of the opponent rather than any profound sense of continental amity.[6]

From this cautiously calm scene came two delegations within four years: a Cherokee envoy in 1730 and a Creek envoy in 1734. Both continued the popularity secured by the Four Iroquois Kings in 1710. Both aroused interest from dignitaries at court as well as plebeians on the street: they each met the reigning monarch, attended official functions of state, undertook specific tours of the capital, and attracted crowds of onlookers. Both also stirred a lively production of squibs, broadsides, articles, and portraits. As with the Iroquois before them, the 1730s delegates were always figured as savages. And also like them, such a designation was valued and used in highly varying ways. Positive or negative, savagery in this context yet served a wide range of ideological positions. The similarity of the Cherokee and Creek envoys to the Iroquois in terms of discursive deployment suggests that Britons in the 1730s were no more agreed on their nation's moral trajectory than they had been a generation earlier.

Neither delegation has earned much notice by modern scholars. The Cherokee have no dedicated historian, though they appear in a few general surveys of Native American travelers or of South Carolinian foundation.[7] The leader of the Creek envoy, Tomochichi, has garnered two hagiographies since the nineteenth century, but the group as a whole usually only feature as passing references in the story of the colony of Georgia.[8] Taken together, however, these envoys further demonstrate the peculiar purchase of the New World savage visitor on eighteenth-century British culture. Their stories as well remind of the various counternarratives going on behind the history of reception, which included personal ambition, negotiation, and reinvention.

SEVEN FROM THE CHEROKEE

Both the Cherokee peoples and the Creek peoples had once lived in what was known to Britons by the turn of the seventeenth century as southern Carolina. In many ways, this region exemplified the fragile peace of British North America in the mid-Hanoverian era. While it was one of the most dynamic economies on the continent, Carolina also witnessed frequent flare-ups with vying Spaniards and French and with the various indigenous nations in or around its borders. Most conflicts stemmed from the disastrous repercussions of the Yamasee War of 1715–17, when nearby Yamasees and Lower Creeks had formed an alliance against Carolinian planters in retaliation for excessive land-grabs and labor raids. The Cherokee had eventually sided with the colonists in this war, driven rather more by their older rivalry with the Lower Creek than by any preference for the newcomers.[9] The vicious defense eventually cowed the Yamasee-Creek offensive, but the effect on indigenous relations with colonists and each other was deleterious for years to come. The Cherokee fell into dire internal division, splitting between those who wished to transfer their allegiance to British Virginia and those who wished to abandon Britain altogether and seek a new partnership with the French. Most Yamasee decamped to Florida, while many Creek moved west toward Louisiana. A small faction of the Yamasee-Creek alliance decided to maintain their British connections, moving southward down the Savannah and renaming themselves Yamacraw. Among everyone, resentments and anxieties burbled and bubbled.[10]

In Britain, the Cherokee were better known than other southern Native Americans. At least, by the late 1720s they had come to the attention of a Scottish crank called Sir Alexander Cuming. With a long history of speculation and foolhardiness behind him, Cuming saw in Carolina at this time an opportunity that few others were yet ready to undertake.[11] Some chroniclers have attributed what followed as the consequences of a prophetic dream.[12] Cuming himself only referred to the inspiration of Isaiah 28, explaining that the verse's reference to cumin seed had been an explicit sign for him to rise up on the Appalachians, as the Lord had risen up on Mount Perazim, to "carry out his work, his singular work, to perform his deed, his strange deed."[13]

That deed was to make contact with the Cherokee peoples and bring them fully under British influence away from French temptations. Although it is true that for a long time afterward Cuming pestered Whitehall for a reward for his work in the shape of an "overlordship" in the colonies "at least for three years," he was evidently also motivated by some mystical-xenophobic mania. His correspondence with Whitehall officials spanned nearly forty years and consisted mostly of schemes for the colonial redemption of pagans, debtors, Jacobites, and Jews.[14]

Cuming began his work in December 1729, a few months after South Carolina became a crown colony in its own right. Shunned by most Charles Town residents as a lunatic, he managed to secure only one guide, Ludovick Grant, to take him into Cherokee country.[15] With such a slim resource, it remains a question whether Cuming's later success was due to any serious understanding of Cherokee politics or simply bizarre luck. At a minimum, he must have intuited the deep tensions in the kinsmen he encountered. In one town after another Cuming exploited those tensions—with no small amount of physical intimidation—by promising a new and stronger relationship with Britain and, in consequence, a final redemption from the perennial threat of French attack. No doubt in many leaders' minds these words appealed because they spelled peace, and with it a chance to reunite the nation.[16]

Such motivation probably explained the large turnout of Cherokee warriors at the meeting that Cuming convened on 3 April in the Middle Cherokee town of Nequassee. Only historical serendipity, however, can explain what then transpired. Cuming's openly declared need for a headman through whom he could carry out his plans coincided with the personal ambitions of one Overhill Cherokee chief called Moytoy of Tellico. In Cuming's idiosyncratic determination, Moytoy saw his chance to grab an unprecedented level of local power. He evidently stacked the meeting beforehand, himself playing on internal grievances and grudges. When Cuming demanded a convenient single contact point, the assembly found themselves electing Moytoy to be "emperor" of all the Cherokee. Moytoy in turn was only too happy to say that Cuming was now the nation's "lawgiver" and King George II its sovereign—neither of which terms overly impressed him. What Cuming read as his own extraordinary magnetism in making the event run his way was rather the result of canny opportunism and clever behind-the-scenes politicking.[17]

The British annual chronicle, *The Political State of Great Britain*, later retold the story this way:

> [Cuming] required Moytoy and all the head Warriors to acknowledge themselves dutiful Subjects and Sons to King George, and promise that they would do whatever Sir Alexander should require of them . . . all which they did on their Knees, calling upon every Thing that was terrible to them to destroy them, and that they might become no People, if they violated their Promise and Obedience. Sir Alexander ordered that the head Warriors should answer for the Conduct of the People to Moytoy, whom he had appointed their Head, by the unanimous Consent of the whole People, and to whom at Sir Alexander's Desire, they all gave an unlimited Power over them, and he to answer to Sir Alexander.[18]

But even the *Political State* conceded that this narrative "was not a Thing in itself very credible."[19] Back in April, Cuming had anticipated such skepticism, which was why he immediately began arranging for an envoy of Moytoy's men to travel to Britain "as evidence of the Truth."[20] Moytoy himself declined the invitation but apparently gave his blessing to the six men who did decide to make the journey. The motivations of these men are not clear, other than perhaps a set of personal ambitions to match Moytoy's own. They included four from the Middle town of Tassetchee and two from the Overhill town of Tennessee. The Tassetchee Cherokee were Ouka Ulah ("the chief that is to be"), Scalilosken (or Skallelockee or Kettagustah, and apparently the secondary chief of the town), Tethtowie, and Collonnah. The two from Tennessee were Clogoittah and Oukanaekah. This last man later became the famous leader and negotiator known as Attakullakulla.[21] On the way back to Charles Town, a seventh Cherokee called Onaconoa or Ounakannowie—presumably from a Lower town—asked to join the group, to which Cuming assented, though he claimed to have declined "several other" later requests from would-be adventurers.[22]

Cuming and the seven Cherokee set sail on 4 May 1730, arriving in Dover one month later. Like the Iroquois party of 1710, the envoy also included an interpreter—this time, experienced colonial fur trader, Eleazer Wiggan.[23] But also like the predecessors, such an addition proved of minimal use to posterity. The history of the Cherokees' own experience of their journey remains a relatively murky presence behind the remaining documents.

THE CHEROKEE IN BRITAIN

Upon arrival in Dover, Cuming quickstepped to London alone in order to inform an unprepared Whitehall of his accomplishments. He was acutely conscious of the unauthorized nature of his venture, though evidently confident of its ultimate reception.[24] Whitehall proved amenable, encouraging Cuming to go ahead with arrangements to meet George II, who was residing in Windsor that summer. The Cherokee arrived in the castle town in mid-June.

The visitors met with the king four times over the next six weeks, signifying either a greater determination on the part of Cuming and the Cherokee than their 1710 forebears had mustered, or a keener royal interest in the New World than had pertained earlier—or both. From the beginning, the press was sure that these visitors were savages: "the King had a scarlet jacket on, but the rest were naked, except an apron about their middles, and a horse's tail hung down behind; their faces, shoulders, &c.

were painted and spotted with red, blue, and green, &C. they had bows in their hands, and painted feathers on their heads."[25] Another account called them "feather'd chiefs" who "compared the King and Queen to the Sun, the Princes to the Stars, and themselves to Nothing."[26] Cuming himself constantly referred to them as savages. No doubt George II thought the same, though this did not dampen his enthusiasm to formalize the envoy's position and grant them one hundred guineas for their enjoyment of "all the Curiosities here."[27]

Arriving in London on 1 August, the Cherokee quickly confirmed their connection to the earlier 1710 envoy by staying in the same guesthouse. Cuming evidently learned of Thomas Arne Senior's prior hospitality and lodged them at the Two Crowns and Cushions for the remaining two months of their stay. The newspapers of the time similarly recalled the precedent, though the *Daily Courant* fancifully imagined that it was the Iroquois themselves who had recommended the place.[28] Other, later examples of the connection between the two envoys included a revival of the *Four Indian Kings' Garland*, which had concocted a love affair between one of the Iroquois and a British maiden: in August 1730, the *Daily Post* spread a rumor that one of the Cherokee had likewise fallen for a local girl called Miss Busch.[29] The connection also reverberated when an anonymous pamphlet called *Royal Remarks* appeared around October: in homage to Joseph Addison's 1711 *Spectator* piece, this work opened with the conceit of having found "a Bundle of Papers" left behind by the Cherokee Ouka.[30] Unfortunately, the pamphlet did not then go on to simulate Addison's wit—it degenerated rather quickly into a diatribe about the decline of the English language—but its existence added to the powerful sense of reenactment undergirding the Cherokee's visit.

From their Covent Garden address, the party ventured into a city even more bustling and discombobulating than it had been twenty years ago. Like the Iroquois, the Cherokee toured Greenwich, the Tower, Parliament, Bedlam, Christ's Hospital, and a great many parks and theaters. They were said to be "highly delighted" and "diverted" by it all.[31] Unlike their predecessors, however, the Cherokee also visited a number of the local spas, a few city fairs, and the Society of Archers, who were apparently pleased to meet folk "reckon'd very expert at Bows and Arrows" themselves.[32] The additional sites on the travelers' itinerary reflected the ever-burgeoning wealth and sociability of London. Spas were iconic symbols of advancing commercialism in the early eighteenth century: centers of luxury and consumerism, they often retailed the goods of overseas trade to patrons newly accustomed to having public leisure time.[33] Fairs were

an older institution, though undergoing notable revival in this period
due to the increased affluence and preponderance of the urban middling
orders.[34] Finally, the Society of Archers, although itself established in the
late seventeenth century, represented the new profile of clubs and societies in the British capital. By the 1730s, London boasted around 2,000
such organizations, all formed to promote the new commercial values of
conviviality, self-improvement, and social vigor. Several modern scholars have claimed that clubs and societies, together with the growth of the
press, were the two most important factors in the creation of the polite
society that commerce both required and fueled.[35]

Everywhere the Cherokee went they provoked broad-based fascination. From the king down, Britons seemed to respond to this latest delegation with the same if not more attention than they had shown the
Iroquois. When strolling through St. James's Park, the Cherokee were
said to be "accompanied by several Persons of Quality and Distinction . . .
Persons of all Ranks and Distinctions being admitted to see them that
behave with Decency and good Manners."[36] At the various merchant
houses (including the Carolina Coffee House), they were "regaled in a
handsome Manner" by a "great Number of Gentlemen."[37] At the various,
lesser public venues there was always a "numerous Crowd of Spectators"
or a "vast Concourse of People" to see them.[38] At their own residence, they
daily fought off a huge variety of callers.[39]

What exactly attracted these followers to the alleged savages is not,
of course, transparent, but their views may be inferred from the myriad
commentaries published on them throughout the Cherokee's stay. Most
reports at this time appeared via newspaper print—an unsurprising fact
given the great boom in newspapers of the mid-Hanoverian era.[40] Like
the commentaries on the Iroquois, they were mixed in their depiction and
deployment of the so-called savages. Even more than in 1710, though,
they seemed marked by polemical disagreement over what savagery said
about contemporary British society and its agreed correlate with the
greater commercialization evident throughout the city.

Early in July, the *Grub Street Journal* kicked off observations with a
satirical-critical approach. It first laughed at the way Ouka Ulah presumed to "preserve his superiority" over his "naked subjects" even in his
sleep by lying on a table while the other Cherokee rested on the ground.
But it then observed that in doing so he probably keeps "better state than
[our] European Princes" and at least is safe from all "bed-tester plots"—
a reference to a popular contemporary joke that had George II blame
Jacobites for the collapse of his bed when it was really due to the gross

weight of his mistress.[41] In a later edition, the same journal observed that the *St. James's Evening Post*—a well-known beneficiary of governmental press subsidy—insisted on giving the Cherokee the title of kings. *Grub Street* took pleasure in correcting the mistake, though cattily conceded that "this is not the first time that Kings have been confounded with their Ministers."[42] The journal's generally pragmatic and cynical reputation probably occludes any especially ideological interpretation of these remarks, though it certainly knew how such jabs would resonate with Britons still uncomfortable about the increased powers of parliament over monarchy in the eighteenth century.

A more genuinely oppositional publication of the time was *Fog's Weekly Journal*. On 22 August 1730, *Fog's* ran a lengthy parable about contemporary British politics which featured the Cherokee at its center.[43] The parable began with some disaffected city merchants, bored by the "dulnes of Trade," resolving to take a trip into the country. At Windsor they "behold the comely Presence of that Sun-burnt Potentate, King *Oricioulah [Ouka Ulah]*, High and Mighty Sagamoor of the *Cherrikees*." The merchants are "not a little pleas'd" to meet the Cherokee chief, for he is surely the archetypal savage, "affected to shew the modern World a true Copy of a primitive . . . in the simple State of original Government." In appearance he has savage-like "Scarifications in his swarthy Face, wrought first with some sharp Instrument and then inlay'd with Gunpowder to add a further Terribility to his awful Countenance." Such a savage, however, to the merchants, is also still surely a king: "his presence was not in the least incoherent with his Royal Dignity, for he had a great Sagacity in his Looks as well as Majesty in his Deportment."

As a savage monarch, Ouka is admirable through what he lacks. He has no "fawning Courtiers to secrete Aims from the Publick," no "cringing Sycophants to tickle his Ears with Flatteries whilst they pick'd his Pockets," and no "Guards to attend him for the securing of his Person" since he was "martial" and "fearless" enough to defend his own body. The critique here of Britain's increasingly opaque system of governance, its acquiescence to monied interests, and its formalization of a standing army was hardly subtle.

The parable went on to distance the targeted Hanoverian court from the generality of British people by adding how much the "nut-brown majesty" enjoyed eating "good old English" food. An example, served in a pub later on in the story, apparently suited the Cherokee's "abstemious Way of Living" and complied with their effort not to "guttle the Public Purse." These were the same reasons that such food had also suited "primitive

British kings in the early Days of Government . . . in those untax'd Ages, when every Man sat under his own Vine and enjoy'd the Fruits of his own Labour."

As in 1710, there were of course also apologist mobilizations of the visitors. On 10 September 1730, the loyalist *Daily Post* began one article, much like the earlier *Grub Street Journal* article, with a derogatory smirk about the visitors' intellect: "yesterday the Indian Chiefs were carry'd from their Lodgings in King Street, Covent Garden to . . . the Lords Commissioners . . . whereupon they were let known [why] they were sent for."[44] After a note on the Cherokee's feather-based greeting rituals, the report then recorded their supposed words to the Board of Trade: "We came here like Worms out of the Earth . . . naked and [you] put fine Cloaths on [our] Backs." Unlike *Grub Street*, though, the *Daily Post* piece proceeded to list all the ways in which the British were *not* like such savages: they know "good protocol" and run their events like clockwork; they are fearsome warriors with imposing and orderly "files of musketeers"; and they deal with inferiors "kindly" like a "Father" treats a "Son." As a result, they achieve the best imaginable trade agreements. For this newspaper, the Cherokee were useful as foils in the praise of progress.

Britain's boom in news culture was accompanied by a similar explosion in graphic media. The only surviving image of the seven Cherokee in London is, in fact, a printed engraving (figure 3.1). The original painting by an artist known only as "Markham" is now lost.[45] The engraving was made by Isaac Basire, who, as a well-known plagiarist at the time, may not have been the authorized copyist.[46] Like the Simon engravings of the 1710 Verelst images, Basire's work probably circulated at several levels: first as a pricey piece for the well-to-do, then as a cheaper mezzotint for more plebeian tastes, then as a copy made by other artists—flogged to undercut the original versions. The general crush of people milling about the Cherokee whenever they wandered the city was no doubt the designated market—a plentiful prey to enticements to purchase a memento of their fascination.[47]

The image itself is unusual, halfway between a formal group portrait and a more informal conversation piece.[48] It is certainly cruder than Verelst's collective depictions and much less detailed. But in most respects, the Markham image works similarly to those of Verelst: the subjects' savagery is easily secured by certain key flags but the ferocity potential in it hardly alarms or threatens. As in the Verelst images, the background suggests a sylvan New World more than the actual Old World, and the tattoos and feathers augment this idea. Also like the Verelsts, each subject

FIGURE 3.1.   The Cherokee delegation of 1730, engraving by Isaac Basire after Markham, London, 1730. © The Trustees of the British Museum.

carries a powerful weapon of some kind: swords, a club, a rifle, a bow and arrow, a tomahawk, and a dagger. The furthest subject (probably Attakullakulla) holds aloft a heart, which is the clinching determinant of the direction of the piece. The signals to savagery come together here as promises of comforting strength: however fierce these warriors appear, they indicate that their efforts will always act *with* British plans rather than against them.[49]

The overall print response, then, to the Cherokee visit panned out similarly to that shown the Iroquois: all assumed the visitors were representatives of savagery, though commentators were mixed in their valuation of savagery as well as in the ways they used it to reflect on British society. If anything, these reflections proved more pointed than they had been twenty years earlier because the expansionism at the heart of public concern had only escalated in the meantime. Amidst a cautious stability, the Cherokee highlighted some of the enduring, and even increasing, anxieties among ordinary British urbanites of the mid-Hanoverian age.

One marked difference between the Iroquois envoy and the Cherokee envoy, however, was the way the official agreements ended. While Anne's pledge to the Iroquois had been taken down as a minute, the formal pact between Cherokee and British was written up into a treaty. For its part, the Office of Trade and Plantations was keen to establish a proper agreement. After both an extra twenty years of experience with Native Americans and the percolation of more serious meditation on the benefits of alliance, the Office figured that the Cherokee not only promised critical military advantage but also the chance to make important territorial claims at some later date. In its correspondence to then Secretary of State, the Duke of Newcastle, the Office noticed that, like "the 5 Indian Nations" of New York, the Cherokee "are a warlike people and can bring Three Thousand Fighting Men, upon occasion, into the Field." Moreover, "words may easily be inserted . . . acknowledging their Dependence upon the Crown of Great Britain, which Agreement remaining upon Record . . . would greatly strengthen our Title in those Parts, even to all Lands which these People now Possess." The Office was confident that the process would be a synch: "as this treaty is to be only with Savages," it concluded its letters to Newcastle, "we presume His Majesty's Orders . . . may be a sufficient power for us to act."[50]

For the Cherokee, treaty-making had become so much the norm in the colonies that they simply assumed it when in Britain's metropolis.[51] More than likely, they had instructions from Moytoy to consent to any British overture at formalizing his position. Whether they had also been told to accept other proposals in his name was evidently cause for some contention. Nearly fifty years after the event, the colonial historian James Adair recorded his personal interview with the interpreter Eleazer Wiggan, who claimed that the Cherokee had fought fiercely among themselves over the wording of the final draft. They had "held a very hot debate in the dead hours of the night of September the 7th, 1730, whether they should not kill [the interpreter], and one of the war-chieftains, because, by his mouth, the other answered *To e u hah* [it is true] to his Majesty's speech, wherein he claimed . . . their land . . . as his right and property."[52] If there was such a debate, it still ended in Britain's favor, with the Cherokee eventually signing the treaty as it was on 9 September. How such resolution was achieved remains a mystery. The signatories may have been swayed by a late intervention by Cuming—as many newspapers believed—or they may have been driven by Ouka Ulah himself—perhaps making a play, in cunning imitation of his own leader, for the position that Moytoy had just created.[53]

Certainly the eventual "Answer . . . to the Propositions," given by the

Cherokee on 9 September, appears an awkward, even tight-lipped, document. While the respondents claimed to have come from a place "where nothing but darkness is to be found," they also pointed out that "you have everything, and we that have nothing must love you and can never break the Chain of Friendship that is between us."[54] Subservience and resentment mingle in disconcerting fashion.

Resent indeed they might, since the final treaty was hardly balanced. It demanded that the Cherokee trade exclusively with the British, that they never fight the British but always offer assistance against their enemies, that they help to capture any runaway negro slaves of the British, and that they obey common law in the case of murder. The British for their part pledged merely a vague "friendship," and granted them living space on lands they already possessed: "as the King has given his Land on both sides of the Great Mountains to his own Children the English, so he now gives to the Cherrokee Indians the privilege of living where they please."[55] The original six Cherokee blessed by Moytoy put their names to the piece, after which there was an exchange of gifts.

The Office of Trade was keen for the Cherokee to return home as soon as Whitehall had finished with them. Though Cuming protested that Ouka Ulah seemed to want to stay in Britain with him, the Office was firm: "their Lords Opinion [is] that it will be for His Majesty's Service that all the said Indians should return back to South Carolina . . . and their Lordships do desire you would persuade them all to return together."[56] The seven delegates set sail from Portsmouth on 7 October, accompanied by the new governor, Robert Johnson. Cuming was not with them: disappointed by the lack of gratitude shown him in Britain, the maverick adventurer now set his sights on an unsuspecting Jamaica.

The afterlives of the seven Cherokee are sketchy in the records. Returning home with a mostly weapon-based cache of gifts, the Cherokee met a decidedly mixed reception. Many leaders were furious to learn about the concessions made in their name; more were skeptical about the authority under which they had traveled in the first place. Certainly none acted as if their national sovereignty—or national problems—had changed in any fundamental manner. Nevertheless, the general inclination toward Britain over other European rivals remained with the Cherokee for the next three decades. The 1730 treaty had been an important refresher of the tie, and was referred to by factions of both parties at several junctions in the following years.[57] In 1756, Attakullakulla, then one of the most eminent leaders of the nation, reminisced that "I am the only Cherokee now alive who was in England or that saw the Great King George . . . Sir

Alexander said that it would be a much better effect if some of us would go with him."[58]

NINE FROM THE CREEK

The success of the 1730 mission was fresh in the mind of at least one other British entrepreneur when he set sail for the southern colonies in 1732. General James Oglethorpe, however, leading the first party of settlers to the new colony of Georgia on HMS *Anne*, was quite a different figure to Cuming. As a member of Parliament yet also fervent critic of Britain's thrusting commercialism, he was both more and less acceptable than his Scottish predecessor. Oglethorpe was traveling to Georgia as one of the founding members of the Georgia Trust Council, a body of twenty-one relatively idealistic leaders who wanted to establish Britain's first phil-anthropic colony. Following Oglethorpe's official exposé of British pris-ons in 1728, the MP had led a group to dream of creating a refuge for the nation's burgeoning number of debtors and other criminal victims of Hanoverian economics. Georgia was to embody the simple values of the stoics, share its land equitably, refuse all forms of slavery, and offer asylum to any persecuted Protestants from elsewhere in Europe. A more perfect vision of English republican principles at the time would be hard to find.

Arriving in January 1733, Oglethorpe and the 114 prospective colo-nists eventually settled near to where the tiny tribe of the Yamacraw—the exiled creations of the doomed Yamasee-Creek alliance—had established their township. Oglethorpe was quick to extend friendly relations to the Yamacraw mico, or headman, Tomochichi. Tomochichi was by this time a very senior elder (many contemporary reports put his age at over ninety, though later historians have lowered it to around sixty), who was prob-ably part Yamasee and part Creek himself.[59] Most Yamasee were long gone, but a large contingent of Creek had built up in the Yamacraw region postwar. Though living in formal exile from them, Tomochichi yet maintained warm relations with his "mother" nation. Oglethorpe knew the mico's goodwill was imperative, not only for Yamacraw consent to build his new utopia at Yamacraw Bluff but also to make contact with the 10,000 or so surrounding Creek, whose permission for settlement beyond the Savannah was actually entailed in South Carolina law.[60] For his part, Tomochichi was attracted to the security that Georgia offered his people against the ever-threatening encroachments of French and Spanish colonists, and, more important, of their various Native American allies. He gave his oral consent to Oglethorpe and agreed to help him negotiate with the Creek.

In May 1733, at the new British settlement, Tomochichi headed a meeting of all the Yamacraw families and about fifty Creek leaders. Within three days the Creek had agreed to a treaty that echoed to a significant degree the document that the Cherokee had just signed in London. In return for advantageous trading rates, the Creek allowed Georgians to keep the land they were now on, though they limited any future growth to lands that the Creek did not themselves use.[61]

Compared to some earlier colonists, Oglethorpe's legal problems seemed to have resolved in remarkably swift manner. But the General, being a keen student of contemporary history, knew that one additional act might bring significant rewards. "It is a policy of considerable benefit to our colonies," he noted, "and an expense well laid out, at proper Distances of Time to persuade some of the chiefest savages, both for Authority and Understanding, to visit Great Britain." The purpose of such an undertaking was to "awe" the visitors with the "high idea [of] our Metropolis" and thus secure friendliness and "even assistance" from them for at least one generation. "Such was the journey of the Iroquois chiefs in the reign of Queen Anne," Oglethorpe went on, "and such was lately the visit from our Indian Neighbours of Carolina. The good effects of these visits are well known to the Planters of those colonies respectively, and probably will be felt with pleasure for an Age to come."[62]

Oglethorpe's own relationship, however, with the "high idea of our Metropolis" was extremely mixed. The son of a brigadier to King James II, his family had experienced exile for some time after the Revolution of 1688. Oglethorpe retained quasi-Jacobitical leanings all his life, but as a servant of the crown and confirmed Protestant this was mostly expressed in general classical critiques of the debilitating luxury and political corruption that he believed all post-Revolution governments had encouraged. He often voiced his hatred of trade "as a thing low in its nature"—supremely exemplified by the "French in America." The economy he envisioned for Georgia was agrarian and sustainable. Small, self-sufficient landowners would circumvent the need for manufacturers and financiers. With no ravenous commerce to serve, no standing armies would be required; citizens imbued with frugal virtues would be able to defend themselves against enemies and maintain peace with each other. Unlike some earlier republicans, Oglethorpe did not see a contradiction between this ancient ideal and modern colonization. He believed that his own endeavors in the

New World followed the early Romans, who had "reduced the establishing of colonies into an art," because they were neither "pressed by poverty nor clogged by luxury." He evidently felt no threat from the example of the later Romans, who had—as many fellow classicists believed—allowed the wealth that came with expansion to corrupt their original values. Oglethorpe's understanding of Native Americans was also colored by the early ancients. He thought that the Creeks anointed their bodies and wore togas just like the Greeks. He admired what he saw as their disdain for movable property and acquisitiveness, remarking at one point that "I am a red man, an Indian in my heart, that is why I love them." Both his variety of colonial ambition and representation of New World indigenes were, then, implicit retorts to the methods of many British contemporaries and indeed of the British government. He must have harbored some ambivalent feelings as he readied Tomochichi and his entourage for the journey over to his home country.[63]

The entourage in the end numbered nine. The mico was accompanied by his wife, Senauki; his young nephew and heir, Tooanahowi; his brother, Hillispilli; his Creek cousin, Hinguithi; and four other attendant Creeks—Umphichi, Apokutchi, Santachi, and Stimaltechi.[64] The envoy could reasonably be called "Creek" in makeup, which is how Oglethorpe and most commentators referred to it. The ten set sail for Britain on 7 April 1734, additionally accompanied by John Musgrove—the husband of half-Creek Métis, Mary Musgrove—as interpreter.

THE CREEK IN BRITAIN

Whether triggered by knowledge of Oglethorpe's own philosophies or not, the Creek envoy inspired numerous critiques of British expansionism along roughly classical-republican lines during their four-month stay. Of course, they inspired many stirring defenses too. In other words, the delegation acted very much like their eighteenth-century predecessors, both in highlighting the ideological divisions in Britain's early commercial society and in enabling a degree of mutual expression on them.

Before the Creeks hit the urban press, however, they enjoyed a short stay at Oglethorpe's family estate in Surrey while the Georgia trustees hurriedly arranged accommodations for them in their Westminster offices. Arriving as a charge of a chartered trust rather than of the crown directly proved a far better deal for New World visitors: in contrast to the stipends presented to either the Iroquois or the Cherokee, Tomochichi and his group were showered with gifts and monies worth upward of £1,000.[65] As with the earlier delegations, they were exhorted to spend the cash in pursuit of "whatever is curious and worthy [of] observation."[66]

As they were observing, needless to say, they were also being observed. One of the most important discussions of the envoy came in the form of an ode, possibly written by a young Thomas Fitzgerald, Westminster local and friend of the now ageing Alexander Pope.[67] Though printed on quarto pages—evidently meant for binding—*Tomo-Cha-Chi: An Ode* soon gained wide popularity due to its retailed association with other, well-known poems about Georgia.[68] The eleven verses begin with an exclamation over the main visitor: "What Stranger this? and from what Region far? / This wond'rous Form; majestic to behold?" The ode retains a gaping admiration of "uncloath'd [and] artless" Tomochichi throughout. Its ultimate purpose, though, is to put his host into dark contrast. Britain in 1734, the poet believes, has "sunk down from its Meridian Height / The noblest Ardors now no more inflame." The cause is simple: the rapacious greed that led British explorers to plunder the lands from which Tomochichi has himself just come.

> Wealth without End, from such Exploits as These,
> Crown'd our large Commerce, and extended Sway;
> And hence dissolv'd in soft luxurious Ease,
> Our ancient Virtue vanish'd soon away.

In its wake are "inglorious times . . . our degenerate race . . . a prostituted age." Oglethorpe's exact politics are invoked, nostalgically, in the sixth stanza:

> Rare to be found is the old gen'rous Strain
> So fam'd amongst us once for Patriot Zeal,
> Of try'd Good Faith, and Manners staunch and plain,
> And bold and active for their Country's weal;
> Clear from all Stain, superior to all Fear;
> Alas! Few such as These, few OGLETHORPES are here.

The final boot comes in the acknowledgment of the virtues that the poet most admires in contrastive Tomochichi: "aw'd by no slavish fear, from no vile passions blind," this visitor reminds of all that most concerned the disaffected of Hanoverian society. Hardly a work of "praise" or glorification, this ode sat firmly within the critical camp of eighteenth-century Britain.[69]

The press was slightly more subtle when it decided similarly to employ the latest savage envoy for national critique. The *Edinburgh Caledonian*

Mercury also figured Tomochichi's simplicity in favorable manner, but piled on his supposed admiration for British achievement to such a degree that it coyly implied excessiveness. Upon seeing "the grandeur of the British court . . . the richness of the inhabitants, the magnificence of the buildings, [and] their extensive trade and commerce," Tomochichi was said to wonder why "the English should go out of such a land of plenty to seek support in a foreign country"?[70]

Of course, the press also reported more allegiant versions of the envoy. The newly established *Gentleman's Magazine* applauded the way in which "the British nation" handled the latest dispatch of savages. "They have been entertained in the most agreeable manner possible . . . nothing has been wanting . . . to give them a just idea of English politeness." The article noted particularly how impressed Tomochichi was with British displays of military might: no wonder that they seemed "heartily attached" by trip's end.[71] The *Monthly Intelligencer* likewise took the opportunity to note the "handsome" hospitality and "respectful" generosity shown by Britons when dealing with savages, and was pleased to see that Tomochichi also recognized "the Power and Greatness of the King and Nation."[72]

Congratulatory responses to Tomochichi were also found, as with his predecessors, in pictorial form. In one of several uncanny twists in this story, it was the son of the 1710 Iroquois' portraitist who painted the two most enduring images of the envoy. Like his father before him, Willem Verelst was a moderately successful painter in London. Whether he was requested to paint the official group portrait of the envoy (figure 3.2) because of his father's prior work or because his brother, Herman, happened to be the trust's accountant remains unclear.[73] After the official undertaking, and probably also paid for by the trustees, Willem as well painted a half-length of Tomochichi standing beside his heir (figure 3.3).

The group painting, commonly known as *The Trustees of Georgia*, was commissioned to hang in the trust's Westminster offices.[74] Some copies were made, though their distribution is difficult to calculate. The work was intended primarily to confirm the trust's vision of itself and assure the king of his well-judged patronage. It includes thirty-five figures—twenty-seven Britons and eight Creek. Tomochichi stands with right arm extended to the boy Tooanahowi. The interpreter Musgrove stands behind him. Oglethorpe is in black giving Tooanahowi a book. Senauki is under the window wearing a salmon-colored European dress.

Despite the quotation of one of his father's Iroquois portraits in the placement of a small dark bear at bottom right, Willem Verelst created in this painting quite a different image of Native American visitors than

FIGURE 3.2.   Willem Verelst, *Trustees of Georgia*, 1734. Acc. no. 1956.0567.
Courtesy of the Winterthur Museum.

had been seen earlier in the century.[75] Most obviously, the setting is for
the first time identifiably Old World. The sumptuous décor of the trust's
offices, with glimpses of Westminster Abbey out the window, firmly
establish emphasis on the British side of the transaction. The Creek are
depicted with enough flags to an essential savagery for the viewer to
know what they are (the tattoos, the nakedness, the feathered accoutrements, and the animal totems), but the focus is rather more on what the
British can offer than on what savages can promise. As several critics
have noted, the British figures vastly outnumber and outpose the Creek
figures.[76] Elevated in position and larger in stature, they appear an admirable collective, united by their virtuous ambitions. The Creek mostly
hold classical stances—continuing Oglethorpe's understanding of them—
but are categorically the more marginal, supplicant party.

That said, from within the circle of eight Creek, it is Tooanahowi who
holds most attention. The brilliant blue of his jacket makes him appear
brighter than Tomochichi. That Tomochichi is gesturing to his nephew at

FIGURE 3.3.   John Faber II, *Tomo Chachi Mico or King of Yamacraw, and Tooanahowi His Nephew,* after Willem Verelst, 1734. Acc. no. 1946.9.763. Yale University Art Gallery Mabel Brady Garvan Collection.

the same time as Oglethorpe is bestowing the book confirms the focus on the heir over the present mico. Tooanahowi's youth, drawn in a comfortably humble pose with completely European dress, foretells a long and peaceful future for the Georgian settlers. Oglethorpe had been careful to outline the situation to his fellow trustees, mentioning numerous times that Tomochichi called Tooanahowi his heir.[77] The painter evidently understood the implication, and focused on the figure most likely to protect British interests into the proceeding decades.

Verelst's second painting from the visit (figure 3.3) was much more quickly and widely circulated. Copied in affordable mezzotint by John Faber Junior (the son of another imagist of the 1710 Iroquois), it returns to the more typical style of depicting Native American envoys. Surrounded by the wooded foliage of the mythical New World forest, uncle and nephew are covered in the usual signs to a savage lifestyle. Their lack of martial equipment make their intentions—if proudly figured—all the more straightforward. Like the group portrait, it emphasizes the possible longevity of the British alliance by including the youthful, pliant Creek heir. The eagle that Tooanahowi holds was perhaps the actual bird given to the king's son, Prince William.[78] At the least, it stands for the strange yet peaceful culture understood by such a gift.

The mezzotints of this print, like the engravings of the 1730 Markham Cherokee, probably sold in their hundreds to the crowds that were said to follow the retinue all over London. A "prodigious concourse of people" clamored around them when touring Westminster Abbey, St. Paul's Cathedral, and the Royal Exchange, while a "great concourse" formed when they took in Hampton Court, Windsor Castle, and Eton College.[79] (At the latter, the visitors won some everlasting friends when Tomochichi "begg'd" the schoolboys a holiday, "which caused a great Huzza."[80]) During a brief later spell at Oglethorpe's Surrey estate, "a great Number of the Country People," too, were said to have "flock'd in to see them."[81]

Other venues on the envoy's itinerary included the Archbishop's house at Lambeth, the Tower of London, Christ's Hospital School, Bartholemew Fair, Hyde Park, various merchant clubs and the usual theaters and pubs.[82] New on the list for Native American visitors was the Royal Society, Chelsea's veterans hospital, and Oxford University. As ever, the delegates were mostly assumed to be delighted or impressed.[83] Some contrary observations were made, however. The chair of the trust, the Earl of Egmont, learned that they were displeased by the "naughty" language of the "rude multitude" overheard when traveling on a barge down the Thames. They were similarly disapproving of the display of Henry VIII's codpiece at the Tower: "there were many women that crowded in and liked the sight," recorded Egmont, "but [Senauki] turned her head away. [Tomochichi's] reflection on it was that to be sure that man had more wives than one."[84] Likewise, when visiting the Royal Society, the *Grub Street Journal* caught wind that the mico was "so afrighted at the sight of [Dr. Desaguliers'] magick lanthorn . . . that he will hardly be prevail'd on to see any more curiosities of that nature."[85]

The envoy was probably more satisfied than not in the end, since its official engagements were—at length—quite successful. Its first meeting with the trustees on 3 July laid out the priorities. Tomochichi made clear his desire for Christian instruction and peaceful relations, but Egmont as Chair responded rather vaguely that the trust certainly wished for a "strict Alliance and Friendship with You."[86] In later meetings, Tomochichi got more specific. He asked for a missionary, fair trading agreements, the prohibition of rum, favorable rates of trade over that given other native nations, and a kind of ombudsman for the settling of disputes. The Trust tried to stall. Only after they learnt that Tomochichi had detailed knowledge of how earlier treaties between Britons and Native Americans often went awry at the latter's expense did the trustees give their formal consent. Egmont mused that it seemed the "Indians [really did have] great reason to complain of hard wage."[87] The Trust helped Parliament pass an Act the following year that addressed most of Tomochichi's concerns.[88]

The Creeks met twice with King George II. Their apparel on both occasions was cause for some discussion. The *Gentleman's Magazine* had it that the delegates wanted to appear "in the Manner they go in their own Country, which is only with a proper Covering round their Waste, the rest of their Body being naked." Oglethorpe thought better of this idea and evidently tried to get them into breeches and shirts. These, however, were roundly rejected by the Creeks.[89] The final compromise was a fantastical invention that some commentators likened to the "Moorish Fashion."[90] Tomochichi wore a scarlet coat edged with gold lace and white rabbit's fur; the other men wore similar articles in blue; Senauki wore a scarlet wrapper, "except that she had no stays"; and Tooanahowi wore "a waistcoat of silver tissue"—possibly as painted in Verelst's group portrait.[91] Previous Native American envoys had experienced similar problems regarding official clothing. No party had ever been allowed to wear entirely their own dress, though all had retained something that was familiar. The resultant hodgepodge, or fantasy, spoke to British desires for a balance between contemporary modesty and a display of the essential savagery that made each visitor attractive in the first place. But it also spoke of the elaborate negotiations that each envoy underwent with Whitehall protocol.

The first royal meeting was an introduction, marked by an ostentatious ceremony of Native American arrival in the king's carriage, driven by Sir Clement Cottrell (the son of the courtier who had driven the Iroquois back in 1710). George II was more than aware of the precedents involved, declaring that the Creek must be welcomed in Britain "on the same foot as the Irocquois [sic] Indians were treated in Queen Anne's reign."[92] The second meeting was longer, involving both Queen Caroline and Prince William as well. Tomochichi declared his wish to "renew the Peace which [the Creek] long ago had with the English."[93] George II responded that he would always be ready to "cultivate a good Correspondence" with the Creeks. The subsequent exchange of gifts involved some eagle feathers on the part of the Creek, "as a sign of everlasting Peace," and a gold watch and pistol on the part of the British, symbolizing perhaps more than they realized.[94]

Only eight of the nine Creek attended the king—the same eight who were eventually memorialized in Verelst's painting. The ninth man, Tomochichi's cousin Hinguithi, suffered from small pox during most of the party's stay in Britain. Despite the ministrations of the reputable Hans Sloane, he died a few days after the last royal conference. The *London Magazine* was amazed to report that while the rest of the envoy "sat up all night" after Hinguithi's death, "crying and bewailing," they did not afterward hold a recognizable funeral ceremony. The cousin was buried between two boards held together with a cord in a small churchyard with only Tomochichi and a couple of others present to witness his final departure. The presiding Creek threw in the man's clothes with his body, "for the customs of those Indians is to bury all their Effects with them." The starkness of the event seemed a timely reminder of the savagery that these increasingly accomplished delegates were after all meant to embody for Britons.[95]

The death put a dampener on the whole venture for Tomochichi: he was soon requesting a berth back to his people at the nearest opportunity. The eight survivors, minus Oglethorpe, duly sailed on 30 October 1734. Tomochichi found a mostly favorable reception upon return, though there were some reports of anger over his "selling" of the Creek to the British and the envoy's incessant "lyes" about their journey.[96] In 1735, however, at a major conference of Creek in Savannah, one of the leaders noted that "altho' Tomo Chachi has been a Stranger, and not lived in [Creek] towns, amongst them, yet they See that in his old Age, he has done himself & them good because he went with Esqr. Oglethorpe to See the great King and hear his great Talk, and has brought it to them, and they have heard it, & believe it."[97] Thus, Tomochichi's place in larger Creek history was secured. His solicitations had led to the foundation of workable relations with Georgia and his overseas trip had assured their immediate future.[98]

While Christianity never really took with the Creek—not even with Tomochichi—the good will that the envoy had primarily sought maintained for nearly a generation. Tomochichi died in 1739—some say at the age of 97—while his heir followed him four years later, fighting for Britain against Spanish colonists and allies. Tooanahowi's death spelt the end of the Yamacraw as a political entity, though the tribe's recent reconciliation with their mother nation, the Creek, made its demise seem less a tragedy than a kind of closing of a chapter.[99]

. . .

The two delegations of Native Americans from Britain's southern New World colonies during the 1730s continued patterns of reception and experience first established by the Iroquois of 1710. In terms of reception, they met with similar dignitaries, ventured on similar itineraries of the metropolis, and provoked similar reactions from observing locals. These reactions—like those in 1710—figured the Cherokee and Creeks as various embodiments of savagery, which were in turn used to commentate on issues as different as the status of monarchy, the health of parliament, questions surrounding decadence, defense, and the growth of polite spaces and culture. When viewed from an eighteenth-century perspective, trained in both ancient and modern attitudes toward profound economic transformation, these issues easily came together under the general rubric of commercial expansion. However stable the 1730s were in comparison to the 1710s, these years shared the same pervasive—and corrosive—popular debate about the implications that might arise from such an ongoing contemporary phenomenon.

In terms of experience, the Cherokee and Creeks shared with the Iroquois a similar knack for internal power-play and traveler endurance, though the circumstances surrounding the different envoys need not be reduced to strict comparison. Their abilities in opportunism and stoicism would soon also be equaled by the next significant arrival from the New World, a man called Ostenaco, come on a mission almost entirely driven by his own hopes and desires.

4. Ostenaco and the Losing of America

By the time the Cherokee warrior Ostenaco and his small entourage arrived in 1762, Britain was once again mired in war and political upheaval. The relative peace of the 1730s had ended with Walpole's declaration of war against Spain in 1739 in order to maintain prior trade agreements and especially the lucrative *asiento* agreement that allowed British slave-selling in Spanish America. Despite the massive popularity of Admiral Vernon during the subsequent War of Jenkin's Ear, anxieties over the cost and effects of increased militancy never went away. One journalist in 1745 spoke for many when he decried this "cruel, bloody, expensive, and unnecessary WAR" against the Bourbons.[1] As the War of Jenkin's Ear bled into the continental War of Austrian Succession (in which Britain sided with Austria and Holland against Prussia, France, and Spain), the military and especially the financial consequences spiraled. Defense-spending crept up again to 1710 levels while the national debt by war's end was more than double its figure in 1713.[2] As with all of Britain's military commitments in the eighteenth century, war soon spread to the New World. Most hostilities in America during this period fell under the general rubric of "King George's War" and included particularly bloody fighting by the southern colonies of Georgia and the Carolinas against Spanish and French interests.

Before the mixed peace treaty at Aix-la-Chapelle in 1748, the British people also experienced another serious Jacobite uprising—in retrospect a threat with very little chance of success but, as many historians have realized, one that was nonetheless "perceived [at the time] as a crisis throughout the British Empire."[3] In less than eight years the nation was at war again; this time with Prussia and against Austria but as ever fighting mainly their chief foe of France. Indeed, hostilities between Britain and France had established in the New World a full two years before the official start of the Seven Years' War. By 1754 the two major European powers were in open conflict in various North American hotspots over issues of territorial and commercial control. This war saw an explosion in defense-spending and another near doubling of Britain's indebtedness.[4]

One especially gruesome theater of the Seven Years' War was the Anglo-Cherokee conflict of 1759–61. The Treaty of Friendship and Commerce signed by the Cherokee visitors of 1730—though hardly a binding document for either colonists or natives—played an indirect role in the outbreak of this conflict. Its trading terms had encouraged a strong Cherokee dependence on British goods over the years, channeled chiefly through South Carolina. Though Cherokee leaders always sought to maintain decent relations with French traders and other British colonies, precisely to mitigate against overdependence, the Native American nation was through the 1730s and 1740s deeply implicated in Carolinian fortunes and, as a consequence, in Carolinian conflicts with other peoples.[5]

The 1750s demanded ever-increasing military assistance from the Cherokee, which the Cherokee came to believe was accruing ever-lessening returns or appreciation. In early 1759 a small band of Lower Cherokees rebelled, slaughtering two Carolina settlers who had encroached too far into their hunting grounds. Within months, South Carolina responded by banning its trade in ammunitions and threatening a full-scale offensive. Several native leaders journeyed to Charles Town to call for calm but were captured instead and held as hostages in Fort Prince George. Attakullakulla, now an important leader in his own right, managed to get the most senior chief, Oconostota, released, though Oconostota in turn staged an attack on the fort's commander, which led—in fatal domino sequence—to the massacre of all the remaining prisoners. Total war ensued. Cherokee warriors held the upper hand for at least the first twelve months. Their ferocious campaigns on colonial settlements, especially in the Overhill region, necessitated a request from Charles Town for aid from neighboring northern colonies. Even with Virginian help, however, the Carolinians had retreated by September 1760 from most Overhill towns. But now focused only on Middle and Lower towns, the colonists gradually regained control through the following year. By July 1761, with their lower villages in tatters and the majority of their crops burned, Cherokee leaders finally began making overtures for peace.[6]

Attakullakulla, ever the diplomat and marked by many as an Anglophile, negotiated a treaty with the Carolinian army through the fall of 1761. His fellow leaders back in the Overhill capital of Chota, however, felt that an additional peace should be made with Virginia. They duly asked for a representative from Virginia to come to Chota to secure terms. No doubt seeing their own opportunity for a special alliance, the Virginians hurriedly sent Ensign Henry Timberlake, accompanied by one sergeant and an interpreter.[7]

Rather like Cuming thirty years before him, Timberlake was a naïve and fairly brittle character. Like Cuming, too, he had little experience of Cherokee people before his appointed (or self-appointed) meeting with them, even though Timberlake had been born in the colonies not far from Cherokee country. His perception of his colonial birth turned out to make him just as paranoid and striving as the unstable Scottish baron had been in 1730. Fortunately, both men left records of their adventures: Timberlake's was published, to little acclaim, in 1765.[8]

After a grueling trek up to Chota, Timberlake was received by a warrior called Ostenaco, whose name Timberlake had probably already heard due to his several well-known stints aiding earlier Virginian battles.[9] Timberlake called Ostenaco the Cherokee's "commander in chief," which was not an unfair estimate of the man's position.[10] By birth an inferior to such leaders as Attakullakulla and Oconostota, Ostenaco had nevertheless earned his prestigious title of Outacite (man killer) through exemplary service in both battle and diplomacy.[11] As it happened, both Attakullakulla and Oconostota were away in December 1761 when Timberlake arrived, so it fell upon Ostenaco to host the Virginian for the duration. Timberlake always insisted that his reception in Chota was the kindest imaginable, for, "tho savage people, [the Cherokee] always pay a great regard to any one taken notice of by their chiefs."[12] The talks were protracted, involving a wait for Attakullakulla's return in February 1762 as well as several requirements of assurance that South Carolina was not secretly planning a resumption of hostilities. Finally, in April 1762, the Overhill Cherokee felt satisfied with the intentions of both South Carolina and Virginia not only to halt fire but also to reopen trade, and so they ratified both treaties.

Ostenaco was chosen to escort the Virginian home. As the historian John Oliphant notes, the Man Killer could not have been forced to carry out this task by his Chota council.[13] Certainly in Timberlake's memoirs he appeared reluctant to do so—not least because of the colonists' deserved reputation for nabbing foreign peacemakers and turning them into hostages. But Ostenaco evidently found reason, and courage, enough in the end—perhaps figuring, as a warrior, that a personal connection with

British power would secure his well-being in the coming era of peace. The party set off after a formal valediction that involved cannon fire and song, attracting fluctuating numbers of fellow native trekkers along the way. By the time the party arrived in Williamsburg in May, Ostenaco and Timberlake were accompanied by nearly seventy other Cherokee, which "somewhat displeased" the receiving governor.[14]

Governor Fauquier nevertheless arranged for proper accommodations and presents for the travelers, as well as a formal ceremony to confirm the recent agreements. The following evening, Timberlake and Ostenaco were hosted at the College of William and Mary, where Ostenaco fatefully caught sight of a picture of King George III. Probably to Timberlake's considerable surprise, Ostenaco turned to him and said that he had long wished to see "the king my father"; that though this was his resemblance, he desired to witness the man himself. Since he was so near the sea now, was this not his best chance of satisfying his desires?[15] The governor was informed of the warrior's request. Though at first reluctant, Fauquier soon came around to the same understanding of potential advantage in sending Ostenaco to Britain that Ostenaco himself had seemingly so recently acquired. As Fauquier wrote to the secretary of state, it could only do the colonies good for such a powerful man to see "the Grandeur of our King, and the great warlike power we had at our command." Moreover, Ostenaco had grown up with Attakullakulla's boastings of his time in London, and wished "permission . . . to judge whether the Little Carpenter [Attakullakulla] had not told them lies."[16]

Timberlake was prevailed upon to switch roles and now become the escort. He agreed morosely, with extended grumblings about the sacrifices entailed, fearing—rightly, as it happened—that he would end much the poorer for it.[17] The expedition also included the sergeant who had earlier trekked to Chota, a young Thomas Sumter; a new interpreter called William Shorey; and two other Cherokee, known now only as Stalking Turkey or Cunne Shote and Pouting Pidgeon or Woyi.[18] A young Thomas Jefferson, then a student at the college, recalled the "great farewell oration" that Ostenaco gave to the remaining Cherokee on "the evening before his departure for England. The moon was in full splendor, and to her he seemed to address himself in his prayers for his own safety on the voyage, and that of his people during his absence. His sounding voice, distinct articulation, animated actions, and the solemn silence of his people at their several fires, filled me with awe and veneration, altho' I did not understand a word he uttered."[19]

REPEATING PATTERNS

Disastrously, Shorey the interpreter died during the voyage to Britain, inadvertently assuring a repetition of some of the worst communication problems that earlier Native American envoys had endured. On 16 June 1762 the reduced party docked at Plymouth, where Timberlake says a "vast crowd of boats, filled with Spectators" instantly drew around them, curious to identify the source of the "solemn dirge" that Ostenaco had broken into upon arrival. Though unheralded, the seaport crowd was captivated enough to follow the party after their disembarkation, "thronging" so heavily that they made it "almost impossible" for the Cherokee to enter a nearby inn.[20]

Timberlake was eager to get his charges to London as soon as possible, hoping against hope that Fauquier's letter of explanation had preceded him. Unfortunately, it had not, though Timberlake was lucky to find a secretary of state who seemed to understand the importance of Native American alliance. Lord Egremont had only just come into office at the end of 1761 when he learned of the Cherokee peace treaty. At the time he had written to the British commander-in-chief in North America, Jeffrey Amherst, in order to request his "Humanity and proper Indulgence" toward all conquered natives.[21] Upon hearing of Ostenaco's arrival, Egremont arranged for lodgings with an apparently well-patronized landlord on Suffolk Street near the Haymarket. Timberlake was to ensure that both the Cherokee and he himself "wanted for nothing"—which the soldier correctly took to mean that he should distract the visitors for the time required to organize a royal audience.[22]

When Egremont finally received the formal letter of introduction of the Cherokee from Fauquier, he replied with typical assurances of appropriate care but included as well an unprecedented note of irritation. "You rightly observe," he told Fauquier, "that such visitors are always troublesome, and these Chiefs are become more so after from the Death of their Interpreter . . . [Yet they will be] treated with all possible civility and Attention, and it is to be hoped they will return to their Country fully confirmed in their good Intentions."[23] No previous British official had in fact ever complained about the burden of caring for New World envoys. Egremont's impatience—though coupled with an astute comprehension of the significance of Native American allies to current British interests— foreshadowed a new aspect to the phenomenon of Native Americans in Britain. While Ostenaco's trip repeated many of the patterns established by earlier envoys, it also occasioned some fracturing of those patterns—to such an extent that it became effectively the last popular envoy of Native Americans to Britain.

Before the fractures, however, there were continuities. The most obvious was the way in which popular commentary marked the Cherokee as savages as soon as they arrived. The majority of reports focused on their numerous wild accoutrements. "Their Faces are painted of a Copper Colour," observed one, "and their Heads are adorned with Shells, Feathers, Earrings, and other Trifling Ornaments. They neither of them can speak to be understood . . . which obliges them to make their wants and desires known as well as they can by dumb signs."[24] "They seem to have no hair on their heads," said another, "and wear a kind of skull-cap adorned with feathers; their faces and necks are besmeared with a coarse sort of paint, of a brick-dust colour . . . their necks are streaked with blue paint . . . there seems to be a mixture of majesty and moroseness in their countenances."[25] Both the *London Chronicle* and *St. James's Chronicle* named them "savages" in the first instance. Rougher publications like Henry Howard's scurrilous ballad on *The Cherokee Chiefs* stooped to call them "Monsters" and even compared them to "Monkies."[26]

Like earlier envoys, too, the Cherokee were taken to many of the sites of power and magnificence around London. They saw St. Paul's Cathedral, Westminster Abbey, Kensington Palace, the Houses of Parliament, the Temple Bar, and the Lord Mayor's Mansion, as well as the Tower, the Artillery, the Arsenal, Greenwich, Woolwich, and Deptford. Their more leisured tour included the same theaters, spas, taverns, and sporting venues as their predecessors had seen but also the newly fashionable pleasure gardens within the city—especially Vauxhall, Ranelagh, and Marylebone. Of their standard itinerary, they were said to be, as usual, "highly delighted" and to some even "utterly astonished."[27] The practical Timberlake concurred at least on their views of the armaments: "their ideas were . . . greatly increased by the number of ships in the river," he wrote, "which I did not fail to set out to the greatest advantage, intimating that our Sovereign had many such ports and arsenals round the Kingdom."[28]

And even more than for previous New World delegations, the Cherokee of 1762 stirred huge spontaneous crowds. The port mob at Plymouth was in retrospect only an augury of the public sensation that these latest arrivals would prove. Their residence in Suffolk Street was soon surrounded day and night by locals striving to catch a glimpse of them— "at which they were so displeased," Timberlake commented, "that home became irksome to them."[29] Among those who waited for hours outside their door was the literary star Oliver Goldsmith. He queued all morning to gain a chance to meet them in person; when Ostenaco finally emerged, the Cherokee apparently kissed the writer on both cheeks, leaving his face covered in ochre and Goldsmith more than usually grumpy.[30]

At public venues, the crowds swelled in their hundreds, one paper reporting 10,000 persons at Vauxhall.[31] Not only large, these crowds were also frenetic in their eagerness to witness New World savagery. Observers described them as "a gaping multitude," who were "ungovernable," "intrusive," "mad [with] avidity," and "a hazard to health and life."[32] The *St. James's Chronicle* reported that when in Vauxhall, "a Songstress of the Grove attempted the Honour of traversing the Walks with the swarthy Monarch dangling on her Arm; but the Press was so much, as to Oblige him to retire . . . into the Orchestra." The paper was careful to add that once the Cherokee had stepped into the orchestra area and started "scraping" and "sounding" the instruments in animalistic fashion, the crowd was even more thrilled.[33] Without doubt, it was the supposed savagery of these guests which attracted this intense attention.

The Cherokee's popularity was not lost on the various commercial vendors about town. After Ostenaco's visit to Sadler's Wells spa, an advertisement appeared assuring patrons that they "would frequently come there" again.[34] A rival spa, Bagnigge Wells, responded that the Cherokee would also soon be touring its premises.[35] The Haymarket Theatre advertised that all its performances in July were put on "by Desire of the CHEROKEE King and CHIEFS," hinting at their at least sporadic attendance.[36] Perhaps the most telling proof of their appeal was that three "imposters" started appearing at all the same venues that the Cherokee frequented. With faces painted to look like the Cherokee, these men were assumed to be after a share of the moneys now being offered to secure a view of visiting savagery.[37]

Above all, though, it was the way in which Ostenaco and his entourage inspired deeply polemical commentary on Britain's contemporary situation that connected them to previous New World travelers. As ever, the Cherokee found themselves employed to further both critical and loyalist agendas. The critics largely followed a by-now traditional course, using the visitors' savagery as a launch into diatribes against Britain's warmongering, its excessive trade, and its descent into luxury. The *London Chronicle* was one of the most vehement in this period, publishing one letter by "Craftsman" (referencing the famous country-party journal from mid-century) who wanted to know what exactly could "apologise for peoples running in such shoals . . . to see the savage chiefs that are come among us?" Craftsman then likened the frenzy whipped up around "these poor wild hunters" to the frenzy that the British people always now evinced for "running after fights; a folly that foreign nations reproach us with but too justly, and which undoubtedly is pernicious as well as ridiculous."[38]

Later, the same journal published another letter by someone called Philo Britannia who wondered about the extent of Britain's overseas commercial commitments. While the writer believed that some trade is "useful"—such as that which had been enjoyed in the ancient world—he was sure that Britain today engaged in "too much" and thus opened itself up to "dangerous . . . luxury." He believed that the recent agreements with the Cherokee were yet another instance of excessive and unnecessary trade. The Phoenicians, Carthaginians, and Flemish had all been too fond of trade, the writer warned, "and they were all ruined." In anticipation of the cry that without a trade in luxuries there would not be enough merchant marines in Britain and consequently not enough sailors in time of war, Philo Britannia answered that "if we were not by commerce in pursuit of trifles round the globe, we should not need to station fleets in every part of it."[39]

Some less programmatic critics similarly took the Cherokee's visit as a cue to let off political steam. The well-known squibster Henry Howard produced a popular broadside that scolded British crowds for their decadent behavior:

> Who the Duce wou'd a thought, that a People polite, Sir,
> Wou'd ha' stir'd out o'Doors to ha' seen such a Sight, Sir?
> Are M[onster]s so rare in the British Dominions,
> That we thus shou'd run crazy for Canada Indians[?][40]

While Howard himself did not draw a straight line between excessive trade and an excessive culture (though he did connect trade's polite society with craziness), the link was more obviously made in a newspaper article by "You Know Who." This piece understood that trade was at the core of the mission to bring the Cherokee to London but played on the irony that it was also the reason why Britons now acted like a "Pack of Idiots, Beasts, and Barbarians" when presented with a view of authentic savagery. This writer also believed that the whole thing had been cooked up by the previous prime minister, William Pitt, in a sneaky, whiggish attempt to infect the "Dregs of the People" with the Cherokee's apparently well-known "dislike to Monarchy."[41]

The loyalist reaction to the Cherokee was slightly less typical. There was certainly the usual number of positive reports about the visitors' views of British might. When the *Public Register* waxed congratulatory about the Cherokee's amazement at the ships lined up at Woolwich, for example, it was only repeating the stance of many organs.[42] But loyalism itself was undergoing important redefinition in this period. The traditionally whiggish apologists for the Hanoverian regime were splintering between those who maintained their support unconditionally and those who were still pro-expansionist but now critical of some of the new king's proclivities—namely his professed antiparty politics and his unfathomable preference for the particular courtier Lord Bute.[43] George III's anti-ideological stance, together with his introduction of personal favoritism to a parliamentary system—and with a suspiciously Scottish peer, no less—caused many loyalists to reconsider the relationship between incumbency and patriotism. In other words, the 1760s witnessed a significant widening of the base of disaffection among ordinary Britons, even while the older schism over the question of expansion yet maintained.[44]

The majority of whiggish commentaries on the Cherokee, in fact, turned around the contentious issue of Bute. Appointed prime minister just two months before Ostenaco's arrival, this inexperienced northern royal intimate provided a timely focus for general anxieties about the king's commitment to Revolution principles. The aggrieved *St. James's Chronicle* was one of the first to use the Cherokee's presence to lash out at recent changes embodied in the figure of Bute. "Everyone knows that the reason why the Savage Cherokee King came over hither was on Account of the Antipathy, which [his] nation bears to the two chiefs that accompany him, one of whom is *Creek* and the other a *Catawa*," the paper claimed, implying that Ostenaco's mission was to create an alliance with Britain in the event of an uprising from his people. "When Kings chose Foreigners for their Favourites," the paper then tutted, "the Nation is sure to be undone."[45]

The *Royal Magazine* made a similar dig, though protected itself partly by transposing the current situation onto the meeting of Attakullakulla with George II thirty years earlier: "King George himself, as I have been told, once asked him, whether the people in his nation were free? Yes surely said Attakullakulla, for I who am their Chief, am free. The King was silent and a certain Prime Minister left the room."[46] A popular broadside entitled *Without/Within*, and priced affordably at just sixpence, exemplified the discontented whiggish cause at an even grittier level.[47] Dedicated to "the King of the Cherokees a Lover of Englishmen," the sheet was split in half. The top half offered a caricature of around a dozen kilted

Scotsmen all asking for places in the ministry. The bottom half offered doggerel:

> With Shame O BRITONS here behold
> Sly SAWNEY Pocketting your Gold . . .
>
> See here the STATE turn'd upside down
> The BONNET triumphs o'er the [crown]
> The half starv'd CLANS in hopes of Prey
> Come o'er the Hills and far away
> But let us still our Rights maintain
> And drive the LOCUSTS home again.

In the history of British representations of New World visitors, this piece held the unusual position of defending both English liberty and English wealth against the government of the day.

The polemics on British destiny occasioned by the Cherokee—however disparate they may seem out of context—were the strongest link between this envoy and earlier delegations of New World peoples. Ostenaco's envoy was similarly tied by its repetition of itinerary, popularity, and general representation.

FRACTURING PATTERNS

In 1762, however, some cracks in the eighteenth-century story of receiving New World peoples were also starting to appear. The first major divergence was the way in which the royal encounter played out. Previous delegations had met with relatively enthusiastic monarchs within a week or two of their arrival. Although always a highly staged occasion, royal audiences had proved important openers to, and legitimizations of, later popular discussions of New World visitors. This time, George III appeared reluctant to bother with the new arrivals. Egremont was evidently working hard behind the scenes, but it was up to Timberlake to field Ostenaco's complaints. "What is the reason that we are not admitted to see the Great King our Father, after coming so far for that purpose?" the chief asked his escort. Timberlake bluffed his reply, saying that His Majesty was "indisposed and could not be waited on till perfectly recovered."[48]

Eventually, the king capitulated. After more than three weeks of delays, he saw them at St. James's Palace, conducted by the familiar Sir Clement Cotterel, who had led the Creeks in 1734. As most before him had endured, Ostenaco was outfitted for the occasion in a bizarre mixture of apparel—a "rich blue mantle covered with lace" but also "scarlet sashes" and a heavily "ornamented" headdress.[49] But unlike his traveling forebears, Ostenaco seemed neither to receive nor offer any gifts of friendship at the court meeting. Unlike former monarchs, George III made no reference to their place in the royal tradition of receiving New World delegates.

George III granted them a ninety-minute audience, during which Ostenaco delivered a prepared oration. In the absence of the interpreter, Timberlake offered a garbled translation which he claimed to have recalled hearing from Shorey before his untimely demise. Whether coherent or not, the speech seemed to render the British king mute. "The man who assisted as Interpreter was so much confused," offered the *Annual Register* by way of explanation, "that he [George III] could ask but few questions."[50]

Despite the obvious awkwardness of the event, Timberlake reported that the Cherokee were pleased with the "youth and person" of His Majesty. The Virginian himself was probably happy to conclude the proceedings, after discovering with horror that Ostenaco wanted to smoke his pipe with the king: "I told him that he must neither offer to shake hands or smoak with the king, as it was an honour for the greatest of our nation to kiss his hand."[51] Ostenaco relented peacefully, agreeing to disagree about their respective customs.

Other incongruities in the reception of the Cherokee emerged during the official tour of British political sites. The usual review of military organization in a parade in St. James's Park went off script when the Cherokee panicked upon spying some grenadiers fixing their bayonets. The sight "threw them into such an Agitation," reported the *Public Register*, "that it was with the utmost Difficulty they were persuaded to advance a Step on the Parade. They had a suspicion of Treachery, were exceedingly Impatient to be gone, and when they got Home desired to see no more Warriors with caps."[52] The more dispassionate *Annual Register*—compiled at this time by a young and earnest Edmund Burke—observed that the Cherokee were taken to places that "could serve to inspire them with proper ideas of the power and grandeur of the nation; but it is hard to say what impressions these seights made on them, as they had no other way of communicating their sentiments but by their gestures."[53] Burke was one of the first commentators in the eighteenth century to reflect publicly on a central problem in the British tradition of hosting New World envoys: their journeys were always supported and welcomed in the name of advancing better relations with native allies but their effects and afterlives were rarely followed or analyzed. The strategy behind hosting New World peoples was always more gamble than well-considered policy.

The immense crowds that formed around the Cherokee—although in themselves a mere escalation of the popularity that previous envoys had inspired—also introduced a note of disquiet. For the first time, some commentators worried seriously about the justice of treating such people as archetypal spectacles. This was most evident in the outrage that flared over the crush of viewers at the Cherokee's residence. Rumors quickly spread that Timberlake was charging a fee for public admission. The Virginian remarked that the experience of being so accused was akin to a sheep's fate before "the wolf of rapine." He added with unintended piquancy a reflection on the state of being a stranger in a strange land: "a blunt Virginian soldier cannot know the laws of England, as little can he bear an insult from so mean a quarter."[54] Timberlake nevertheless set out to find the truth behind the accusations, and discovered that fees were indeed being charged, not by his party but by the shady landlord, nicknamed "Cacanthropos."[55] Timberlake's complaints, coupled with the growing general fury, forced Egremont to issue a formal decree against any future admissions to see the Cherokee without an order from him or his undersecretary.[56] The secretary of state's instructions revealed a fresh concern about dehumanizing—and indeed, commodifying—Native American visitors.

A publican writing in to *Lloyd's Evening Post* in late July shared a similar worry. Calling himself "Old Honesty," he lamented that his unscrupulous wife had become determined to lure the Cherokee into their tavern in order to attract more drinkers He protested his disgust at the notion, arguing that "I think no man has a right to make a property of them."[57] Oliphant has since called the publican's letter a cynical advertising ploy, but its claims for the Cherokee's liberties heralded an association between Native American visitors and certain legal rights that had not been present before.[58] It joined the growing air of discontent amassing around the Cherokee in 1762.

Discontent was likewise evident in the unprecedented musings that appeared post-visit about what Britons had failed to deliver to their guests. The question of legacy had rarely bothered previous commentators on New World visitors. The satiric ballad *Royals Strangers' Ramble* of 1710 had gestured to the inanity of returning the Iroquois home with none of the "advantages" of British enterprise, but few others had cared even to note the absence.[59] Now some newspapermen were fretting about what London had not provided. The widely distributed *Jackson's Oxford Journal* pondered whether Ostenaco should not have been "carefully instructed in the Principles of the Christian Religion? Should not he and his Attendants have been taken frequently to our Cathedrals to hear the grand service there?"[60] The *St. James's Chronicle* knew more certainly that the failure to evangelize had been a grave mistake. Had the "Savage Americans" been taught the "Excellencies of our Religion," it opined, "then indeed might his Cherokeean Majesty have entertained a wonderful opinion of our Wisdom." As it was, Ostenaco took back with him only impressions of spas and prostitutes and drinking, spreading the view across the ocean that a once mighty nation now revolved entirely around the frivolous products of luxury.[61]

The mixture of continuity and discontinuity that the Cherokee engendered in 1762 marks this envoy as a significant turning point in the history of New World travel to Britain. Of the few historians to discuss this delegation, Troy Bickham has recently made a similar point. He argues cogently that it was the imperial contexts of the visit that made it distinct from predecessors. "Emigration, evangelism, greater economic integration, and a more regular flow of communications [had] all helped to bring North America to the forefront of British attention," Bickham writes. Now that war threatened this increasingly recognized enterprise, the whole region was viewed in much sharper and more "pragmatic" light. Central to this new interest, Bickham goes on, were Native Americans—for the first time seen to be "real people living in real places" because only now were they understood by the general metropolitan population to be crucial in determining who won and who lost.[62]

The Seven Years' War undoubtedly did change the way that Britons thought about North America and all its inhabitants. But Bickham pushes for too clean a break, and for too neat a reason. The "pragmatization" of the region in British imaginations was not fully completed until the American Declaration of Independence in 1776. And it was not only the growing appreciation of Native Americans in this process that eroded their ideal status (for that had been partly existent for many decades) but also the massive elevation in the stakes of Britain being in North America. The size of the victory in 1763 and the consequent size of the loss in 1776 made the region seem not just newsworthy but now fundamental to Britain's very identity.[63]

In 1762, the shift to a more pragmatic view of America was still in its infancy. This is why the Cherokee delegation occasioned a combination of responses rather than a complete about-turn. Bickham argues that, in stark contrast to the Iroquois of 1710 who were seen as "little more than exotic curiosities" and used merely to "critique British society," the Cherokee of 1762 were viewed in a realistic way and treated instead as serious "players" in imperial politics.[64] His clinching example of this extreme switch is the exhibition of wax models made of the Cherokee twelve months after their visit. These "presses" of the delegates, exhibited in Mrs. Salmon's famous Waxwork Museum, were supposed to strive for an "accurate" portrayal, shunning past indulgences in stereotypical representation.[65] Not only does this example raise its own questions about what passed for an accurate portrayal of Native Americans in the era but it also ignores the numerous counterexamples of stereotypical representation that Ostenaco and his companions yet endured—the many references to their savagery, the myriad ways in which they were made foils for imperial argument, and, as we shall soon see, the several instances of careless attribution in the images drawn of them.

The vagaries of empire did make the Cherokee delegation of 1762 different to the foregoing Native American envoys to Britain in the eighteenth century. But the transformation of imperial context was itself long and complex, so this difference was uneven and incomplete.

LOSING AMERICA

Before sailing home at the end of August, Ostenaco's party inspired a number of likenesses from British artists. Some of the pricier periodicals included rough prints of the Cherokee leader: the *Court Magazine* carried a pipe-smoking caricature bust, while the *Royal Magazine* offered a full-length portrayal of "Austenaco . . . Commander in Chief of the Cherokee Nation."[66] Even the sixpence broadside by Henry Howard included an engraving of the three visitors, named respectively "Stalking Turkey," "Pouting Pidgeon," and "Man Killer."

One print of the Cherokee became especially popular. Entitled *The Three Cherokees, Came Over from the Head of the River Savannah to London, 1762*, it shows three and a half figures (figure 4.1).[67] Only some of Shorey is evident—his shaded, slightly menacing profile, apparently attacked by a Cherokee wolf, signifies his lamentable death. All four men are blithely misremembered in the print: the artist claims to depict "1. Their interpreter who was poisoned. 2. Outacite or Man Killer who sets up the War-Whoop, as Woach, Woach, ha, ha, hoch, Woach; 3. Austenaco or King, a great Warrior who has his Calumet or Pipe; 4. Uschesees, Ye Great Hunter, or Scalpper." Shorey, of course, was not poisoned but died of natural causes. Outacite—Cherokee for "man killer"—was another name for Ostenaco himself: the figure named so here borrows from the image given of Ostenaco by the *Court Magazine*. The figure named Austenaco—second from the right—plagiarizes the image of him given by the *Royal*

FIGURE 4.1.   *The Three Cherokees, Came Over from the Head of the River Savanna to London, 1762*, engraving, London, 1762. © The Trustees of the British Museum.

Magazine. Neither the name nor the stance of the final fourth figure can be traced, though as Stephanie Pratt observes "on the basis of the foregoing it may be presumed to originate in a recycled print [and hearsay] rather than observation."[68]

The casual attitude to accuracy in the print is also evident in the many allusions to Jan Verelst's earlier portraits of the 1710 Iroquois. The wampum offering of "Outacite" and the stance of "Uschesees" both copy strongly from Verelst's image of Tejonihokarawa while the wolf refers instantly to the image of Onigoheriago. Together with the preponderance of feathers and tattoos, the namings and borrowings in this image suggest that the presentation of the idea of savagery far outweighed any concern for authentic documentation.

As for the politics of the idea of savagery in this piece, it is harder to judge. On the one hand, the gorgets and demure positioning of the weapons imply a peaceful role for savagery in British affairs—much as the heart did in Basire's engraving of 1730. On the other hand, the dark half-image of Shorey adds a confusing counterpoint. Does his squint-ing, damning posture commentate on the Cherokee's destiny? Or does it indicate the diminished and fading nature of British claims to be worthy chaperones of such people?

Two other images of the Cherokee envoy survive that also broached some troubling questions. Both are substantial oils, painted by artists who exhibited in London's emerging art-show calendar. Francis Parsons was an aspiring portraitist who soon moved onto shopkeeping and art restoration.[69] In 1762, however, his rooms in Queen's Square were well enough known as a haunt for famous people eager to acquire a likeness of themselves that crowds kept a watch on comings and goings. When one of the Cherokee visited Parsons's studio in early July, there was such a press of would-be spectators that one woman fell down the stairs and required the assistance of two surgeons.[70] How or why the Cherokee came to sit for Parsons is not known. Parsons named the portrait *Cunne Shote*, which probably referred to the visitor known as Stalking Turkey (figure 4.2). In an elaborate disentangling, Pratt conjectures that *Shote* was an approximation of the Cherokee capital, Chota, from whence Ostenaco and Timberlake had most recently come. She further suggests that *Cunne* estimated the name of the last-but-one chief of Chota, Standing Turkey or Kunagadoga.[71] Whether Parsons believed that his sitter was Kunagadoga or whether he derived the name on the basis of the shared reference to Turkey is unclear. It is evident that Parsons had some knowledge of Cherokee history but how much and from whom remains a mystery.

Like most depictions of New World visitors, *Cunne Shote* included many references to the portraits of past visitors. The exotic-looking trees in the background resemble the attempt at New World foliage in Basire's engraving of the 1730 envoy. The upright, even haughty, pose of the sub-ject recalls the martial posture painted by both Basire and Jan Verelst. And the subject's prominent display of a knife echoes the positioning of weaponry in a range of earlier pictures.[72] All these aspects worked toward signaling an indisputable notion of savagery. What is new in Parsons is the detailed facial expression. Both more realist than in any previous portrait of a New World visitor and yet curiously also more distant and inscrutable, the face disrupts any straightforward reading of the function of savagery in the piece. Is the blankness of the expression merely a com-mentary on the simplicity of savagery, implying that even emotion is too complex a property for the type? Is it instead a warning of the power of savagery, hinting at the untold damage that such a freedom from senti-ment might wreak? Pratt has concluded that the painting was "terrifying"

FIGURE 4.2. Francis Parsons, *Cunne Shote Cherokee Chief,* 1762. Reproduced by permission of the Gilcrease Museum, Tulsa, Oklahoma, acc. no. 0176.1015.

in the eighteenth century.[73] A counter-argument could be made, however, that the centrality and brilliant shine of the subject's gorget overruled doubts in the end, turning the piece in favor of British loyalty. The work's final irresolution makes it another example of the instability found in the reception of this particular envoy.

Parsons exhibited *Cunne Shote* in the annual Society of Artists' show of 1763, for which he received some promising reviews.[74] Afterward, it was copied by the successful engraver James McArdell, whose print versions ensured a wide dissemination of the image through the 1760s.[75] Less is known about the distribution of the second oil produced from Ostenaco's visit. Ironically, this work was executed by the famous Joshua Reynolds. Although Reynolds had not yet become the inaugural president of the Royal Academy, or published his influential views on the proper purpose and hierarchies of art, he was by 1762 already one of the most respected

FIGURE 4.3.   Joshua Reynolds, *Scyacust Ukah*, 1762.
Reproduced by permission of the Gilcrease Museum,
Tulsa, Oklahoma, acc. no. 0176.1017.

portraitists in Britain. But his likeness of Ostenaco, entitled *Scyacust Ukah* (figure 4.3), was never exhibited in Reynolds's lifetime.[76] The artist clearly regarded it as a failure—though not so much, it should be noted, that he destroyed it.

Despite its lack of public profile, *Scyacust Ukah* is worth analyzing for the anxiety it caused the creator. Why did the work disappoint Reynolds so much? One short answer points to the way in which the painting failed to fit Reynolds's personal theory of art. According to his later publications, Reynolds believed that art, and especially painting, had an important role in reviving classical virtue in Britain. By "rais[ing] the thoughts, and extend[ing] the views of the spectator," painting in his so-called grand style would "be among the means of bestowing on whole nations refinement of taste," which in turn would obviate the worst excesses of appetite, "till that contemplation of universal rectitude and harmony which began by Taste, may . . . conclude in Virtue." Elevation was achieved, Reynolds went on, by questing always for the "general and intellectual" over what he variously termed "actual nature," "common nature," or the "vulgar and strict historical truth."[77]

Portraiture—Reynolds's own genre of choice—presented an obvious problem to this theory: its necessary attention to the particular sat uncomfortably with dictates about universality.[78] Reynolds's response to this challenge was twofold. On the one hand, an artist could include certain "single features" if they were minor or "innocent" enough to provoke neither "disquisition nor any endeavour to alter them."[79] On the other hand, an artist should work to make particularity serve the creation of "character." Character was an ideal notion, but at least as one of a "certain number" it promised some variety or texture to the otherwise rather monotonous story of human universality. At all times, diversity was only to be admitted in so far as it nurtured the overall ideal of an ultimate integrity, *not* for the sake of celebrating diversity itself.[80]

Following this elaboration, a Reynolds portrait of a Cherokee might reasonably be expected to portray—amid some minor or innocent details of cultural difference—a general idea about the character of savagery, designed to instruct a British audience on a universal theme. Considering Reynolds's neoclassical politics and aesthetic commitment to beauty, this general idea would no doubt include a noble savage, whose qualities compare favorably with those of Britons, and thus teach of the admirableness of their shared ancient virtue and the consequent interconnectedness of humanity. Had Reynolds's politics and aesthetics been otherwise, perhaps this general idea would have entailed a noble savagery reprimanding British waywardness from virtue, or an ignoble savagery congratulating or castigating contemporary Britons. Whichever the perspective, the subject would have been made into an allegory about savagery and contemporary British life—in much the same way, that is, that previous New World visitors had been represented for the past fifty years.

No such grand rendition of a general idea, however, is apparent in *Scyacust Ukah.* All the usual early-modern signs to the character of savagery are here reduced or muted. The smudged clouds in the background obscure any clear reference to savagery's primordial forest. There are no scarifications, no feathers, and no hide. The regal mantle—though similar to cloaks worn in other portraits—seems here crumpled and perfunctory. The implement held aloft is unidentifiable—it could be a Native American calumet or tomahawk, but from the manner of carrying, it likewise suggests a European scepter or baton.[81] Finally, the wampum around the subject's neck reminds of those shown in earlier works but its incorrect positioning in this piece (for a belt) once more disrupts any straightforward connection.

In place of any firm conceptual anchor, the main focus of the work becomes instead the complex individual gaze. Dignified, weary, bemused, and defiant, this sitter is his own person. We do not know if this was a fair likeness of Ostenaco, but we do now that this was precisely the kind of problem—together with portraying individuals as their own persons— that Reynolds shunned. As a Reynolds exemplar, thus, *Scyacust Ukah* was clearly a flop. Reynolds's notebooks reveal only a single line about the artist's meeting with Ostenaco. On 1 June 1762, it reads simply "The King of the Cherokees."[82] Whatever his reasons for wanting to paint the visitor's portrait, Reynolds evidently found the work had mutated into something unexpected by the end. The equivocation reverberant in the general reception of Ostenaco's party had somehow crept into his own representation of the leader at the deepest level. Where *Cunne Shote* had been ambiguous about its understanding of savagery, *Scyacust Ukah* appeared ambiguous about whether its subject was truly savage or not. A longer answer to the question of Reynolds's disappointment, then, is that the work not only failed to fit the artist's personal notions about art but it also tugged uncomfortably at the whole tradition of representing New World visitors as instructive savages. As influential as he was, Reynolds never sought the role of iconoclast or revolutionary. He would not have wanted his version of the phenomenon to cause any controversial reconsideration of its basis.

Of course, even if displayed, *Scyacust Ukah* would hardly have been the sole precipitant of a radical change in the British portrayal of Native Americans *generally.* The famous representations by Benjamin West from this very period, for example, continued far more than they ruptured older ways of imagining such people.[83] But in retrospect, Reynolds's portrait does appear as a kind of confirmation of the way that the British portrayal of Native American *visitors* was changing in the 1760s. Its ambivalence echoed the uncertainty evident in many graphic images of Ostenaco's envoy and symbolized the introduction of new anxieties now circulating around the group. *Scyacust Ukah's* unwitting realism finally undid the correlate between Native American visitors and paradigmatic savagery. No Native American visitor after Ostenaco—for at least the next century— suffered the same absolute association with this particular stereotype. Ironically, it was just as Britain was adding to its clutch of American territories that it seemed to lose one of the key elements in its cultural stock—

the eloquent image of savagery by which all its efforts at expansion had thus far been most succinctly debated.

. . .

Ostenaco and his fellow Cherokee companions finally departed England on 24 August 1762. Egremont arranged for them to stop at Winchester on their way to Portsmouth in order to witness a few last monuments to British achievement: they saw there the cathedral, college, and castle, including at the latter some French prisoners of war, who were said to provoke cries of "detestation" from the visitors.[84] The letter that Egremont sent with Ostenaco for the new governor of South Carolina, Thomas Boone, was a last testament to the anxiety that had sprouted around this latest envoy of Native Americans. In it, the secretary of state sought to find out whether the Cherokee had been offended by the unruliness of the crowds at their lodgings, and if so whether Boone could "conciliate" them sincerely for it.[85] Upon meeting their ship at Charleston, the governor duly asked after the Cherokee's impressions of London. Ostenaco voiced no displeasure about any part of his treatment abroad, but then he offered little praise or wonder either. Boone wrote back to Egremont that "whether from policy or constitution [he] appears to me astonishingly reserved and silent upon everything he has seen."[86]

In the historical records, Ostenaco's voice remains fairly quiet from here in.[87] Few scholars have traced his life after his visit to Britain, though he continued to be an important figure in Cherokee society till the very end. Upon returning to the Overhill region in December 1762, Ostenaco found that his daughter, Sokinney, had given birth to Timberlake's son, Richard Timberlake. His beloved grandson came to stand as a kind of metaphor for Ostenaco's mixed politics in later life. Ostenaco was among the few Overhill Cherokee to withstand the offers of the Transylvania Land Company to purchase their lands in 1775. A transgression of Britain's Royal Proclamation of 1763, which forbade the private purchase of Native American property, the purchase was condemned by various colonial governors but soon lost in the vortex of the American Revolution. The purchase may have contributed to Ostenaco's decision to side initially with the British when the War of Independence started, which in turn caused him to split from his once fellow leaders, Attakullakulla and Oconostota. In 1776 Ostenaco joined the Cherokee rebels of a younger generation, led by Attakullakulla's unfilial son, Dragging Canoe, who denounced the revolutionary-supporting older chiefs as all "rogues and

Virginians."[88] These rebels quitted the Chota area in defiance and resettled in Ultiwa (Ooltewah) near Chickamauga (Chattanooga).

Later, Ostenaco was a personal signatory to a peace treaty with several newly formed states, perhaps signaling most of all a desire to withdraw from the fray.[89] Though he had worked with Europeans his whole life to further Cherokee interests, Ostenaco was no doubt exhausted to find in his eighth decade that his people had become only further divided by their continued encounter with the newcomers. His political and martial spirit grew increasingly "reserved and silent" on multiple fronts: he died around 1780, ensconced in his new estate in Ultiwa, fondly remembered by family members as a proud and adventurous chief.

5. Passing the Mantle

From America to Oceania

Ostenaco's return to America was not the end of Henry Timberlake's involvement in New World travel to Britain. Two years later, Timberlake found himself escorting another party of Cherokee to London, this time under private patronage with no official sanction. Timberlake's *Memoirs* weave a pathetic tale of wrong turns and misfortune. Finding himself bankrupt in Virginia in early 1764, the ex-soldier connived a free passage back to London from a wealthy friend called Aaron Trueheart in the hopes of establishing a personal trade in tobacco. On the eve of his departure, he was visited by five Cherokee who had been searching for him for days. Believing Timberlake a special friend of enterprising Cherokee, they requested his help in gaining an audience with the Virginian governor. Timberlake duly introduced them to Francis Fauquier, whereupon he learnt that they wanted official berths to Britain—just as Ostenaco had been granted—in order to protest the "encroachments daily made upon them, notwithstanding the [recent] proclamation issued by the King to the contrary."[1]

Fauquier promptly refused them, saying that they "should have applied to [the] Superintendent for Indian Affairs; [and] that if the white people encroached, he saw no way to prevent it, but by repelling them by force."[2] This new willingness to dismiss indigenous applications for travel should have been a warning bell to Timberlake: if he had been able to read the auguries of change in his last visit to Britain more carefully he may have doubted the chances of any future envoy. As it was, he became unwittingly entangled in a second, far less successful, Cherokee bid to travel to the heart of the British empire.

Upon discovering Timberlake's own travel plans, the rejected party naturally turned next to him for assistance. Timberlake protested his financial incapacity, though he did approach his wealthy friend, True-heart, who turned out to be sympathetic. Trueheart paid for the Chero-kee's collective passages, joining the motley crew in the voyage out in September 1764. Tragically, two of the Cherokee and Trueheart himself died before the party reached London. Timberlake endeavored to help the remaining three Cherokee secure a meeting with the latest secre-tary of state, Lord Halifax, but soon received the first of many rebuffs. He wrote to Whitehall again and again, first emphasizing the visitors' important political position, then emphasizing his own mounting debts on account of colonial business. Halifax was not only immovable but also cagey about his reasons for refusal. Close to despair, having taken on the burden of accommodating the unwelcomed guests, Timberlake spewed forth a grim prophecy for metropolitan power: "should these people com-mence a war, and scalp every encroacher or even others, to revenge the ill treatment they received while coming in a peaceable manner to seek redress before they had recourse to arms, let the public judge who must answer it."[3]

Eventually Timberlake gathered that Halifax was concerned about both the Cherokee's lack of colonial endorsement and Timberlake's own growing reputation for scurrilous showmanship. Timberlake's earlier im-plication in the furor over Ostenaco's privacy had "made such an unfa-vourable report of me, that either his Lordship believed, or pretended to believe, [that I had the Cherokee] brought over for a shew." Two years on, the anxiety about commodifying Native American visitors seemed only to have intensified. Timberlake thought that the situation was made even worse by the recent popular memory of "three Mohock Indians [who] were . . . made a shew of in the Strand and immediately confounded with the Cherokees."[4] This comment probably refers to the two Mohawks who had been displayed for profit briefly in early 1764 by two unscrupulous New York entrepreneurs. Their plight had roused some outrage at the time, though not for long as they were whisked off after only a few weeks to The Hague to suffer similar indignities.

While these Mohawks became an issue again in later British commen-tary, Timberlake and his benighted Cherokee fell from all consideration by the end of the year. The Virginian was apoplectic about the accusations against his character, pointing out that had he "showed them, I should not have been under such anxiety to have them sent away; I should have wished their stay, or been able to have them sent back without any inconveniency in raising the necessary money for that purpose." He man-aged to scrape their living together into 1765 and found a berth for the

Cherokee to return home by March. While in Britain, the Cherokee kept an almost invisible profile as Timberlake's circumstances "would not permit their going . . . to public diversions as they should have done."[5] Once back in America, they faded completely from historical view. Halifax did eventually reimburse Timberlake a small fraction of his costs—probably out of relief that the problem had finally retreated—though its miserliness was cold comfort. Timberlake died in September 1765 after a short stint in debtor's prison for failing to pay the last of his lodging bills.[6]

By this time, the Mohawk scandal that Timberlake believed had abetted his downfall had returned with a vengeance. In retrospect, it was the occasion that formalized Britain's disenchantment with Native American visitors. During the rest of 1764 the two Mohawks had remained in the Netherlands. Their hasty dispatch from Britain had been in fact a low move by one of the colonial entrepreneurs against the other. Lawrence Blasius had stolen the Mohawks away from his partner-in-scurrility, Hyam Myers, in February 1764 in order to become the sole beneficiary of their unfortunate display in numerous Dutch towns. Myers tracked Blasius down in Amsterdam with the help of the British ambassador to The Hague, who ordered him to return the Mohawks to America forthwith. Myers defied these official orders and continued to display his charges in both Amsterdam and London so as to recoup, as he later claimed, his doubled expenses.[7]

On 4 March 1765, London's *Gazetteer* was advertising "two Indian Warriors of the Mohawk nation" at the "Sun Tavern . . . from ten in the morning till six in the evening" for one shilling per person. The next day, "complaint was made" of the advertisement in no less an establishment that the House of Lords. Myers as well as the proprietor of the Sun Tavern, John Schuppe, were ordered to stand before Parliament. Here Myers explained that the Mohawks had originally approached him for passage to Britain to "see their father [King George III?]." As he had inadequate funds, he resolved to afford their venture by showing them for gain.[8] It is not recorded what the Mohawks thought of this idea.

The Lords' response, on top of forbidding Myers to continue his venture, was to issue a general twofold resolution: "1. That the bringing from America any of the Indians who are under his Majesty's protection, without proper authority for doing so, may tend to give great dissatisfaction to the Indian nations, and be of dangerous consequence to his Majesty's subjects residing in the colonies. 2. That the making a public shew of Indians, ignorant of such proceedings, is unbecoming and inhuman."[9] The first part of the resolution chimed with the rhetoric of the 1763

Proclamation in North America, acknowledging long-standing anxieties about indigenous allegiance—especially when it came to potential or former allies of the French. Ironically, earlier manifestations of these same anxieties had led Britons to aid Native American travel to the metropole. Now their fear of a traveler's poor opinion during such a trip had the reverse effect, reflecting perhaps more than anything else a new, creeping self-doubt about the ability of London to live up to its ballooning imperial reputation. The second part of the resolution had almost certainly never been articulated in this way before—though like the first part it continued the gist of some older beliefs. Britons had always believed that savages were human, despite their supposed ignorance, and were therefore entitled to be treated as such. What was new was the explicit reference to a protocol for humans, couched in the emerging language of individual-based humanitarianism.[10] The Lords' pronouncement tipped Native American visitors fully into late-Enlightenment realms of British thinking.

Together, the recognition both that Native American visitors could unravel increasingly sensitive imperial structures and that Native American visitors could now be full agents in individualist discourses exploded the myth of such people exemplifying archetypal savagery. In somewhat perverse consequence, Native Americans after the mid-1760s never inspired quite the same level of interest in quite the same way as had their predecessors. Previous interest had been based explicitly on the Native American epitomization of savagery; later instances of interest—rarer as they were—were based more on idiosyncratic or unique factors.

Of course, Native Americans continued to turn up in Britain after 1765. Alden Vaughan has counted at least eight delegations arrive before the American Revolution from places as far apart as Labrador and the Mosquito Coast.[11] But these delegations were either one of two things: they were quiet affairs of diplomacy that made little mark on popular or official minds, *or* they were celebrated events though now for completely different reasons than had animated earlier visits. In neither case, that is, did they continue British fascination with Native Americans as savage ideals. Examples of the former group included the two Narragansett brothers from Rhode Island who traveled to plead land rights in 1768; a Chappaquiddick who came for the same reason in 1772; and a grand total of twelve Inuit—scattered over four separate delegations—who arrived as traders' guides from 1768 to 1774.[12] All visited to undertake political business of a sort but none stirred much response from general or local audiences.

Examples of the latter group—the celebrities—include the Mohegan Samson Occom, who came in 1766, and the Mohawk Joseph Brant, who arrived in 1775. Both these visitors, it is true, attracted significant attention: Occom as an evangelical preacher determined to raise funds for the establishment of Dartmouth College, and Brant as a captain in the British Indian Department sent over to reassure the government of Mohawk allegiance against revolutionary colonists. Neither Occom nor Brant, however, were linked primarily with the idea of savagery—their appeal was not phenomenal but rather individual. Occom—like Pocahontas more than a century before him—was feted as a demonstration of complete Christian conversion. Brant—the reputed step-grandson of one of the 1710 Iroquois—was so hailed as a loyalist that he was "easily . . . mistaken for a white man."[13] By the late 1760s, the day of the Native American envoy as New World savage exemplar was well and truly over.

This is not to say, however, that the concept of New World savagery was also dead.[14] Late-Enlightenment humanitarianism did not penetrate everywhere for everyone at the same time. The idea of New World savagery thrived well into the next decade, and indeed into the one following, but it was now shouldered by a different set of people. If they had not been so busy dealing with the changed complexities of politics at home, Native Americans would no doubt have been relieved to find themselves free of the mantle of paradigmatic human simplicity that had folded over them for nearly three centuries. But they could not have guessed that it was now to be passed on to people living between two and twenty thousand miles west of their divided continents. From the late 1760s to the outbreak of the American War, the various peoples of the far-flung Pacific Isles gradually came to stand as the new bearers of the burden of savage exemplification for a British public still mixed in their views of overseas expansion.

THE AFTERMATH OF PEACE

In many ways the Peace of Paris had been the true origin of the shift in British thinking about the center of the New World. Its confirmation of Britain's victory in 1763 assured both the full historicization of America, which in turn severed the region finally from useful fantasy, and the concerted exploration of Oceania, which opened up new opportunities for idealization.

As many historians have noted, the stunning success of 1763 precipitated only the briefest of celebrations. The sheer size of the spoils, together with the final costings for their attainment, soon generated keener anxiety about empire than had been felt in Britain all century. The victory had indeed been huge. Britain ousted all serious European competition from North America, gaining control of Canada and most territory east of the Mississippi. In return for the small concessions of Guadeloupe, Martinique, St. Lucia, Gorée Island, Cuba, and Manila to France and Spain, Britain secured dominance in all European-affected areas of Asia, Africa, and the New World. But the price tag was also overwhelming: by 1763 the national debt had nearly doubled to a staggering £132 million. After initial gasps of self-congratulation, British governors and subjects alike had to face the moral and practical consequences of their achievement.[15]

Many anxieties were voiced in the familiar terms of the classical anti-expansionist. One angry pamphleteer echoed long-held concerns about the economic implications entailed in overextension when he spluttered about a peace which, "under the Name of Security, we sought with Eagerness extensive and unprofitable Empire."[16] In this regard, he was joined by the well-known editor of *The Critical Review*, Tobias Smollet, who ventured "to say that we have already made more conquests than it is our interest to retain . . . our very existence as a . . . nation, seems to be at stake . . . the public credit is drawn so fine as to threaten cracking at the very next stretch."[17] Some members of Parliament were more exercised by the political effects of excessive acquisition. While Edmund Burke pondered that old nugget of how the "strong presiding power" necessary to command an "infinitely diversified empire" was to be reconciled with traditional English liberties, another harder-line politician, the Earl of Chatham, stated flatly his fears about Britons' now increased exposure to "Asiatic principles of government."[18] It was no coincidence that the great Enlightenment historian Edward Gibbon resolved to embark upon his influential study of the decline and fall of the Roman empire just one year after the peace was signed. Nor that the writings of the famous seventeenth-century republican critic Charles Davenant—who had argued against any ambition for more provinces in America "than we can either cultivate or defend"—were published as a collection in 1771.[19]

But traditionally pro-expansionist pundits were also anxious in 1763. However much some were proud to have "over-run more world" in one war than the Romans had conquered in a century,[20] they had still to deal with the pressure that a massive influx of non-Protestants exerted on their toleration principles; with over 200,000 demobilized soldiers returned unemployed to the metropolis; and with an unnerving estimate by government advisers about what the new colonies were going to cost to maintain. It was these more practical concerns that generated the actions that would eventually help to de-idealize America, for they in turn would inspire a colonial backlash which, no matter how unexpected, started the gradual recognition of the colonies as a separate political entity.

Together with increased administrative attention to existing controls such as the Navigation Acts, Whitehall introduced into the colonies two significant revenue-raising measures in the form of the Sugar Act of 1764 and the Stamp Act of 1765.[21] The "fierce and ominously concerted colonial resistance" to these developments, and the story of radicalization that followed, is well known.[22] Less appreciated, though, is how "genuinely surprised" Parliament was to solicit such an angry reaction.[23] Despite the depth of their division about imperial expansion—and despite later popular controversies about American independence—most ordinary Britons would also have been surprised in the mid-1760s.[24] Their shock was no reflection of a united sympathy for government action but rather a sign of how tightly bound the peripheries and center still were in the minds of most metropolitans at the time. Just as an MP like Edmund Burke— an early supporter of the American revolutionaries—yet believed in the 1760s that the colonies should be treated like a "corporation" under one constitution, so a popular novelist like Frances Brooke—in her patriotic *History of Emily Montague* (1769)—was sure that all imperial outposts were as "infant" children to dowager elders.[25] Indeed, the terminology of companies and families had been rife through British discussions of New World colonies since the mid-seventeenth century.[26]

By the early 1770s, however, official and popular rhetoric about America was beginning to evince a subtle but significant shift. Instead of discussions about corporations under constitutions, Burke was now articulating his support in declamations about the right of "countries" to be free from slavery.[27] The feisty *London Evening Post* was talking of America's just cause for "SELF DEFENCE" while the more cautious squib, *A History of the Old Fring'd Petticoat*, was writhing with distress over the idea of American "sovereignty." In place of metaphors about parts within wholes were now admissions about separate states. [28]

To understand the American colonies as a separate state was in effect to grant that state full status as a historical subject. No more a land as productive of origin myths and morality tales as of raw materials and foodstuffs, America in the British imagination now acquired all the economic, provincial, and demographic peculiarities recognized in any other foreign power. The *Realpolitik* of imminent colonial secession—whether supported in principle or not—put an end to all the promising aspects implicit in America's old reputation as a "New World." No one articulated this loss after the event with more pathos than the social theorist William Robertson. His 1777 epic about the clash of commerce against savagery in America had taken the reader up to the turn of the seventeenth century.[29] Though he vowed to discuss the eighteenth-century period in later volumes, Robertson never delivered. "I long flattered myself that the war might terminate so favourably to G. Britain, that I might go on with my work," he explained in 1784. "But alas America is now lost to the Empire and to me."[30] Robertson was less stumped by British defeat than by the ruination of his hypothetical canvas for philosophical thought. After all, a revolution by British descendants hardly damaged his general thesis about commercial progress. Instead, Robertson—ironically best known today as a historian—was thwarted chiefly by America's historicization.

The same practical concerns that had led to the imagining of American separation also rejuvenated British interest in Pacific exploration, and with it the conjuring of a new realm for speculation. Though long touted by isolated advocates, the commercial prospects of Oceania came to serious government attention only after the accounting of 1763. The suspicion that France might begin its vengeance on Britain in hitherto unclaimed territories of the globe also spurred officials into a reexamination of Antipodean potential. The shift regarding New World epitomes, therefore, had as much to do with the reopening of the Pacific vista to British observers as it did with the contemporary fight to maintain the thirteen colonies.

If interested, British officials would have had an old file to consult for arguments supporting Oceanian annexation. As early as 1692 the explorer William Dampier had urged the Admiralty to consider the riches that might be found in the region: "so great a part of the World," he assured, could not be without "very valluable commodities."[31] In 1711, the pragmatic journalist Daniel Defoe guessed that the region could "probably" yield "the Greatest, most Valuable, most Profitable, and most Encreasing Branch of Trade in our whole British commerce."[32] At the time, Defoe had been promoting investment in Chancellor Harley's joint stock South Sea Company. But even after the SSC crashed appallingly in 1720, Defoe continued to believe in the general gist of the enterprise. In 1724 he "laid it down as a Foundation; that whoever Sailing over the South Seas . . . shall never fail to discover new Worlds, new Nations, and new inexhaustible Funds of Wealth and Commerce, such as never were yet known to the Merchants of Europe."[33] The bursting of the South Sea Bubble, which affected hundreds of Britons from university dons to soldiers' widows to the king himself, marred the name of the region for several years. Together with the reputation of joint stock companies themselves, however, all was mostly forgiven by the 1740s.[34] By 1744 confidence in Oceania had returned to the extent that historian and government loyalist John Campbell could declare that "whoever perfectly discovers & settles [the unknown south] will become infallibly possessed of Territories as Rich, as fruitful, & as capable of Improvement, as any that have been hitherto found out . . . in the West."[35]

That officials had ignored this persistent call for most of the eighteenth century was not simply a reflection of pragmatic concerns to soothe a jumpy Spain or France, or an instance of greater preoccupation in contemporary warfare.[36] The steady critique of expansion that had continued unabated since 1688 had also affected official thinking about new enterprises—even if it appeared in retrospect to have made little impact on the maintenance of existing holdings. Ironically, at a time when that critique was at its most shrill, official anxieties about the cost of *not* expanding seemed finally to compel Whitehall to act.

Thus in 1764, when the balance of power in Europe could not have been a tenser issue and when the government was least in a position to fund it, the Admiralty commissioned an expedition to the Pacific to "make Discoveries of Countries hitherto unknown."[37] Captain John Byron set sail in July 1764, making a record-breaking circumnavigation of the globe but hitting upon little of interest in the expanses of Oceania (it was later found he had steered a course that dodged nearly every significant island between the Falklands and the Philippines). By the time of his return in May 1766, a second voyage had already been planned, based primarily on Byron's earlier dispatched "belief" that a large southern continent probably lay to the "west of the magellanick Streights."[38]

Captain Samuel Wallis turned Byron's *Dolphin* around in less than a month, sailing it out to the Pacific again in June 1766, this time charged more specifically to make discoveries of lands "or Islands of great extent . . . in the Southern Hemisphere . . . convenient for Navigation and in Climates adapted to the product of Commodities usefull in Commerce."[39] Though Wallis, too, failed to find the long-sought Great Southern Continent, he did hit upon an important island group in the middle of the Pacific Ocean by sailing just five degrees south of Byron's route. These he named "King George the Third's Islands" but they would soon become known as the Society Islands, with its central prize known as Otaheite.

Tahiti became famous for two intertwined reasons. First, the tales of its abundance and pristine condition, with which Wallis regaled his patrons when he returned back home, concentrated those British minds set on establishing new avenues for wealth. Second, the news that Louis-Antoine de Bougainville, sailing under the auspices of the French king, had reached Tahiti only ten short months after Wallis suddenly made Britain's Pacific enterprise seem to many to be a race for unclaimed spoils. Rumors of Tahiti's great promise were heightened by the fear of losing it at the same time as the threat of renewed rivalry with France helped to make the island seem precisely what was now required.

It was the worldly Bougainville who first saw the connection between the riches of Tahiti and the supposedly idyllic nature of the Island's society. His *Voyage autour du monde*, published in 1771, was certain that the inhabitants were *sauvages* like those in America, but they were beautiful, hospitable, innocent, and most of all happy savages—reckoned by its well-read author to be representatives of both the ancient Elysian heroes and a more modern understanding of the state of nature. It was thus also Bougainville who was the first to say explicitly that Oceania in toto amounted to a *new* New World. The *Voyage* named Tahiti "la Nouvelle Cythère" and made frequent references throughout to Oceania's echo, and indeed even replacement, of America as the optimal site for European philosophizing.[40]

Pirated editions of Bougainville's *Voyage* soon flooded British reading markets. In turn, British accounts of Tahiti began to incorporate what Britain's own Wallis had been rather too prosaic to grasp—namely, that the recent discoveries provided the metropole with a new set of savages in a newly ideal region just as its old contenders were becoming overly problematic. The idea of a radically alternate social simplicity had survived intact in the transfer of attitudes about New World exemplars from America to Oceania.

THE PACIFIC CRAZE

Excitement over Tahiti precipitated what one eminent historian has called a full-blown "Pacific craze" from the 1770s to the French Revolution.[41] The popular hunger for all things Oceanic was in fact foreshadowed, or undergirded, by two key titles from the 1760s. The first was a racy, bowdlerized translation of Charles de Brosses's magisterial *Histoire des navigations aux terres australes* (Paris, 1756). Published in London in 1766–68 by John Callender under the confident title *Terra australis cognita*, it summarized the early-modern voyages of famous navigators such as Magellan, Mendaña, and Quiros. Its simplified accounts of the great explorers' impressions of "rough," "wild," and "perfectly independent" peoples took on fresh significance to a readership now looking for alternative New Worlds.[42] A year later, the Royal Society fellow Alexander Dalrymple published a small book on *The Discoveries Made in the South Pacifick Ocean Previous to 1764*, which advanced his pet obsession about the probability of a great southern continent to "counterpoise" the landmasses of the north. The theory was expounded at greater length and to a wider audience in his *Historical Collection of the Several Voyages and Discoveries in the South Pacific Ocean*, published in 1769–71.[43] Callender and Dalrymple set the scene for a decade of frenetic publishing about Oceanic exploration.

That frenzy was stimulated most of all by the third major British expedition to the Pacific—the *Endeavour* voyage of 1768–71. This was the first expedition to be significantly funded, and thus heavily influenced, by the Royal Society. However, while the rising scientific body managed to get multiple naturalist objectives tabled alongside the by-now standard commercial aims of the voyage, it failed to convince the Admiralty to allow one of its fellows—none other than Dalrymple himself—to captain the enterprise. The society had to concede leadership to middle-aged and highly experienced naval officer James Cook, though it was pleased to secure several scientific positions onboard, including a young Joseph Banks and the Swedish Daniel Solander as botanists. The *Endeavour* visited the Society Islands (where Banks learnt the indigenous name of its centerpiece), as well as lands previously unknown to Europeans in what is now Australia and New Zealand.[44]

The *Endeavour's* return was greeted with instant acclaim, from the demimonde to the daily news reader. "The people most talk'd of at present are Mr Banks and Doctor Solander," twittered noblewoman Lady Mary Coke: "I am told . . . their Voyage round the world . . . is very amusing." These "ingenious gentlemen," remarked the *General Evening Post*, have been encountering "unknown species," including most of all savages who are "well-made and well-featured . . . extremely lascivious . . . [and who] paint their posteriors jet black."[45] As Nicholas Thomas comments, it was hardly the scientific aspect of the voyage that first intrigued metropolitan followers. Newspapers were soon elaborating stories of virgins who could be bought for "three nails and a knife," "nut brown sultans," and "women danc[ing] in the most indecent manner, performing a thousand obscene gesticulations."[46] Within weeks, an unauthorized and anonymous *Journal of a Voyage . . . in his Majesty's Ship the Endeavour* had appeared that added to the circulation of stories about Oceanic licentiousness.[47]

By 1772, the *Monthly Review* at least was looking forward to something a bit more substantial. It is with "real pleasure," the journal thus announced, that an official reckoning of the "discoveries and enquiries [made by] Mr Banks and Dr Solander" will soon be available.[48] In the end, readers had to wait another year for the Royal Society's formal production—though for most it proved to be well worth the forbearance. John Hawkesworth's three-volume compilation of the voyages of Byron, Wallis, and Cook became one of the literary sensations of the eighteenth century. While expensive to purchase, the work went through multiple editions in its first year alone. By the end of the 1770s it had been borrowed more times from many local libraries than any other title that decade.[49]

The attraction of the work turned out to have not a little to do with the prurience already established by the earlier reports about Cook's voyage. Initial responses—mostly anonymous broadside squibs—tended to concentrate on Hawkesworth's revelations about Oceanian sexuality. *An Epistle from Mr Banks, Voyager, Monster-hunter, and Amoroso, to Oberea, Queen of Otaheite* (1773) declared that "one page of *Hawkesworth*, in the cool retreat, / Fires the bright maid with more than mortal heat; / She sinks at once into the lover's arms, / Nor deems it vice to prostitute her charms." It went on to recount the adventure between Banks and Oberea implied in the compilation, but was coy enough to point the finger of blame at the European, since Oceanians are apparently so "untaught in guilt" that they cannot recognize virtue. *An Epistle from Oberea, Queen of Otaheite to Joseph Banks* (1773) was not so forgiving: it also reimagined the dalliance between Tahitian royalty and the now notorious naturalist but decided that it had been caused by Oberea's own zealous nymphomania. Finally, *An Heroic Epistle from the Injured Harriot, Mistress of Mr Banks to Oberea, Queen of Otaheite* (1774) added a melodramatic element to the cycle when it imagined the poor fiancée of Banks, Harriot Blosset, reading Hawkesworth in a rage against the "inveigling harlots" and "savage sluts" of Oceania.[50]

Censures of the work by more respectable quarters of course only fueled the salacious interest in it. "A Christian" writing in to the *Public Advertiser* was scandalized to find "Stronger Excitements to vicious Indulgences" in Hawkesworth than in the worst French novels.[51] John Wesley preferred disbelief, remarking that Hume and Voltaire might well want to trust Hawkesworth's account of "men and women coupling together in the face of the sun and in the sight of scores of people . . . but I cannot."[52]

Later responses revealed some more ponderous considerations, though the chief theme remained surprisingly constant. The anonymous *Otaheite:*

A Poem—sixteen pages of tortured angst about the consequences of Tahitian passion—decided that Hawkesworth had made plain the need for European intervention. While the savages' lawless sensuality appears a form of "past'ral Love," the author opines, it will inevitably spiral into lawlessness per se if left unchecked—including a descent into the spectral act of infanticide.[53] The pretended *Epistle (Moral and Philosophical) from an Officer at Otaheite* could not have agreed more. After his own weighty discussion of Oberea's "Love empire," its author also professed that Tahiti would ultimately unleash a Medea: "O dire effect of passions unrestrain'd, / O dire effect of Nature's laws profan'd."[54]

Somewhat unpredictably, the name of Oceania as well as the reputation of all the key explorers managed to survive the shocking elements of the Pacific craze until at least the 1780s. The fall instead was taken by Hawkesworth himself—up to that point a figure unrelated to New World adventuring. The Admiralty had chosen him to compile their accounts on the rather flimsy basis of his prior journalistic efforts and cursory connection to celebrated literary circles. Though ecstatic to receive the astonishing advance of £6,000—equivalent now to over £1 million—he soon regretted his role as scapegoat for thousands of overtitillated readers. He died six months after the accounts' publication, driven to his grave—in the opinion of the writer Frances Burney—by the "livid . . . abuse he has met with."[55]

The Pacific craze thus continued unabated through the reports of Cook's second voyage, which departed in 1772 and returned in 1774. By this time it had further consolidated the turn from America to Oceania as the primary source of wonder about global newness. Now, geographers confidently claimed that Oceania represented the "terra incognita of America."[56] Museum curators gave as much, if not more, space to Oceanic artifacts in their ethnographic halls on New World people as to Native Americana.[57] And, most tellingly, published writers of all stripes started to assume that the word "savage"—as well as its common eighteenth-century twin "Indian"—could indicate a person from the Pacific as easily as one from Iroquoia, Appalachia, or Savannah.[58]

One area of cultural expression succinctly exposed the turn from America to Oceania in the third quarter of the eighteenth century. This was the genre of conjectural history, practiced primarily by moral philosophers in Scottish universities at the time. Though seemingly a small and exclusive body of writings, conjectural history in fact informed a wide range of social actors in this latter period. Its peculiar articulation of a "four stage" approach to human history soon became "something very like an orthodoxy" in Blackstonian law, Beattiean science, and Reynoldsian art.[59] The way in which conjectural history employed the figure of the New World savage—first in the shape of Native Americans and then in the form of Oceanians—reflected a common pattern in much contemporary culture.

Conjectural history flourished among philosophers for about a generation from mid-century. The term was coined retrospectively in 1790 by the philosophical biographer, Dugald Stewart, when describing the kind of approach fostered by Adam Smith at the University of Glasgow. Smith had been interested in the development of human morality and posited that the key to its understanding lay in that period before "men [thought of] recording their transactions." In order to study an era with no written sources, Smith called for a new form of history that "conjectured," from both "nature" and current "circumstances," which events were "likely" to have happened. Such an enterprise would reveal the mechanism by which humans had moved from a state of "uncultivation" to the present state of "artifice and complexity."[60] In turn, this would establish the key driving contexts of the major moral forms of humanity.

The crushing problem for such history, though, was how the hypothesizing implicit in conjecture went so corrosively against the empiricist tradition of most British *philosophes*. Smith's fellow Glaswegian philosopher, Thomas Reid, had famously called all "traffic in conjecture" to be "contraband and illicit."[61] The conjecturalists' solution was a rather coy melding of two otherwise strongly empirical practices. On the one hand, practitioners were to mobilize the insights of a near century of systematic observations about nature. On the other, they were to assemble all observations available about those peoples said to be living *like* the earliest men. Together, these two fields would somehow deliver workable estimates about an erstwhile untouchable era. As the scholar H. M. Höpfl has rather dryly remarked, "our philosophers evidently thought they had avoided fanciful speculations and unsound 'hypotheses' by founding conjectural history on the rock of the 'experimental method.'"[62]

By the 1760s, the consensus in the two respective fields was, first, that society naturally progressed through stages from savagery to commerce, and, second, that the peoples most like those of the earliest stage were definitively the savages of the American New World. In lectures through the 1760s, Smith demarcated the stages of society into those of "hunters" or "savages," "shepherds" or "pastoralists," "agriculture," and "commerce." He was similarly sure in his belief that "the age of hunters subsists . . . in North America."[63] In 1767, Smith's celebrated pupil, Adam Ferguson, published his version of the stages in his *Essay on the History of Civil Society.* Though he gave slightly different names to the stages—calling them ages of "savagery," "herding," "agriculture," and "polished art"—Ferguson was just as firm as Smith about the way in which Native Americans most perfectly "mirrour, the features of our own progenitors."[64]

Though believers in progression, it was never a straightforward given that conjecturalists would also always favor progressivism. Smith had been clear in his worries about the potential of commercial society to erode the classical values of courage, curiosity, and the "heroic spirit" (which apparently resided as a matter of course in savage societies), though in the end he decided that the sophistication of such an order would compensate amply in the arenas of political stability and, thus, of morality.[65] Ferguson, in contrast, remained ambivalent.[66] "The boasted refinements . . . of the polished age," he noted, "are not divested of danger"—which for Ferguson meant specifically "corruption and baseness," "envy," and "servility."[67] Such dangers were not, it seemed, prevalent among savages. On the question of savage versus commercial, Ferguson ultimately offered only another question: "Is it not possible, amidst our admiration of art, to find some place for . . . institutions that fortify the mind, inspire courage, and promote national felicity [?] . . . Let statesmen, who are intrusted with the government of nations, reply for themselves."[68]

The conjecturalist stance on the capacity of contemporary Native Americans to represent the savage state was less contested. For at least the first twenty years of conjecturalist practice, Native Americans stood as the primary example—and thus indeed the primary legitimization—of history's "rudest form."[69] In a sweeping review, the *Scots Magazine* summarized that "the nations of North America . . . give us the spectacle of savage life in a more perfect form than it is any where else to be found."[70] During the 1770s, however, this stance underwent some reform. Conjecturalists never wavered in their conviction that New World folk could serve as likenesses to savagery, but they did start to revise their understanding of the provenance of such people. Increasingly, Native Americans were joined by, and in some cases replaced by, Oceanians as the best example of original rudeness in conjectural history. Even as early as the late 1760s, the influential Smith pupil John Millar was lecturing that the stage of "hunters . . . or mere savages" could be seen not only in "the Indians of America" *but also* in those of "Terra Australis."[71] In 1773, in his important *Of the Origin and Progress of Language,* the judge and linguist James Burnett (Lord Monboddo) stated his preference for using Oceanians over Americans, since the "manners" of the latter had become so contaminated by European interference. Thinkers in search of savage examples, Burnett went on, "are now to look . . . in the South Sea."[72] In 1774, fellow judge and intellectual, Henry Home (Lord Kames) took his recommendation, despite a famous personal antipathy to Burnett. In his *Sketches on the History of Man,* Home referred to Tahitians more often than to Native Americans when expounding on the particulars of "savage society."[73]

The conjecturalist switch to Oceanic examples over or in complement with American examples in any discussion of the New World was typical of general British metropolitan thought. Importantly, the role of the New World did not alter in this switch—it remained a synonym for savagery, which in turn remained central to debates about Britain's national destiny. What had changed was the chief flag bearer for this complicated concept.

While a few recent scholars have paid special attention to the "historicization" of Native Americans in British culture during the 1760s, none has considered this process as part of a larger intellectual rearrangement regarding the New World.[74] Despite the demands of war and rebellion in America, Britons at this time were not ready to give up the rhetorical idea of the New World: the promise of pristine simplicity did too much work in a contest that was still too unresolved. Consequently, they came to substitute Oceanians for Native Americans in their public imaginary. The flipside to American historicization, then, was Oceanic idealization. Only when these two moves are taken together does the full history of British attitudes to Native Americans come into focus—not to mention the preconditions for later attitudes to Oceanians. The driving notion of New World savagery framed and linked both together.

By the summer of 1774, Oceanian fever was as high as it had ever been. In this crucial moment between Britain's impending loss of America and the full European discovery of Pacific lands, the first representative of Oceanian society disembarked at Portsmouth Harbour.

6.   Mai and the Finding of Oceania

On 10 July 1774, the great gossipmonger of the age, Horace Walpole, declared in a letter to a friend that "Africa is, indeed, coming into fashion. There is just returned a Mr Bruce, who has lived three years in the court of Abyssinia . . . Otaheite and Mr Banks are quite forgotten."[1] Just four days later, the first native representative of Oceania, Mai of Raiatea—an island near Tahiti—arrived in London. The magnitude of the sensation that Mai created in Britain for the near two years of his stay suggests that Walpole had badly underestimated the reach of Pacific fascination. He had assumed that the interest in "Otaheite and Mr Banks" was merely one more manifestation of a perennial European fascination for the exotic, easily replaced by another version. He had failed to see that there was something specific about Oceanic exotics. Mai's celebrity showed that New World peoples were still particularly interesting to Britons. In its freshly revived incarnation, now free from the demands of an advancing *Realpolitik*, New World savagery continued to speak powerfully to ongoing British concerns about expansion.

In fact, Mai turned out to be the most popular New World visitor of them all. Like many of his earlier Native American predecessors, Mai met the monarch, dined with numerous dignitaries, toured the sites—both patrician and plebeian—and inspired a flurry of productions, from ballads and satires to poems and letters to paintings and engravings. In addition, however, Mai was the muse behind one of the most successful pantomimes of the eighteenth century, his portraitists were some of the most famous in the country, and his activities were followed avidly by thinkers from all over the continent. For various reasons, Mai's star shone more brightly and widely than that of any who had come before.

As a result of his lustrous impact, Mai is the only New World visitor of the eighteenth century to have generated a substantial historiography. Almost all of this scholarship has proceeded from a belief that Mai constituted a unique case in British history, appearing as a popular "savage" with neither predecessors nor successors. As well, the majority of this work has pursued either a critical analysis of the cultural productions of Mai's trip or an ethnographic history of his persistent agency against the forceful structures of British power.[2] Very little has attempted to place Mai within a larger historical tradition or to understand why, really, Mai became so popular among a people who were apparently so dominant.

If pushed on this question, both strands of scholarship on Mai would seem to argue that Mai proved a sensation because he embodied the centerpiece of a particular fashion raging in Britain at the time—namely, a kind of popular Rousseauism that favored a primitivist reading of the French *philosophe*'s writings, whereby noble savagery shows up the ignobility of civilization.[3] For the cultural critics such Rousseauism then becomes the chief subject for analysis while for the ethnohistorians it turns out to be an example of the colonizing structures that acted against Mai's individuality during his stay. Either way, great chunks of the response to the visiting Oceanian go missing. Certainly Mai was seen as an embodiment of a European idea, but popular Rousseauism was only one way of mobilizing it at the time. The tendency to castigate European civilization via a notion of noble savagery was just one angle in a debate that had been coursing through British public discourse for several decades. As witnessed during the many previous visits of New World peoples, other angles included the tendency to praise civilization via noble savagery as well as tendencies either to congratulate *or* to criticize civilization via conceptions of ignoble savagery. Though the length of his stay and the playboy status of his patrons certainly helped, Mai was popular in Britain because he enabled *multiple* ways of debating the problem of contemporary direction.

Further, though Mai was indeed seen largely through European conventions, such an imposition revealed more about the cracks in British power than about its hegemony. By seeing Mai as an embodiment of savagery—however wrought—Britons could continue their disagreement with each other regarding the future of the nation. In the mid-1770s, this disagreement still turned generally around the question of expansion, even though at this particular time—on the cusp of American cessation—popular debate was figured especially as a conflict over the costs to "happiness" that expansion effected. Older concerns about the expense, corruption, irreligiosity, and decadence potential within expansion also continued to simmer. Mai's celebrity suggested that the conflict over expansion was at least as intense—or as unresolved—now as it had been all century.

Although Mai fitted the model of New World savage visitor so well, his two-year sojourn in Britain introduced some new elements to the phenomenon, too. Mai toured further around the country than any predecessor; he was also the first to be inoculated against smallpox. Both these developments were due to his far greater immersion in British intellectual circles than any earlier New World visitor had experienced. Mai's odyssey from Raiatea to Tahiti to Britain and then back to the South Seas was both a rehabilitation of and momentous addition to the phenomenon of the New World person in Britain.

MAI IN TAHITI

Mai's motivation to journey across vast seas to another world came from personal anguish. He had been born in about 1753 in Raiatea, a tiny island to the northwest of Tahiti. Although sometimes proclaimed a prince or a priest, he was probably from the second order of Raiatean society, high enough to own land and stock but lower than the *arii*, or chiefly class.[4] In the early 1760s Raiatea had been invaded by warriors from the even tinier neighboring island of Borabora, who were acting out age-old dynastic rivalries. Mai's father was killed in the ensuing struggle and his ancestral lands dispossessed. The rest of the family managed to escape to Tahiti, where they were welcomed as refugees given their honorable Raiatean status. Raiatea was acknowledged by most at the time as the source of much Tahitian religious culture.[5] Without land, however, Mai would never rise to the status of his birthright. Throughout his teenage years, the young Raiatean harbored dreams of revenge and restitution. As some later British friends recalled, Mai "would never listen to any other mode of settling than that of violent possession of his father's lands."[6]

Mai knew of British weaponry from firsthand experience. He claimed to have been wounded by Captain Samuel Wallis's men when the *Dolphin* had anchored in Matavai Bay in June 1767.[7] Wallis had entered the bay with guns literally blazing. Convinced that explorers should always meet new people with a conquering attitude, he had ordered his men to open fire on the canoeists who had come to greet the *Dolphin* as well as on the men, women, and children who ran to the hills to escape.[8] Mai was apparently one of the latter number. Though only a boy who must have been bewildered by such a display of unprovoked aggression, he was evidently old enough to begin calculating the uses to which this kind of military capability might be put.

There is no evidence to say that Mai met with the next voyaging vessel from Britain, Cook's *Endeavour* in 1769, but he probably heard of it on the fast-moving Polynesian grapevine. The *Endeavour's* naturalist, Joseph Banks, had decided on this voyage to take home with him a "specimen" of Oceanic man. His chosen candidate was Tupaia, another Raiatean refugee as it happened, who perhaps saw the same opportunity in the British as Mai would later. Cook himself refused to take responsibility for Tupaia, but allowed Banks to do so if kept by the naturalist's own means. "Thank heavens I have a sufficiency," Banks wrote, alluding to his considerable fortune; "I do not know why I may not keep him as a curiosity, as well as my neighbours do lions and tygers." Unfortunately, Tupaia died from dysentery during a stop at Batavia on the way home. Banks's ambition, however, to obtain and relocate a New World savage for his own observational purposes did not die with him.[9]

Cook's second voyage to the Pacific, beginning in 1772, had meant to include Banks once again, but at the eleventh hour the scientist and the captain fell out over the issue of accommodation. The former withdrew in disgust. The Royal Society intervened long enough to get Cook to agree to an attempt at fulfilling Banks's desire for a Oceanian returnee—if not to make him welcome the rakish hothead back onboard. Probably Cook agreed because of the opportunity that a local informant would provide to his voyage—a chance to check navigational decisions and to learn otherwise hidden quirks about other Oceanic cultures. But Cook also understood his place in history. Unlike many later historians, he did not regard his mission as the beginning of a new phase in world exploration. He knew that it was instead a continuation of the search through New Worlds for avenues to ever more commercial growth that his government had sponsored for nearly a century. Cook had been directly involved in many of the bloodier American campaigns of the Seven Years War: he was an eyewitness to the riches that can flow from the creation of trade monopolies overseas. And as Nicholas Thomas has remarked, during his trips back to Greenwich Hospital, Cook would have encountered every day the magisterial painted ceiling of James Thornhill, inscribed with the deeply held maritime belief that "Our Trade, Commerce, and Public Wealth are chiefly owing to our Navy."[10] Like all earlier British expeditions to the New World, then, the captain of this enterprise would be looking out for potential brokers with whom later emissaries might negotiate an exchange agreement.

At Huahine—an island in between Raiatea and Tahiti—Cook's officers, at least, thought they had found the right man for the job. Mai had evidently moved to friendly Huahine in the last few years, possibly as one further step toward realizing his vengeful goals. He now appeared to the British as an easygoing youth, prepared to chip in with the sailors on deck and obviously keen to make the journey for his own reasons. One officer, James Burney (brother of the famous novelist), described the new recruit in approving terms: "The Indian who came on board is named Omy; though we commonly call him Jack . . . he is possessed of many good qualities—is Strong, Active, healthy, & as likely to weather the hardships of a long Voyage as any of us." Burney also recounted that Omy, or Mai, was "going to *Britannia* to get poopooe's (guns) of the Aree of that country . . . to kill the people of Borabora."[11]

Cook himself thought little of Mai: "dark, ugly, and a downright blackguard," is how the captain described him.[12] He was also bothered by the Oceanian's political attachments. One of the main chiefs of Huahine sought a special audience with Cook when he heard of Mai's intentions, in order to explain that the island's peace depended on its delicate relationship with the chiefs of Borabora. All could be compromised, the chief insisted, by an external boost to the ambitions of one former Raiatean, sometime Tahitian, angry young man.[13]

The captain's concerns in this instance, however, were not enough to override the determination of his escort ship's leader. Mai was accepted among the crew of Tobias Furneaux's *Adventure*, listed as "Tetuby Homey . . . 22, AB" on 9 September 1773.[14] The twinned enterprise of Cook's *Resolution* and Furneaux's *Adventure* then began the long voyage westward. Unlike his immediate Polynesian predecessor, Mai survived the journey, arriving at Portsmouth on 14 July 1774.

MAI IN BRITAIN

As soon as he reached British shores, Furneaux was eager to report Mai's arrival to the Admiralty. The First Admiral, Lord Sandwich, was in turn just as hasty to invite Banks to Whitehall to greet his desired prize. Banks was delighted, reassuring all of his commitment to wear the entirety of Mai's costs while in Britain. In the newcomer, Banks recognized the longed-for example of what he called "natural man," to be studied and molded as contemporary scientific principles dictated. For his part, Mai recognized Banks rather more specifically. Banks's sister, Sarah Banks, recorded afterward that "when he first heard my brother's voice . . . he cryed there's tapano the name the South Sea Islanders always called him."[15] Although unlikely ever to have met in person before now, Banks had become so well known in Polynesian Oceania that a youth like Mai knew him on sight.

Banks quickly settled Mai in his own home in London. Communication in those first few weeks, however, must have been difficult. The young Fanny Burney, moving within Banks's circle of acquaintance, observed that Mai had "few English words" and that neither Furneaux nor Banks much Tahitian. "Our *Jem*," however, she noted, referring to her beloved brother James, "speaks more Otaheite than any of the Ship's Crew . . . [Mai] is very fond of *Bunny* [Mai's word for Burney], who spent a great part of his Time in Studying the Language with him."[16] Later accounts of Mai's English vary: some lamented that he never gained sufficient language to be "intelligible" while others maintained that he could eventually "jabber" enough to "hold a conversation."[17] One certain casualty of the lack of communication was the official rendering of Mai's name. It quickly became standardized to Omai, integrating the formal Tahitian "O" for "it is" in with the personal moniker.[18] Mai may have liked the accidental aggrandizement of his title that resulted, which could explain why he never appeared to protest the mistake.

Within days, Banks had arranged an audience with George III and Queen Charlotte. The ease with which this royal appointment was made represents the first tangible sign of Mai's rehabilitation of New World visitor norms. Sarah Banks recorded that Mai "kissed the Queen's hand and behaved decently."[19] The press, only now alerted to the visitor's presence, was more than happy to imagine the rest. The *London Chronicle* claimed that Mai had been instructed in court protocol beforehand, but "forgot" most of it when faced with His Majesty, mustering only a simple *"How do ye do?"*[20] Amplifying, a letter-writer in the same journal decided that this was nonetheless "not only a kind question, but [one which] would be extremely pertinent to be put to many other Monarchs in Europe." How did Catherine of Russia do, for instance, the author wanted to know, "after breaking all her solemn engagements with Poland"? Likewise, how did Frederick II of Prussia do "after all the oppression and bloodshed he has been guilty of"?[21] The verve with which the press began mobilizing Mai for polemical comment was the second key sign of his incorporation into the eighteenth-century phenomenon of New World visitors. Recent concerns about both the propriety and the bother of hosting exemplary savages vanished in the face of this luminous fresh model.

A second letter-writer to the *London Chronicle* confirmed Mai's gift to

British polemicists. He imagined Mai reading a newspaper report about his arrival and noting that it described him as a savage. The visitor then apparently asked for an explanation of the word. A learned friend obliged him by recounting how a savage is a person from one of "those barbarous nations that are uncivilized, and that do not live in a regular manner or method of policy or religion." Mai is given to retort:

> You had better have said, that all those who are not conversant with European manners are Savages, for your definition, Sir, is as injurious as it is unjust. We practice those virtues you only teach; are enemies to luxury . . . never go to war but from a principle of self-preservation or self-defense . . . and whilst we entertain the most sublime ideas of an Almighty Being, do not cut the throats of each other for differing in the manner of worshipping him . . . Let me beg of you for the future, Sir, never to call us barbarous, you deserve the appellation yourself.[22]

Before the printed response to Mai really flared, however, the visitor was whisked away from London to receive inoculation against smallpox and to undertake an initial, minor tour of some provinces around the capital. The *General Evening Post* gave conflicting reports about the origins of the proposal for Mai's inoculation. On 21 July, it claimed that Mai himself, so fearing the disease that was "almost always fatal to the people of his Country," insisted on having the procedure performed on his body. A week later the same paper declared that it was George III who ordered inoculation, His Majesty noting that "it would be imprudent to expose him to the crouds that curiosity would incline to see him before he was secure from that disease so fatal to all his complexion."[23] Most likely it was Banks's idea: he moved within a circle where inoculation was a matter of course, and indeed where renowned inoculists moved as well. Of the range of European diseases already introduced to Oceania, however, Mai probably feared syphilis more than smallpox, the former having wrecked quicker and starker effects in the Tahitian archipelago than the latter, perhaps due to its greater capacity to lie dormant and invisible in some carriers for long periods of time.[24] That the press were claiming knowledge of smallpox's effect on peoples of Mai's "country" and "complexion" was another proof of Oceania's assimilation into a general conception of the New World: smallpox had been notorious since the sixteenth century as a deadly problem for Native Americans.[25] Although inoculation had been available in Britain since the visit of Cuming's seven Cherokee, Mai was the first New World visitor to undergo the measure.

The procedure, in the end, was performed by Baron Thomas Dimsdale in Hertford, a friend of Banks and famous as the inoculist of many European aristocrats. "Mai understood thoroughly the disease he was to expect," pronounced Banks, "& we are certain that he did understand it." Banks's sister, however, thought otherwise. "Mai misunderstood," said Sarah, "for he thought by those precautions instead of having the expectation of the illness in consequence of which when it came out he was very low spirited & said he would dye." Fortunately, the visitor recovered from his ordeal within a few weeks. "We are informed," reported the *General Evening Post* on 25 August, "that the native of Otaheite has undergone the operation of the small-pox much better than was expected, and will set out this week with Lord Sandwich and Mr Banks on a tour into . . . England."[26]

This was another first for a New World visitor: none had ever been taken out of greater London for extended periods of time. All, of course, had traveled to London from one of the major ports—Portsmouth, Plymouth, or Dover. But few had stopped for more than a quick rest along the way, the exception being Ostenaco who was delayed at Winchester for a couple of days to witness the pomp of its cathedral, college, and castle. After his inoculation, Mai was taken to see and be seen at Leicester, Huntingdon, and Cambridge. A year later, Banks took him on a journey through Yorkshire, travelling as far north as Scarborough. The purpose of these trips was manifold. First, Banks enjoyed an itinerant sort of life—he was often on the move, seeing friends or "botanizing," as was the expression, in the countryside. No doubt he also wished to show off Mai to his eager and powerful friends: at Huntingdon, for example, resided Lord Sandwich, an obvious enthusiast; at Cambridge, "many Doctors and Professors" clamored to meet Banks's charge. Scholarly colleagues who wrote to Banks for news of all things Oceanic—although they never met Mai—included Lord Monboddo and William Robertson.[27] Finally, the turn to the country away from the city in part reflected a particular vogue at the time for the rural picturesque over the bustling urban: Banks was ever at the forefront of fashion, making the most of the current trend by staying in some of the nation's most sumptuous country estates.[28]

Observers in the provinces were largely tickled by what they saw in Mai, although few yet turned that delight into any particularly weighty reflection about either savagery or civility. At Leicester, a journalist remarked that "Mai . . . behaved with great politeness, allowing for his short acquaintance with manners": he sat and conversed with "ease" and "familiarity."[29] At Huntingdon, the literary memoirist Joseph Cradock, who was also staying at Sandwich's house, recounted how Mai was asked to cook for the party one night. The Raiatean accepted willingly because "he always wished to make himself useful." He apparently prepared some mutton in the customary Polynesian manner, wrapping it in leaves and burying it in a makeshift underground oven. "The meat was . . . much commended," wrote Cradock. "And let not the fastidious gourmand deride this simple method, for are not [certain foods] now frequently . . . wrapped in vine-leaves . . . in St James's-street and the Palais-royal?"[30]

At Cambridge, an obscure student wrote to his brother, the artist George Cumberland, from his "Cell in Maudlin" that Mai had been presented at Senate House. There he was "introduced to all the Drs &c & behaved with wonderful ease." The student, an eyewitness, also noted an incident that found independent reportage elsewhere. Upon being offered some snuff, Mai was said to have replied "No tank You, Sir, My Nose be no Hungry": to the student, this was "a severe satire on Snuff Takers."[31] A London newspaper claimed more prosaically that "Some one offered [Mai] a pinch of snuff, which he politely refused, saying that his nose was not hungry."[32] If Cumberland did not go straight to the press with his letter we may assume that Mai indicated something of the kind related above, which also suggests that the visitor spoke more English than many sources have let on. At the same time, the story in the student's letter may have been crafted specifically to please the reader: George Cumberland was, his brother notes, a devoted Rousseauist, keen to learn that savages were as pure and wise as the *philosophe* had early claimed. "You cant conceive how you oblige me by your account of Omiah," Cumberland wrote back. "Every little anecdote of a man born in [innocent nature] with all the Facultys of understanding . . . is well worth remarking."[33]

Mai's appeal to famous Rousseauists such as Frances Burney, James Boswell, and Banks himself has become well known. Less appreciated is both the way in which Rousseauism in Britain had a more popular base than often believed and the virulence with which it was simultaneously attacked—again, in generic literature as frequently as in literary discourse. When Mai returned from his provincial tour to London in November 1774, he began in earnest his employment in metropolitan discussions about the value of contemporary British society. It was an employment that lasted at least until 1785, nearly a decade after his return to Oceania. Just because this employment was now often couched in the language of romantic naturalism (or antinaturalism), it does not follow that such polemical mobilization signaled a fresh departure in the reception of New World people. Though studded with remarks about "nature," "art," and "heroes," the discourse on Mai during his stay in London was mostly a continuation of the eighteenth century's contest over the moral, economic, and political effects of Britain's commercial expansion.

OF PHILOSOPHERS AND THE COMMONLY CURIOUS

In many ways, Rousseauism in Britain was itself a continuation of the decades-long critique of modern commercialization. Though of course the vogue entailed some elements peculiar to its period and namesake—such as an emphasis on deism, pastoralism, feelings and the self—Rousseauism was at core a political expression of hostility to the growth of art in human governance. Since the growth of art in eighteenth-century British governance was intimately tied to the growth of a credit economy, and with it an expanded state and greater sociability, Rousseauists in Britain were to some degree all torchbearers for the general classical-republican case against expansion.[34]

The range in degree of torch-bearing, however, was fairly wide. British fanciers of Rousseau could be as strictly idealist as the young George Cumberland in believing that savagery was the best condition for humanity and contemporary commercial society the worst. Such followers favored the more strident sentiments of Rousseau's *Discours sur l'inégalité* (1755), which had circulated widely in Britain since the late 1750s. Or they could be more reform-minded critics, believing with the Rousseau of the 1760s that so long as the savage can guard against "the passions and prejudices" of society, standing more as "spectator" than as "participant," he should grow "wise and reasonable in towns," serving to improve art along natural principles rather than to encourage a total rejection of art.[35]

Sitting squarely in the former camp was the young and impressionable Frances Burney. The Burney family saw a lot of Mai upon his return to the capital due to their close connection to Banks's own social set. While Jem was entertaining Mai in the Burney home one November day, Frances declared herself dazzled by the "great personage." Mai seems to "Shame Education," she gushed in her diary, "for his manners are so extremely graceful, & he is so polite, attentive, & easy." She went on to compare Mai to the son of Lord Chesterfield, whose father had just that year published a book advocating an elaborate and cynical style of living.

> The 1st with all the advantages of Lord Chesterfield's Instructions, brought up at a great school, Introduced at 15 to a Court, taught all possible accomplishments from an Infant, & having all the care, expense, labour & benefit of the best Education than any man can

receive—proved after all a meer *pedantic booby* . . . the 2nd [Mai] with
no Tutor but Nature appears in a new world like a man who had all
his life studied the Graces . . . I think this shews how much *Nature*
can do without *art*, than *art* with all her refinement, unassisted by
Nature.

Frances concluded that Mai was "far superior to the common race of *us
cultivated gentry:* he could not else have borne so well the way of Life into
which he is thrown."[36]

An example of the latter camp of Rousseauists was Joseph Banks.
Though certainly an enthusiast of nature in its many guises—geographic,
botanical, sexual, and anthropological—this dilettante heir to a merchant's
estate was not quite as prepared as Frances to eschew the cornerstones of
commercial culture. Banks evidently reveled in proclaiming Mai's manners, habits, and insights as those of a true natural—and indeed often in
holding them up as apt models for society—but he also believed his duty
as Mai's patron included the inculcation of some European ways. Banks
was behind Mai's sartorial and conversational preparation for elite company. He was committed to teaching him the basics of botanical analysis.
And he wanted him to take back to Oceania the rudiments of European
carpentry, cooking, and music.[37] Banks was most of all a disciple of ratio-
nal Enlightenment thought, keen to reform society along natural principles in some measure, but only in so far as nature itself could be defined
according to his account of rationality.

The key to understanding Mai's attraction to Rousseauists in Britain,
however, is to recognize how the primitivist inclination went far beyond
the privileged circles of Burney and Banks. The impulse to idealize Mai
as a noble savage in order to criticize contemporary British life was as
evident in the cheap squibs and hack journalism that abounded in his
wake as in the ponderings of the literati. Mai did not become a sensation because he proved a darling of "patrician Britons" but because he
appeared to speak to multiple sectors of society.[38] The *St. James's Chronicle* saw as much when it noted how "every circumstance relative to the
Native of Otaheite engages the Attention of Philosophers, as well as the
commonly-curious."[39]

The commonly curious turned out to be quite as articulate and in
many instances far harsher than the philosophical when it came to the
subject of Mai. In 1775, one pamphlet appeared that demonstrated a
razor-sharp appreciation of the current Rousseauist stance against commercial wealth, modern militarism, and the liberty of the polite. Entitled
An Historic Epistle from Omiah to the Queen of Otaheite, it recalled the

cycle of pretended letters that had appeared two years previously in response to Hawkesworth. The narrator is supposedly Mai, who begins with his initial views of London: "Where'er I turn, confusion meets my eyes, / New scenes of pomp, new luxuries surprise . . . " He goes on to ask:

> Can Europe boast, with all her pilfer'd wealth,
> A larger share of happiness, or health?
> What then avail her thousand arts to gain
> The stores of every land, and every main:
> Whilst we, whom love's more grateful joys enthral,
> Profess one art—to live without them all.

From a consideration of the effect of commerce on personal well-being, the narrator then turns to the way it necessarily commands systematic violence:

> [Europe's states] in cool blood premeditately go
> To murder wretches whom they cannot know.
> Urg'd by no injury, prompted by no ill,
> In forms they butcher, and by systems kill;
> Cross o'er the seas, to ravage distant realms,
> And ruin thousands worthier than themselves.

From here, he castigates false claims to freedom:

> Sick of these motley scenes, might I once more
> In peace return to Otaheite's shore . . .
> There fondly straying o'er the sylvan scenes,
> Taste unrestrain'd what Freedom really means:
> And glow inspir'd with that enthusiast zeal,
> Which Britons talk of, Otaheitians feel.[40]

Similar sentiments were expressed in the usually sanguine *Gentleman's Magazine*. In mid-1775, a writer named only H.D. took the opportunity of Mai's arrival to remind readers that Britain's exploration of Oceania in the name of greater wealth—just like Spain's exploration of America two centuries before—had "cost the lives of many Indians." To the "cruelties of discovery," the reporter added, was "that of transporting a simple barbarian to a christian and civilized country, to debase him into a spectacle and a macaroni, and to invigorate the seeds of corrupted nature by a course of improved debauchery." It is difficult to tell whether the author was more "shockt" by the aggression inherent in modern expansionist imperatives or by the decadent culture they had created.[41]

Another middling and otherwise mild journal, the *London Magazine*, also thought Mai presented a chance to drive home some truths about

New World exploration. In Mai's Otaheite, a correspondent was "sorry to assure you we have established a disease which will prove ever fatal to these unhappy innocents, who seem to have enjoyed a perfect state of simplicity and nature till we, a more refined race of monsters, contaminated all their bliss by an introduction of our vices." Thus, what were once "the happiest race of mortals" can now only look forward to "the return of Omiah, who is . . . not a priest nor a man of any distinction among them."[42]

An octavo-printed poem by an obscure Irish writer, Gerald Fitzgerald, peddled the same message as late as 1779. His *Injured Islanders; or, The Influence of Art upon the Happiness of Nature* was sure that readers remembered Mai's recent visit but wondered if any appreciated the effects of Britain's own visit to Tahiti. Where once "kindred Love connected ev'ry Shore," now "Discord and War in dread Confusion rise"; because "Europe's Crimes with Europe's Commerce spread, so all one hears is "Widow's wailings" and "Orphan's cries."[43]

The rougher kinds of commentary that appeared in penny broadsides were admittedly less concerned about the effect of British expansion on peoples elsewhere, but they could be just as pointed in their criticism of commerce at home. Ostensibly an attack on the rakish decadence of the Royal Society circle, *Omiah: An Ode* (1776) took in all of sociable Britain when it imagined Mai's memory of his visit:

> Of wondrous sights, OMIAH tells
> Of asses—and apes—and Sadler's Wells!
> And of our smooth cestinos!
> —How he admir'd a masquerade,
> Was sometimes 'prentice to the trade
> —Of opr'ras—and festinos![44]

The ribald satire *Seventeen Hundred and Seventy Seven* (1777) was equally condemnatory when it fantasized about a complementary visit by British elites to Mai's Oceania:

> Then shall perfection crown each noble heart,
> When southern passions mix with northern art;
> Like oil and acid blent in social strife,
> The poignant sauce to season modish life.[45]

A gentler, more Banksian kind of primitivism appeared in the common reflections on Mai, too. This was mostly evident in the numerous images made of the visitor. Indeed, the first two British depictions of Mai were popular engravings—the first printed as a small half-broadsheet and the other as an illustration in a magazine. The first engraving shows Mai

FIGURE 6.1. *Omiah: A Native of Otaheite Brought to England by Captain Furneaux,* engraving by "Page," *London Magazine,* August 1774, reproduced by permission of the National Library of Australia, nla. pic-an9060939.

meeting George III: the visitor appears dignified and courteous, but then so do all the surrounding British peers. The piece imagines a harmonious mixing of two estimable societies. The second engraving (figure 6.1) shows Mai standing alone, holding under his arm what looks like a Polynesian wooden stool. Dressed in robes and with tattooed hand outstretched, the subject is an open and winsome savage. As an accompaniment to a story about how well Mai has risen to British standards of sensibility and hospitality, it also paints a congratulatory image of cultural encounter.[46]

Mai was the subject of some grander art as well. William Hodges, the draftsman on board Cook's *Resolution,* had sketched Mai when still in

Oceania. He was later commissioned to paint an oil portrait for the Royal College of Surgeons by John Hunter, who was obsessed with documenting the varieties of human anatomy. Both Hodges's sketch (later available as a large engraving for discerning buyers) and his oil are traditional compositions: Mai appears regal if not noble, proud if not commanding. Hodges's long personal association with Britain's imperial project made him sympathetic to the idea of mutually beneficial encounter. He evidently believed that Mai was going to become a key agent for such connection in the Pacific New World.[47]

The remaining three important images of Mai were all probably commissioned by Banks himself, though this does not mean they all remained confined to elite audiences. Nathaniel Dance's 1774 drawing of Mai circulated widely as an engraving by Francesco Bartolozzi. As in the magazine image, Mai is shown standing with a stool under one arm. His features here resemble more Hodges's realist depiction than the general exoticism of the earlier pictures. But his tattoos, accoutrement, stance, and coverings yet remind that this is certainly a savage, come in peace to meet his social alternate.[48]

Joshua Reynolds's full-length oil of Mai (figure 6.2) became even better known than Dance's image when it was engraved by the German artist Johann Jacobe in 1776. Through this reproduction, Reynolds's *Omai* was soon "familiar to [much of] the eighteenth-century public."[49] Reynolds himself, of course, was responsible for a good deal of that fame. By the time of Mai's visit, he was president of the Royal Academy and one of the most sought-after artists by patrons and exhibition-goers alike. *Omai* exhibited to huge crowds in the 1776 annual show of the Royal Academy. The painting figured the visitor as an unequivocal noble savage. Gone was the hesitancy evident in Reynolds's earlier attempt to portray a New World visitor. Where *Scyacust Ukah* (1762) (figure 4.3) had wavered in its belief that Ostenaco was truly a savage, *Omai* confidently asserted not only that this visitor was a savage exemplar but also that such savagery reminded the civilized of what was best in themselves. The sense of savagery was accomplished by a careful erasure of all of the "singular" features that so haunted *Scyacust Ukah*: Mai's head is a generalized exotic, looking away from any scrutiny; his bare feet, tattoos, and wild setting fix his exoticism into the subgenre of savagery but not so specifically that they signify a particular tribe or geography. The favorable link between savagery and British society is made through the work's many pleasing neoclassical attributes. Where Mai's usual savage robes are reformulated to suggest an ancient toga and where his typical standing posture is

FIGURE 6.2. Joshua Reynolds, *Omai*, 1775.

styled into a senator's best *adlocutio* stance, the viewer realizes that this
visitor echoes the virtues of Britain's own supposed past. He may not be
himself accorded the esteem of the ancients, but Mai functions here as a
novel and topical means of underscoring ancient values.[50]

Banks's final commission of Mai was to William Parry, a former pupil
of Reynolds though always a more obscure artist than his master. The
resultant oil of 1776 (figure 6.3) is a large conversation piece showing
a seated Solander, a gesticulating Banks (in remarkably similar pose to

FIGURE 6.3. William Parry, *Omai, Joseph Banks, and Dr. Solander*, 1776. © National Portrait Gallery, London / National Museum Cardiff / Captain Cook Memorial Museum, Whitby.

that of Reynolds's Omai) and a rather pensive Mai. As Harriet Guest has argued, this image was one of the most ambivalent of the contemporary Mai portrayals.[51] Though he still wears his savage robes and bare feet, his tattoos have been removed and his face is nearer again to Hodges's realism. Instead of bearing a proud and regal expression, however, Parry's Mai is decidedly somber—his eyes halfway downcast, halfway outward-looking; his features long and melancholy. Together with his clear spatial remove from the two British subjects, this Mai creates a more worrying atmosphere for the viewer than any earlier version. If a noble savage, it is unclear whether he reprimands or comforts.

Such ambivalence was not an issue for the writer and lexicographer Samuel Johnson. Another member of the Banks and Burney circle, Johnson was nonetheless one of the fiercest opponents of Rousseauism in literate Britain. His hostility to the vogue illustrates the flipside of the primitivist cult of the 1770s: indeed, it was perhaps the zeal of the attack on Rousseauism at the time that helped to raise the fad's profile in public culture. Johnson was repulsed by the notion of taking lessons from savagery. "Don't cant in defense of savages!" he ordered his long-suffering biographer, James Boswell. "There cannot be anything more false [than the idea of the "superior happiness of the savage life"] . . . you are not to talk such paradoxes: let me have no more on't. It cannot entertain, far less can it instruct." He thought Rousseau himself "a rascal, who ought to be hunted out of society." When the deeply primitivist Boswell once floated the idea of going to live in Oceania for a while "to see what nature can do," Johnson snapped: "What could you learn, Sir? What can savages tell, but what they themselves have seen? Of the past, or the invisible, they can tell nothing."[52]

Johnson's brutal pragmatism on this issue was partly tested when he met Mai himself in March or April of 1776. At a private dinner, Johnson was impressed by the quality of the visitor's manners. He explained to Boswell afterward that this must be on account of his tutelage "while in England [by] only . . . the best company." For Johnson, Mai had become interesting because he was *no longer* a savage. Indeed, he joked that when seated before both Mai and the wealthy Yorkshire peer, Lord Mulgrave, with the light streaming in from behind on them both, he was "afraid to speak to either, lest I should mistake one for the other . . . there was [now] so little of the savage in Omai."[53] Doubtless the remark was supposed to injure Mulgrave more than it was to praise Mai, but it also stood as an example of the refusal to glorify savagery that ran equally strongly alongside the more primitivist reactions to the Oceanian visitor.

This kind of refusal—just as with primitivism—found expression at various levels of the public response. The popular squib *Omiah's Farewell* of 1776 hardly thought Mai an embodiment of any worthy ideal. In Mai's voice, it showed only disdain for Oceanian people: "Oft have I tried, but every art was vain, / No colours hid my dark numidian stain. / Oft have I censur'd too the savage race, / To daub ignoble parts—nor mend the face." The ditty then continued with its condemnation of Oceanian tattooing:

> Is it not strange, the Ladies of my shore,
> Whom Heaven favours, and whom you adore—
> That they should use their paints with such disgrace
> And give the tail what they deny the face?
> How customs vary, yet how like each kind
> The man, the Monkey, differ but in mind.

Though the British man here fairs better than the Oceanian "monkey," the squib ends with a dig also at one particular strata of metropolitan society. The First Admiral Lord Sandwich is ridiculed for his well-known affair with the low-bred singer Martha Ray. This "gallant Peer," credited with directing the nation's fleet in time with Cupid's rapturous beat, is sarcastically thanked as well for being Mai's chief example "of the human race . . . To thee I owe my morals and my grace."[54] Though he shared Johnson's skepticism regarding noble savagery, this author was less inclined to believe that some parts of British society were much different.

The same equivocation about Britain's contrast to a despised savagery crept into the 1778 broadside *Transmigration*. It had little time for the "wanton tribes" of "Southern Oceans" who think that "simple fornication / Requires no sort of Palliation." But it turned out to be as unimpressed with British rakes who philander overseas, striving to "dress your Story, and Make (what is your Shame) your Glory."[55] Popular antiprimitivism with regard to Mai indeed often spiraled into despair over elite British behavior, if not over all British peoples. Sarcasm about the visitor's supposed virtues frequently led to ribaldry about the antics of those who associated with, for example, the scandalously transvestite Chevalier D'Éon or, later, the parties involved in the seedy murder in 1779 of Sandwich's beloved Martha Ray.[56]

Mai in Britain, then, was far from being simply "socialite phenomena among an elite class."[57] His appeal lay in precisely his capacity to offer a means of discussing the problems of elitism, as well as the persistently commercial state that was believed to have created it. Though discussion now often emphasized happiness and art more than virtue and decadence, the *langue* of classical-republican hostility remained the primary goad behind all meditations—pushing pundits to agree or defend contemporary expansionism as they saw fit. Mai departed Britain just one week after the American revolutionaries' Declaration of Independence. In this key period, the British metropolitan public were evidently as concerned as ever about the impulses that underlay New World incursions. Whether they believed them worthwhile or reprehensible, Britons had found in Mai another apt means of giving their views a crucial airing.

FINDING OCEANIA

Before his return to Oceania, Mai completed an itinerary similar to that of his New World predecessors. He saw all the major political and military sites as well as many leisure spots, including now art galleries, university halls, and the British Museum. His month-long trip to Yorkshire took in the seashore at Scarborough and a castle near Whitby. Although Banks had vowed to fund all these activities, His Majesty's government eventually agreed to refund most of the expenses, presumably on the grounds of Mai's potential benefit to Britain's Oceanic project.[58] The increasing steepness of those expenses, however, made the Admiralty somewhat relieved to secure Mai's berth back home in July 1776.

Mai returned to the Pacific with Cook's third and final expedition. Against all historical odds, it was the New World exemplar who would survive this particular hemispheric crossing and the Old World captain who would not. Cook was killed by some local inhabitants of Hawaii in February 1779. Britons were deeply shocked when they learned of his fate in January 1780.[59] Through the following decade, that shock seemed to grow only more profound, coming to stand in many ways as a counter-sign for the later comprehensive shift in metropolitan approach to New World expansion. British mourning for Cook coincided with the beginning of the end of the familiar tussle over expansionism and the rise of a new attitude, where questions of right moved instead to questions of mode or best practice. Tellingly, though the first responses to Cook's death often contained some reference to his erstwhile Oceanian charge, latter eulogies had less and less use for Mai or any of his kind.

The satiric pamphlet *Letter from Omai* that appeared in the first few weeks after the revelation of Cook's murder was in fact the only example of an older, pre-return kind of commentary. It began with Mai's supposed acknowledgment to Lord Sandwich for "the powder, shot, guns, crackers, sword, feathers, and watch" that the Royal Society had thought to leave with him upon his repatriation. "Let me thank you also for my conversion to Christianity: I ought perhaps to have mentioned this before the sword and the crackers, but as [they] have commonly taken the lead, I will not dispute their title to it." The narrator then remarked that he "cannot conclude . . . without saying how much real concern I feel for the unfortunate fate of poor Captain Cook, who was certainly very cruelly and inhumanly butchered, for nothing more than ordering his crew to fire on a banditti of naked savages, who seemed to look as if they had a right to the country in which he found them."[60]

Such aggressive wit had few imitators in the years that followed. Anna Seward's phenomenally successful sentimental *Elegy on Captain Cook* of the same year was far more representative of the general tone of the 1780s. It also invoked Mai but gave most space to the fallen British explorer, now elevated to the status of a "new . . . *humane* . . . Columbus."

When the *Elegy* commanded the "Gay Eden of the south" to pay due respects, it also

> Bid Omiah bring his choicest stores,
> The juiciest fruits, and the luxuriant flow'rs . . .
> Come, Oberea, hapless fair-one! Come,
> With piercing shrieks bewail thy hero's doom!

These fairly unhopeful comments were then swamped by pages of hagiography of one who, with "dauntless breast, . . . quit imperial London's gorgeous plains" to "pour new wonders on th'uncultured shore."[61]

Seward's casual attribution of luxury to Mai's Oceania in the *Elegy* may have been a tiny flourish—an inkling of resistance to the standard eighteenth-century consensus on luxury as an effect of decadence rather than of simplicity. But there was nothing casual about the way William Cowper, another Cook eulogist, applied the word in his meditations on Oceania. In his famous poem *The Task* (1785), Cowper was sure that the inhabitants of

> the favoured isles
> So lately found, although the constant sun
> Cheer all their seasons with a grateful smile,
> Can boast but little virtue; and inert
> Through plenty, lose in morals what they gain
> In manners, victims of luxurious ease.

Not even the fiercest antiprimitivists of the preceding century had thought to find the evils of overabundance in a land of acknowledged savagery. Later in the same poem, Cowper addressed Mai in person:

> Rude as thou art (for we return'd thee rude
> And ignorant, except of outward show)
> I cannot think thee yet so dull of heart
> And spiritless, as never to regret
> Sweets tasted here, and left as soon as known.

The sweets of Britain to Cowper were less sumptuous riches than the ancient prize of virtue itself: "Here virtue thrives as in her proper soil; / Not rude and surly, and beset with thorns . . . / but gentle, kind, / By culture tamed."[62] To think that luxury could derive from simplicity was one thing but to say that virtue could derive from art was entirely another. Such a stance went against some of the founding dichotomies of the eighteenth century—whatever a person's political persuasion. To meddle with some of the key concepts of the old debate about expansion augured a major change in its future direction.

The most dramatic expression of regret about Cook was not an elegy at all but a blockbuster pantomime. Every year, the large theaters of London put on a new pantomime with a topical subject. In 1785, the Theatre Royal in Covent Garden commissioned several leading artists to create its annual show around the theme of Cook's last voyage. The established playwright John O'Keeffe wrote the plot, the Royal Academician Philippe Jacques de Loutherbourg designed the scenery and costumes, and the theater's resident musician William Shield composed the score.[63] Though entitled *Omai; Or a Trip Round the World*, this piece also ultimately placed Cook at its moral center. The title character travels to Britain to woo a British maiden, meets beautiful Londina in London, and takes her home to Tahiti so they can together become Tahiti's royal couple. But it is Cook who makes everything possible, including the persuasion of the existing monarch to yield her powers to his preferred Oceanian on account of his superior judgment. That all ends peacefully is due to Cook's example, for the British explorer taught all "mankind how to live."[64]

The *Omai* pantomime was a major success: it performed over fifty times in one season, and survived, uncommonly, into the next two seasons, finally closing in 1788. Reviewers thought the scenery more "beautiful" and the music more "rich" than anything seen or heard on stage before. Many declared it the perfect illustration to Cook's similarly successful posthumous publication of *A Voyage to the Pacific Ocean* of 1784. De Loutherbourg's final scene, named "The Apotheosis of Captain Cook," depicting the explorer's resurrection by the twin beauties of "Fame" and "Britannia," became a well-known image among magazine readers and print buyers.[65]

The pantomime secured the shift in tone of the British response to Oceania. Into the 1780s, attitudes switched from a fascination in New World savagery, best embodied in real-life visitors, to an interest solely in the benefits that Britain might introduce.

. . .

The actual repatriation of Mai was much more tricky than the pantomime or any of the other eulogies suggested. Cook's orders had been vague as to which island Mai should be resettled upon. Once in the Tahitian archipelago, the specific locale was clearly left to the captain's discretion. Though Banks seems to have taken Mai's political pleas seriously, ensuring that he returned with at least some of his requested weaponry and ammunition, Cook was more concerned to find a peaceful situation for the traveler—even if it went against Mai's personal desires. Where Banks had Mai supplied with guns, shot, powder, and even a bespoke suit of armor, Cook was keener that Mai have an opportunity to use some of the other gifts sent by the British government, such as the tools, the iron, and the livestock. What either Banks or Cook imagined Mai would do with the toys, fireworks, perfume, or peacock is not recorded.[66]

After making extensive use of Mai's interpretive and diplomatic services during stops in New Holland, New Zealand, the Cook Islands, and Tonga on the way to Tahiti, Cook finally steered the *Resolution* toward Mai's home islands. On the island of Tubuai, Mai reunited with his sister, which one officer witnessed as "extreamly moving" and "better conceived than discribed." Moving on to Tahiti itself, Cook tried to persuade Chief Tu to accept Mai into his kingdom, but neither Tu nor Mai seemed agreeable. Apparently Mai pleaded around this time to be taken straight to Raiatea, but Cook discovered that Boraboran rule there was as strong as ever and refused to risk a conflagration. The captain decided on Huahine, where Mai had first encountered the *Resolution* nearly four years ago. By now, Mai was resigned, satisfied at least to receive the grant of land that Cook purchased for him and to set out his unusual new possessions before another community of strangers. The farewell to his erstwhile able seamen was notably emotional: "he sustained himself with a manly resolution," wrote another observing officer, until he came to embrace Cook, bursting into tears, "as did most of us who were his Acquaintance."[67]

In less than two years, Mai was dead. Though Boraboran war did eventually come to Huahine, too—and though Mai did fight with the opposition—he supposedly died from disease rather than violence. Britons did not learn of his fate until more than a decade later when an embattled William Bligh, struggling home from Oceania in 1789 after surviving his notorious mutiny, reported what he had learnt when visiting the island the previous year.[68]

Starkly absent upon news of his death was any resurgence of interest in Mai among Britons. Few journalists reported it; no member of Banks's set uttered a word.[69] Though Oceania remained important to Britons, it was no longer accessed primarily through the figure of a native inhabitant. In the metropolitan imaginary, the region was becoming instead a site for prospective whalers, missionaries and convicts rather than for its own indigenes—a space to be transformed by Britons rather than encountered as a means of understanding their own transformation. It is thus somewhat ironic that in their long effort to find Oceania—as a new world of promise and fantasy—Britons came in the end to see only themselves. Unlike the shift away from Native Americans two decades previously, the loss of interest in Mai signaled something larger than the failure of folks like him to fulfill any more the requirements of savagery. Mai's fading coincided with what would become a turning away from the metaphor of savagery altogether.

7. Palauans, Hawaiians, Tahitians

Diminishing Oddities

Ten years to the day after Mai first disembarked at Portsmouth, another Oceanian arrived in Britain. His name was Lebuu, a Palauan heir escorted by an East India Company (EIC) merchant captain. Lebuu resided in Britain for six months, but in that time he generated only a fraction of the interest that had been shown in his New World predecessors. Into the 1780s, some more Oceanian people turned up but each also to diminishing effect. The long streak of fascination for New World visitors that Britain had entertained all century seemed to dry up in the space of one decade.

The explanation for this diminishment involves the same discursive shift that accounted for the depth of the British mourning for Cook. Both phenomena pointed to a significant change in metropolitan attitude toward Britain's overseas activities. While many historians have identified the 1780s as a turning point in the practice of British expansionism, fewer have concentrated on the realignment of debate that followed in the public sphere. Christopher Bayly has probably been most succinct on this issue, arguing that the 1780s inaugurated an "imperial meridian," during which British officials forged a "more vigorous world empire."[1] He has shown that this vigor was prompted by various "world crises"—not only the American Revolution but also the intimations of radicalism and dissent burbling in France and in Asia—and that it was characterized on the ground by both an aggressive political centralization and a hardening social theory.[2] But Bayly, like others, has had less to say about the changes in British public discourse regarding empire that occurred to sustain this move—other than to imply that the contemporary world crises shocked ordinary pundits into developing the appropriate "ideological will" for vigor in the same way as they did officials.[3]

What has often gone unexplored is the effective closing down of the debate about expansion that had animated metropolitans for the last near-century. This is in no small part due to the reluctance of many historians to acknowledge that debate in the first place, preferring to read late-eighteenth-century jingoism back into the century rather than see it as an unprecedented development. Such closing down did not of course herald a new age of consensus in all matters imperial—Britons were notoriously fiery on questions of missionary reach, colonial education, and governmental self-rule in their overseas spheres from this era onward—but it did signify a shift from the problem of imperial creation per se to problems of correct imperial mode. In other words, it entailed a shift from a problem about first principles to a problem about second principles.

The move away from fundamentals turned out to have a profound impact on the reception of peoples who had always been considered as representatives of fundamental difference. Where savagery had once served as the ideal means of articulating views on Britain's basic structures, it proved less eloquent for discussions on the refinement of those structures.

Before proceeding to a narrative of New World visits to Britain in the 1780s, this chapter detours into a further examination of Cook's eulogization through the same decade. My rationale is twofold. First, such an examination provides a neat example of the general move in discourse about Britain's international position. The eulogies after 1780 were all remarkably agreed that Cook's ventures into Oceania had been glorious enterprises for the furtherance of British expansion. Dissent only figured when some questioned whether Cook's Enlightenment values had really been the most appropriate for such a grueling task. Second, the study of Cook's heroization after death provides the flip side to the study of Britain's lessening interest in New World visitors. If the story of Oceanians in Britain after 1780 is largely one of decreasing attention, then the story of Cook's posthumous approbation reveals something of what filled the gap. The difference in the substitution, of course, was its uniformity; where New World visitors had provoked a diversity of opinions, Cook's death solicited only one kind of response.

COOK'S DEATH IN BRITISH CULTURE

The scholar Bernard Smith once commented that "shortly after his death, Cook's reputation was submitted quite consciously and deliberately to a heroizing process, not by his fellow-voyagers, but by academicians, poets, and artists whose imaginations had been gripped by the magnitude of his achievement."[4] While the latter is certainly true, Cook's "fellow-voyagers" were not exactly immune to the heroizing bug. The first publication on Cook's final mission was by Second Lieutenant John Rickman. Though his *Journal of Captain Cook's Last Voyage to the Pacific Ocean* appeared anonymously in 1781 because it contravened the Admiralty's ban on any publication before the official reckoning, the work was yet fulsome in its praise of the fallen leader. Cook was described as being "gallant," "humane," "sensible," and—in Rickman's narration of his farewell to Mai—deeply "sympathetic."[5] Rickman was careful in how he disclosed the events that led up to the killing, since he knew that some more senior officers believed his own gun-toting behavior on the day had contributed to the Hawaiian about-turn.[6] Excising all mention of his own doings, Rickman described a calm Cook going about the business of native diplomacy when, out of the blue, he was struck from behind by "a savage . . . with his club." The attacking Hawaiian then proceeded to "thrust his Pa-ha-he (a kind of wooden poignard . . .) through his body with such force, that, entering between his shoulders, the point of it came out at his breast. The quarrel now became general."[7] In Rickman's account, it is only savage unpredictability that can explain Cook's death.

Although the lieutenant-astronomer, James King, who wrote the introduction to the eventual official compilation of Cook's journals in 1784, likewise had little time for Hawaiians, he neither had much respect for Rickman. It is clearly Rickman who is imputed to have caused the "accident" of firing on a "Chief of the first rank" while Cook was negotiating with the Hawaiian ruler. This "occasioned [a] ferment" that ended with the killing of the British captain: a native was driven to threaten Cook with his "*pahooa*," which in turn led Cook to fire some shot, which in turn led to "a general attack with stones." What followed, King writes, "was a scene of the utmost horror and confusion," with British officers now firing into the flying stones. Cook was said to call out to his men at this point to cease their firing in the interest of "preventing any further bloodshed," but in that same moment was "stabbed in the back and fell with his face in the water."[8] Though he evidently apportioned most blame to the Hawaiians themselves, and some to Rickman, King felt compelled—with all due regret—to conclude that Cook's own "humanity" had also contributed to the tragedy. Those "worthy qualities of the best men" that Cook "possessed in an eminent degree" had "on this occasion, proved fatal to him."[9]

The Welsh surgeon on board the *Resolution*, David Samwell, was yet another fellow-voyager who contributed to the Cook hagiography. His

Narrative of the Death of Captain James Cook came out in 1786. Samwell's admiration of Cook, and near-depression as a consequence of his death, was articulated in page after page: "there is hardly a corner of the earth, however remote and savage, that will not long remember his benevolence and humanity . . . he was our leading-star which at its setting, left us involved in darkness and despair."[10] Such was his attachment to Cook, and to Enlightenment values generally, that he could not share King's equivocation about the cause of death. Like King, he did think some blame went to the minor officers, for "mistaking the signals" of the captain (he did not name Rickman here but rather a Lieutenant John Williamson).[11] But most of all he blamed the violence inherent in the Hawaiians who were with Cook at the time. Though he was neutral on Oceanians throughout much of the text, he evidently believed that savages had a bottomless capacity for horror and could at any time unleash it in madness. Samwell's description of the final moments seemed to take on the obsessive compulsion of the murderers themselves: "[Cook was] endeavouring to support himself . . . when a savage gave him [another] blow with a club, and he was seen alive no more. They hauled him up lifeless on the rocks, where they seemed to take a savage pleasure in using every barbarity to his dead body, snatching the daggers out of each other's hands, to have the horrid satisfaction of piercing the fallen victim of their barbarous rage."[12]

Finally, the image that was used to promote the official publication in 1784, John Webber's "Death of Captain Cook" (figure 7.1), returned to King's ruefully mixed stance. Webber had been the shipboard artist on Cook's third voyage. The popular engraving of his large-scale oil painting captured the decisive moment when Cook turned to address his men. Notably, he is surrounded by scores of naked, ferocious, and identical-looking Hawaiians. Bernard Smith has wondered whether the outstretched arm was meant to get Cook's officers to leave so they could at least save themselves or whether it was about saving the Hawaiians any further harm.[13] Either reading, however, makes Cook's "humanity" seem at least partially tragic. Webber entitled the piece "The Death of Captain Cook in February 1779 by the murdering dagger of a barbarian at Carakakooa in one of the Sandwich Islands, he having there become a Victim to his own Humanity." The equivocation about the safety of Enlightenment ideals crept back in with the most widely circulated testament about Cook of the decade.

These voyager accounts, with all the weighty authority of eyewitness participants, helped to set the tone for Cook heroization in the 1780s. As Bernard Smith suggests, though, by far the greatest share of responsibil-

FIGURE 7.1. *The Death of Captain Cook*, 1784, engraving by F. Bartolozzi and
W. Byrne, after a drawing by John Webber. Reproduced by permission of the
National Library of Australia, nla.pic-an7678355.

ity for this process was taken up by the nonvoyaging scribes of Britain's
maturing public sphere. Following Anna Seward's lead in 1780 with her
bestselling handwringer, writers of all stamps kept up the adoration of the
explorer for a good ten years. The *Gentleman's Magazine*, when recording
Cook's demise, insisted that the captain resembled no less a figure than
Spain's great Magellan, though Cook outstripped him in honorableness
of motive: instead of being an "aggressor," Britain's famed adventurer was
always "on the defensive, and in this, as a voyager, was almost singular,
that he never knowingly injured, but always studied to benefit the savages whom he visited."[14] Whether this same studiousness became the
inadvertent cause of his death, the journal declined to say. Less circum-
spect were some of the poets who joined their voices to the chorus. While
the middling poet William Fitzgerald hailed Cook's "gentle sympathy,"
he was sobered to think that it may have been precisely the quality that
had drawn out, and then fallen prey to, "the ills of savage life." Fitzgerald
was meticulous in listing the latter: "incurious languor, sordid strife,

want rapacious, toil severe [and] sullenness."[15] The sometime-radical poet Helen Maria Williams was also moved to ponder if the "Great Cook," who bestowed only "love, and hope, and joy" to Oceania, had been "deluded" by a "devious" people. His efforts, at any rate, had left him to redden what she now thought a "raging" land.[16]

Other commentators remained focused on Cook's merits alone. From the evangelical propagandist Hannah More to the nonconformist *philosophe* Andrew Kippis, all agreed that the captain had represented the pinnacle of "humane" and "benevolent" achievement.[17] In one of her numerous abolitionist poems, More gushed over Cook's "gentle mind, / Thy love of arts, thy love of humankind; / [and] thy mild and liberal plan."[18] In his influential biography—soon to become the standard account and remain so for the next century—Kippis devoted a whole thirty-page chapter to Cook's character, citing his "genius [not of] imagination merely" but also of the applied knowledges and moral sense. "To all these great qualities," Kippis concluded, was "added the most amiable virtues." It was, in short, "impossible for any one to excel [Cook] in humanity."[19]

Taken together, the outstanding aspect of the public eulogy for Cook during the 1780s was the absence of any seriously dissenting view. Other than the sarcastic *Letter from Omai* (1780) discussed in the previous chapter, which questioned Cook's motives in being in Hawaii in the first place, no commentator doubted the explorer's accomplishment, and thus neither his mission. If there was any instability in the collective script, it came from those who worried that what Britons now unanimously admired was also what might leave them vulnerable to attack.[20] A secondary aspect of the outpouring, of course, was its move to a much tougher attitude toward New World people—at least as they appeared on their own shores in contest with Britons.

How to account for this exceptional homogeneity (and seemingly twinned xenophobia)? No previous explorer had garnered such a response in Britain before. Cook's predecessors in Oceania, Byron and Wallis, had commanded little personal attention, even if their voyages had sparked overall interest. The fascination for Oceania occasioned by Cook's own earlier voyages had likewise focused more on behaviors and things than on a single figure. Early American entrepreneurs such as Frobisher, Raleigh, and Smith had certainly never enjoyed any concerted glorification—until, that is, around about this period. Of course, unique to this instance was the fact of death—but grief alone cannot explain the reaction. Eighteenth-century Britons were not particularly renowned for their adherence to *de mortius nil nisi bonum*, as the descendants of imperial figures like John

Churchill, Robert Clive, and even George II could have painfully attested. The mode of Cook's posthumous heroization was, rather, something new. Set against the long context of antagonism regarding the general issue of expansionism, this agreed adoration of one of the main agents of New World expansion appears especially novel.

As it turns out, one of the key modern scholars on Cook's death in Hawaiian culture, Marshall Sahlins, has probably come closest to explaining its reception in British culture. Sahlins argued that Britons made Cook into an "avatar of a new kind of . . . imperialism" in the same way as Hawaiians made him into a form of their god Lono—both processes were a means of addressing the unthinkable and, in consequence, of reinforcing the ruling cosmology of each society.[21] What Sahlins left unemphasized, however, was the extraordinariness of the rise of Britain's "new kind of . . . imperialism" to the status of ruling cosmology at all. Imperialist impulses of any kind in Britain before the 1780s had always attracted enough dissent as to negate a hegemonic hold. Now, for the first time, they were evidently dominant enough that their current "spirit incarnate" could command a similarly dominating approval.[22]

Certainly Cook was heroized in the service of expansionist ideology. That he was heroized unanimously, however, signified an important change in the balance of ideologies over the question of expansion. Whatever debates continued to unfold in public culture over Britain's push into the New World, they were now carried out under an overarching dome of acceptance about the basic fact of empire. Into this unprecedented environment of acceptance came three New World visitors in the space of nine years: a Palauan in 1784, a Hawaiian in 1789, and a Tahitian in 1793.

LEBUU FROM PALAU

Lebuu arrived in Britain on 14 July 1784. His tiny island home of Palau lies between Guam and the Philippines in what is today known as Micronesia. His British story began with the shipwreck of an East India Company vessel on the reefs of eastern Palau. Captain Henry Wilson of the *Antelope* packet had set out on a secret mission on behalf of the company in 1781, searching for new routes to China that avoided enemy ships lurking around the African Cape. The company had lost five ships to French, Dutch, and Spanish marauders in the last year alone. Although relatively minor casualties of the ongoing war against American independence, these losses nonetheless inspired some reconsideration of regular procedure. The *Antelope* became the first EIC vessel to head west from Britain for China rather than east. While Wilson arrived safely in Macao by following the southern Pacific routes chartered by Cook and others, he hit trouble upon his return journey by sailing along a more northerly parallel. The Palau Islands had been known to Spaniards for nearly a century but they had never been settled by Europeans and were poorly represented in European records.[23] Wilson claimed to have no notion of their presence when his ship tore along their ragged coastal rocks in August 1783.[24]

Fortunately, no lives were lost. The ship's two boats and a makeshift raft got everyone to shore. Within hours, the survivors were surrounded by canoes full of Palau Islanders. By a "singular accident," as the wreck's chief eighteenth-century historian would later remark, one of Wilson's crew was a speaker of Malay and among the Palauans was a Malay castaway: via the interpretations of these two men the two parties were, serendipitously, able to communicate.[25] The British learned that they would be welcomed by the region's leader, Abba Thule.[26] This "king" was indeed pleased to greet them; in exchange for his assistance in rebuilding their ship, he was able to secure additional manpower in his ongoing war with rebels from a rival region.[27] A deal was negotiated between Wilson and Abba Thule, achieving remarkably satisfactory results for both: within three months the *Antelope* was sufficiently recovered and a victory had been scored by the local battalion.[28]

By November 1783, Wilson was ready to recommence the journey home. He recorded that upon informing Abba Thule of his intentions, one of the crew, a Frenchman called Madan Blanchard, declared his wish to remain forever on the island. Wilson at first forbade it, citing his uselessness to "savages" but probably mostly fearing a mutinous insurrection among his other seamen.[29] When Blanchard threatened to ask permission from Abba Thule himself, Wilson relented, agreeing to confer with the king and "make it appear as a favour" instead of as a burden to the Palauans.[30] Abba Thule turned out to be delighted with the arrangement, since he in turn had hatched plans to send one of his sons to Britain with Wilson. An equal exchange could now be brokered. As George Keate, the eighteenth-century historian, remarked, the king had "already hinted an intention of sending two of his people to England . . . [now] he resolved to intrust his second son, whose name was Lee Boo, to Captain Wilson's care, that he might have the advantage of improving himself by accompanying the English, and of learning many things, that might at his return greatly benefit his own country."[31]

While some twentieth-century readers have voiced skepticism about the neatness of this arrangement, even suggesting that Lebuu was a hostage of the EIC or at the least forced to submit while in Britain to Wilson's personal ambitions, the relevant contexts of both Oceanic seafaring and New World travel to the Old World—not to mention Wilson's own personality—work to support more than splinter Keate's explanation.[32] First of all, Oceanians already had a distinguished record of voyaging by the eighteenth century. As a small platoon of scholars in the last generation have proven, the original Oceanians of the middle Pacific (today's Samoa, Tonga, and Fiji) set out about 2,000 years ago on what Greg Dening has called "the most remarkable voyage of discovery and settlement in all human history," finding initially the Tahitian archipelago, then the Marquesas, and then—within no more than one millennium—Rapanui, Hawaii, and Aotearoa (New Zealand).[33] Accomplished in double canoes of around fifteen meters in length, this seafaring heritage inculcated a permanent maritime inclination in Oceanians. The records of British mariners in the region in our period abound with examples of indigenous eagerness to join their vessels: naval captains and trading merchants alike claimed always to be refusing, and occasionally even evicting, Oceanians who wanted a ride to the next island group or, sometimes, a chance to see the now increasingly fabled land of "Britanee."[34] Second, the sixteenth- and seventeenth-century history of New World visits to Britain reminds us that there was a confirmed tradition of rulers sending inferiors over in exchange for a British guaranty. Brazilians, Powhatans, and Miskitos had done it before: Abba Thule was in some way an unwitting successor. He was certainly as lucky as fate would allow with his choice of escort: Henry Wilson turned out to be as solicitous of the youth's well-being as he promised, folding Lebuu into his own family once in Britain in a more complete and uncomplaining manner than any previous Old World escort had ever shown before.

Keate's rationalization did not mean, of course, that the EIC refrained from making as much use of Lebuu as possible when he arrived in Britain, nor does it today cast doubt on the fact of kidnapping in many instances of New World travel to the Old World. It merely suggests that if there was any coercion in this instance it was most likely of a paternal rather than colonizing nature. Accordingly, Lebuu made the exchange with Blanchard and climbed on board the restored *Antelope*. Eight months later he disembarked at Portsmouth. Making good on his oath to the father, Wilson then conveyed Lebuu to Rotherhithe just outside London to settle him with his wife and son as a new member of the household.

By December 1784, however, Lebuu was dead—from smallpox, the disease that had so concerned Mai's hosts. One modern historian now claims Lebuu's six-month residence a "celebrated" and "famous" event, but compared to the fanfare that revolved around his New World predecessors these words seem a stretch.[35] What celebrity Lebuu achieved in Britain, unlike every other New World visitor discussed thus far, was gained posthumously. Only in death, and in some instances quite some time after death, did Lebuu capture British minds.

The publication that kicked off discussion about Lebuu was, indeed, George Keate's *Account of the Pelew Islands*, published in 1788. In many ways, Keate's work resembled that of Hawkesworth published fifteen years before: it had been commissioned by the sponsor of a voyage and was a literary collation of all the relevant and available journals. In some important respects, though, Keate's *Account* differed from Hawkesworth's. Keate's commissioner, the EIC, was not an arm of government but a recent creature in Britain's political economy—a former joint stock company now partially controlled by Parliament, it represented an unprecedented formalization of relations between entrepreneurship and the state with regard to Britain's overseas prospecting. Keate's tone in the work was a significant alteration, too: where Hawkesworth had been bawdy and picaresque, Keate was sentimental and mannered. The former represented mid-eighteenth-century literary trends while Keate foreshadowed the pathos of romantic sensibility.

In terms of popularity, Keate's book did not cause the same stir that Hawkesworth's had—but then again, very little could. It did, however, acquire an instant and respectable readership: it went through four editions within the first year, and soon inspired scores of abridged, and even pamphlet, versions.[36] Much of its popularity was due no doubt to the romance of a shipwreck, such disasters commanding audiences with relentless regularity throughout the early-modern period.[37] Notably, too, the bulk of the work centered on the heroic exploits of Wilson and his men, which fitted well with the emerging mania for tales of great explorers. But some appeal was also found in the affecting tale of Lebuu's death, taking up the whole last chapter. Wilson, Keate claimed, always intended to inoculate his charge against smallpox, as Banks had for Mai, but wished to wait until "he had acquired enough of our language to be reasoned into the necessity of submitting to the operation."[38] Sadly, he waited too long: Lebuu first complained of illness on 16 December and was dead within twelve days.

In dying, Lebuu was to said to exhibit many of the qualities that would go on to characterize the romantic way of death: a pathetic selflessness, a wasting beauty, and an overflowing of emotion.[39] Keate related how Lebuu worried only about his parents, who would somehow sense that he was sick; he tried to protect Mrs. Wilson from the awful truth, too, by telling her that *"Lee Boo do well, Mother"*; and he instructed the surgeon to tell his father how well he had been attended. Caregivers at his bedside apparently displayed similar fortitude and feeling, somehow contracting the virtues of the dying in the moment of his passing. They shed copious tears and refused to leave his room.[40]

It was not just Keate who saw the visitor's death in this way. Lebuu's doctor, James Carmichael Smyth, confirmed the patient's humility and exemplary behavior in a letter: "[he] died this morning without a groan . . . in dying he has given me a lesson which I shall never forget; and surely, for patience and fortitude, he was an example worthy the imitation of a *Stoic!* . . . the maid servant was in tears and every person in the family wore the face of grief."[41]

The EIC offered to arrange and pay for the funeral. It erected a large tomb in Rotherhithe's cemetery, which carried the words: "Stop, Reader, stop!—let Nature claim a tear— / A Prince of *mine*, Lee Boo, lies bury'd here."[42] Nearly a decade later, this inscription, and the story behind it, would inspire various romantic poets to verse. Samuel Taylor Coleridge recalled having visited Lebuu's tomb in his youth:

> Yet though the hours flew by on careless wing,
> Full heavily of Sorrow would I sing . . .
> My soul amid the pensive twilight gloom
> Mourn'd with the breeze, O Lee Boo! o'er thy tomb . . .
> Where'er I wandered, Pity still was near,
> Breath'd from the heart and glisten'd in the tear:
> No knell that toll'd but fill'd my anxious eye,
> And suffering Nature wept that one should die![43]

One critic has argued that these lines figure Lebuu as the "innocence" that is doomed to die "when it comes into contact with a corrupt society."[44] Although a prominent romantic theme, it is probably secondary here to the idea of the poet's own romantic self-realization—even self-maturation given the explicit reference to the remembrance of youth—via the evocation of extreme pathos: Lebuu, in death, was an agent for Coleridge's becoming. Becoming more of himself was evidently the "lesson" that Dr Smyth had learned from Lebuu, too.

Other poets also wrote on Lebuu's death. William Lisle Bowles, a mentor for many later romantics, imagined Abba Thule's grief as he waited hopelessly for his son's return:

But not a speck can my long-straining eye
A shadow o'er the tossing wave descry.
That I might weep tears of delight, and say,
'It is the bark that bore my child away!'[45]

Coleridge's publisher, Joseph Cottle, similarly focused on the now-broken filial bond: "Since to his Father's arms he bid adieu," Lebuu can no longer recount stories "with tears of transport in his eye."[46]

The appeal of Lebuu in all these meditations was qualitatively different to that of his eighteenth-century predecessors. Most obviously, appeal seemed now to be contingent upon the visitor's death. Earlier New World visitors, as living exemplars of alternate ways of social organization, had appealed because they had enabled discourses about Britain's own mode of social organization. Lebuu, as a dead savage, spoke to more private themes. Observers were interested, first, in the feelings of empathy his death aroused in them, and, second, in how those feelings once aroused could help forge their personal identities. Keate had evidently been much moved by Lebuu's dying behavior; the EIC had clearly wanted to evoke a similar sympathy in churchyard passers-by. In feeling empathy, both Dr Smyth and Coleridge had moved toward greater self-realization.

The appeal of this New World visitor, then, lay primarily in his capacity to enable sentimental discourses about the self rather than critical discourses about society. The sentimental turn to the self is of course a well-known characteristic of the late eighteenth century in Britain. The fact that this new way of mobilizing an Oceanian visitor did not cause Lebuu to become as famous as Mai is probably less an indication of the milder influence of this turn than of the greater variety of means current at the time to articulate it. In other words, where savages had proved one of the most vital ways of articulating the problem of an expansionist society, dying savages turned out to be only one of a number of possible vehicles for the expression of the problem of self-realization. As Philippe Ariès has shown, the sentimental turn to the self fed off a range of different death scenes—deaths of children, deaths of women, deaths of the poor, and so on.[47] The death of the savage served contemporary preoccupations, but it could have been easily exchanged with another kind of death. The appeal of this visiting savage was defined for the first time by something other than savagery itself.

One particularly notable aspect of Lebuu's posthumous appeal was the form in which much of it manifested. Even more than romantic poetry, the genre of children's literature constituted most of the commentary on Lebuu's demise. While poets clustered around the story in the 1790s, children's entertainers used it variously from the time of Keate's publication through to the 1820s. Keate's *Account* was rewritten for younger audiences as *The Interesting and Affecting History of Prince Lee Boo* in 1789.[48] Multiple different children's versions followed: the *Pleasing, Interesting, and Affecting History*; the *History of Prince Lee Boo to Which is Added the Life of Paul Cuffee*; and the 16-page pamphlet *Prince Lee Boo*.[49] A version of one kind or another remained in print for much of the nineteenth century. In 1809 an anonymous children's novel appeared called *The Adventures of Madiboo, a Native of the Pellew Islands*, which assumed juvenile familiarity with Lebuu's tragic story: Madiboo befriends and learns English from the deserter Madan Blanchard; touched by civility, he embarks on a journey to find Palau's prodigal son; upon reaching London, however, he comes to understand the futility of his mission.[50] A popular children's colored engraving complemented the burgeoning literature, as did a twelve-piece jigsaw puzzle that devoted more than half of its narrative scenes to Lebuu's dying (figure 7.2).[51]

Before Lebuu's visit, New World visitors had not featured prominently in children's literature. Granted, the genre had only taken off around the mid-eighteenth century, but it is no accident that Lebuu, rather than Mai, would make it as a children's topic.[52] As an agent for discussions about self-formation, Lebuu's death was appropriate fodder for texts that concerned themselves centrally with the shaping of personal identities. Mai's life, in contrast, had been an agent for discussions about social morality and thus had exercised genres more suited to tackling that task.

As the foregoing suggests, what was most distinctive about Lebuu's visit was the lack of commentary by any sector of British culture while the man was still alive. True, he resided further out of London than most of his predecessors, and with a minor host compared to someone like Joseph Banks. Even so, Rotherhithe was a vital town in the eighteenth century; it served as one of London's key ports and was known as a bustling site of voyager exchange. The port was also culturally linked to such great voyagers as the Mayflower pilgrims and the fictional Gulliver. And while Banks certainly played a significant part in Mai's celebrity, others before him had attained renown without major hosts: the four Iroquois, the seven Cherokee, and Ostenaca's delegation had all arrived with unknown escorts but had then quickly found more powerful patronage. Neither the venue of lodging nor the status of the chaperone quite accounts for the quiet impact of Lebuu's visit.

Moreover, Lebuu did in fact frequently go into central London, and associated there with a number of luminaries. Keate noted that "he was

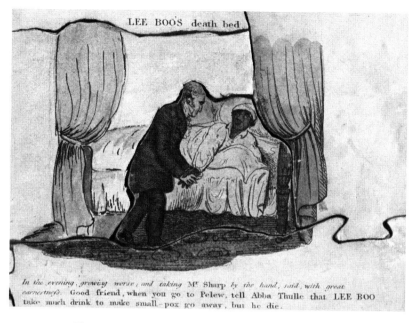

LEE BOO'S death bed

In the evening, growing worse, and taking Mᵣ Sharp by the hand, said, with great earnestness. Good friend, when you go to Pelew, tell Abba Thulle that LEE BOO take much drink to make small-pox go away, but he die.

FIGURE 7.2. *The History of Prince Lee Boo* (detail), 1822, jigsaw (paper engraving on wood). Reproduced by permission of the National Library of Australia, nla. pic-an23113107.

introduced to several of the directors of the India Company . . . and gradually shewn most of the public buildings in the different parts of the town." He was also "several times taken to see the guards exercise and march in St. James's Park."[53] But whenever Lebuu's *predecessors* had ventured to view military parades, some cultural organ had seized on the event, eager to offer a comment through their subject on the question of British might. Now, there was nothing. Similarly, Lebuu was taken to see the first manned ascent of an air balloon in Britain. On 15 September 1784, the Neapolitan Vincenzo Lunardi thrilled London crowds when he successfully navigated his red-and-white striped "aerostatic machine" from Moorfields to Ware.[54] Newspapers, squibs, and gossipmongers focused on little else for some time: most were in awe of the feat, though some likened the mania for ballooning to an influenza. Yet in neither jubilant nor cautious commentaries did the incongruity of a Palauan Islander witnessing this "wonder of the world" present itself as a compelling means through which to offer opinion.[55]

Keate reports that he met up with Lebuu the day after the ascent: "I [assumed] that I should have found him to the greatest degree astonished at an exhibition which had excited so much curiosity even amongst ourselves; but, to my great surprise, it did not appear to have engaged him in the least. He said, *he thought it a very foolish thing to ride in the air like a bird, when a man could travel so much more pleasantly on horseback, or in a coach.*"[56] Admittedly, Lebuu's engagement, or rather lack of engagement, with Lunardi's achievement allowed Keate a subtle voice to speak on present preoccupations, but it certainly failed to grab any other pundits. It is ironic perhaps that this New World visitor proved to be as unimpressed with one of the Old World's most applauded feats as the Old World now was with a living, breathing New World visitor. The absence of reportage on the doings of this latest representative of savagery speaks determinately of the shift in concerns of the urban populace. Before the 1780s, it had been precisely the juxtaposition of savagery with emblems of civilization that had prompted pundits to wonder how either one showed up or vindicated the other. Now, apparently, civilization—or at least its trajectory in Britain—triggered too little controversy to warrant arguments for any end.

When Lebuu was not visiting London, he was participating in two activities that no New World visitor had ever before undertaken: he attended a local school and he became a regular churchgoer. Keate relates that "after he had been awhile settled . . . he was sent to an Academy at Rotherhithe, to be instructed in reading and writing." He was "particularly pleased," Keate goes on, "at going to church, and, though he could not comprehend the service, yet he perfectly understood the intent of it."[57] It is hard to say whether, as a consequence of these two endeavors, Lebuu gained more English than any predecessor or became a convert to Christianity: Keate provides little other information. Lebuu evidently continued at these activities for most of his time in Britain: at his funeral, "all the young people of the Academy joined in . . . and [almost] the whole parish . . . assembled."[58]

School and church attendance reflected general trends in British society as well as a specific trend in the phenomenon of New World visitation. Thinkers of all stripes were reconsidering educational principles in the last quarter of the eighteenth century: some were concluding that regular and accessible schooling for the young was critical to fulfill their enlightened universalist aspirations, while others were finding it increasingly necessary in order to reverse the floodtide of immorality that Enlightenment, among other things, had brought.[59] Educational institutions of several different kinds multiplied around the turn of the century.[60] The increased religiosity of the late eighteenth century is also a well-known phenomenon: alongside a near-quadrupling of membership to Dissenting churches, evangelical Anglicanism burgeoned everywhere.[61] Lebuu's participation in these two major waves of change further points, incidentally, to the larger changes of the era. Both schooling and churchgoing—like children's literature, romantic poetry, and the sentimentalization of death—focused predominantly on realizing selves. Though a visiting savage was now expected to partake of these trends, he was crucially not seen to be an exceptional node for discussion of them.

Lebuu's time in Britain reflected a changed environment for New World visitors. His diminished appeal spoke of new preoccupations among Britons. What appeal he did command was evidently not as crucial to these new preoccupations as earlier New World visitors had been to the issue of expansionism.

KUALELO AND MAITITI

While Lebuu has found one modern biographer since Keate, no subsequent Oceanian traveler has gained the equivalent.[62] Yet examples did exist; they now lie half-submerged in voyager archives, unidentified as successors to an early-modern tradition. In the 1970s, historian Ernest Dodge compiled a list of all the European vessels that officially sailed through the Pacific Ocean after Captain Cook. The list intimates the enormity of the undertaking for most eighteenth-century voyagers, since British vessels averaged only about one a year until 1800.[63] By sifting through the records of each voyage after Wilson, two instances of Oceanian recruitment and subsequent arrival in Britain appear: the first a Hawaiian man in 1789 and the second a Tahitian in 1793.

The Hawaiian, Kualelo, had joined a sloop for the Cadman Etches fur-trading company when it stopped at his island of Molokai in January 1788. Also reckoned a mere "youth" like Lebuu, Kualelo was said to have "begged" Captain Charles Duncan for a chance to see the company's homeland of Britain.[64] Duncan no doubt agreed to the addition for the same reason that had motivated earlier European explorers in Oceania—an opportunity to secure a native informant for both present navigational purposes and possible future alliances.[65] The captain transported Kualelo to China, whereupon the Hawaiian transferred to another company vessel for the final leg of the journey. On the *Princess Royal*, Kualelo befriended the commander

James Johnstone and the surgeon-naturalist Archibald Menzies. The former would give him board during his stay in Britain and the latter would write the only surviving report of it.

Arriving at Plymouth in July 1789, Kualelo settled in the port town for the first year. Menzies writes that he "spent the first Winter & Spring down at Plymouth under the care and tuition of Mr James Johnstone . . . This gentleman's first object was to have him inoculated for the small Pox which he underwent with little inconvenience, & then he was sent to a public school in the neighborhood where great pains was taken to learn him to read and write."[66] Evidently, Kualelo's "care and tuition" was provided in the expectation that he would better serve Cadman Etches in the future: the Hawaiian spent the year of 1790–1791 at sea again on a company trip to Hudson's Bay "to examine the Great Inlets and make discoveries on the interior navigation of that Country."[67] Unfortunately, the only local news organ for Plymouth during the late eighteenth century, *The Exeter Flying Post, or Trewman's Plymouth and Cornish Advertiser* (1779–1804), fails to help ascertain the character of Johnstone, the name of Kualelo's inoculator, or the location of the school that Kualelo was said to attend.[68] No press accounts exist on the Hawaiian at all. As for Lebuu, the advent of a living savage upon British shores no longer seemed to speak uniquely to any pertinent debates going on in metropolitan culture.

Menzies thought the pedagogic attention to Kualelo had produced mixed results. Learning to read, he declared, "could not be accomplished, for though [Kualelo] soon acquired a thorough knowledge & pretty exact pronunciation of the simple letters of our Alphabet, yet no power of art could carry him a step farther & get him to join or mingle these different sounds together in the formation of a word." Learning to write had been slightly more successful. "In writing he made greater progress, that is, he soon acquired a habit of copying whatever was placed before him with great exactness[.] In the same manner he would do a drawing or a picture; indeed to the art of Drawing in general he appeared most partial . . . but in this uncultivated state of mind he seemd fondest of those rude pictures called Caricatures."[69]

Menzies's account ends on an ambivalent note: Kualelo was clearly capable of learning some things—of becoming more of a self—but he hit walls after a certain level of reading and writing. Was this because of a deficiency peculiar to him, or was it because—as a savage—he faced some insurmountable limits? However scathing previous commentators had been on visiting savages, none had ever suggested that savages were destined to be stuck in savagery forever. Indeed, as an inherently social category, and thus one inherently malleable, savagery could never before now have signaled such an essential fate for any of its so-called representatives. Kualelo may have been the first New World visitor to be thought locked, in an absolute kind of way, into what Menzies called "uncultivation."

George Vancouver, the captain of the naval vessel charged with taking Kualelo home, certainly thought him deeply retrograde. Vancouver related that "my orders" in 1791 were to explore the northeastern waters of the Pacific for commercial promise and "to receive on board and convey to his native country, *Towereroo*, an Indian, from one of the Sandwich Island[s]." On board, Vancouver opined that Kualelo "did not seem in the least to have benefited by his residence in [England]." He was, according to the captain, "of weak intellect, of a sullen disposition, and excessively obstinate . . . there was little probability of his service being important to us."[70] Plainly, the experiment in educating Kualelo was thought in the end to have failed. No evidence exists regarding an arrangement to contact Kualelo again, and indeed no later British merchants appear to have met or benefited from him thereafter.

Vancouver was not known for his love of "ordinary savages."[71] When Kualelo tried to jump ship at Tahiti—apparently for the hand of a woman—Vancouver punished him by locking him in confinement for many weeks. In the end, Vancouver forewent his strictures regarding proper repatriation: like Cook with Mai, he decided at the last minute that Kualelo's native Molokai was too unstable so arranged for him to reside—effectively as a refugee—on another nearby island, Kauai.[72]

Kualelo, then, followed in some of the footsteps of previous New World visitors but, like Lebuu, cut mostly fresh paths during his stay. Like his Palauan counterpart, Kualelo came as a potential but never realized go-between, he lived with a mariner's family, and he attended the local school. Unlike Lebuu, though, Kualelo never saw London and, most significantly, he survived to see his homeland again. With the changed preoccupations of the metropole, these two features meant that this visiting savage barely registered with any Britons.

Kualelo was succeeded within a couple of years by a Tahitian visitor called Maititi, who made a still lesser mark on British culture. Maititi journeyed to Britain with the return of William Bligh's second voyage to Oceania. Bligh's notorious ejection from his first voyage in Tahiti in 1789, from which he managed to struggle home twelve months later, had fired him with a determination to return to the scene of the crime and complete his original task. His mission then had been to take a sample of Tahiti's breadfruit tree over to the West Indies in order to propagate a cheap source of food for the colony's slaves. On the second try, launched in 1791, Bligh was successful.[73]

Bligh records that upon leaving Tahiti around July 1792, he was accosted by one of the royal escorts, Tynah, who insisted that he take with him "one of his men, who he said would be of great service to him when I sent him out again, from the many things he could learn and see in England." Although apparently reluctant, Bligh conceded, displaying a peculiar sense of obligation: "I could not help thinking that it was the least that I could do for him, and that whether the Man returned or not it would be no greater burden to our Country than it should bear."[74] Bligh goes on to describe the new recruit: "This Man's Name is Mydiddee . . . about 22 years of Age . . . He is a servant, and therefore a more elligible person for the purpose of learning than if he had been a Chief . . . Such Towtow [a commoner] is more likely to benefit his Country than a Chief who would be only led into Idleness and Dissipation as soon as he arrived in Europe, as was the case with Omai."[75] If it was also at the back of Bligh's mind to secure in Maititi a future native informant, the captain unusually reckoned that an ordinary man would serve his needs better than a high-ranking leader. What is most telling in Bligh's notes, however, is the way that Mai was now imagined as infected with the very decadence that, twenty years before, he had been predominantly employed to critique. Mai's latter-day slide into disrepute was one of the many little manifestations of changing attitudes to Oceanians. Bligh's concern about Maititi's capacity to improve himself was yet another.

Bligh's voyage further exemplified the readiness of Oceanians to jump aboard European vessels. Not only did it carry Maititi as an informant and passenger, but, inadvertently, it also harbored another Oceanian as stowaway. Upon departing from Tahiti, Bligh wrote that "to my astonishment, I found a man who had always been collecting with the botanists secreted between decks and I had not the heart to make him jump overboard. I conceived he might be useful in Jamaica." The stowaway's name, according to Bligh, was "Bobbo," although other seamen's logs recorded him as "Jacket." Whether Bobbo intended to see Britain or its West Indian colony is a moot point: Bligh "selected" him to remain at Jamaica with some Britons to help look after the breadfruit.[76]

Maititi, who did make it to Britain, turned out nevertheless to have less luck than his fellow countryman, and certainly less of a future than Kualelo. While still in Jamaica in January 1793, Bligh arranged for Maititi to receive inoculation against smallpox. Perhaps the captain had taken note of what had been done for Mai and what had been neglected for

Lebuu. In any event, this time the procedure sadly failed. Maititi con-
tracted the full-blown infection while in the Caribbean, remained frail
throughout the journey to Britain, and arrived in Deptford a very sick
man in August 1793. He died a few short months later.[77]

Bligh stated that "our Otaheitian friend was buried at Deptford New
Church Yard in the parish of St. Paul's. I shall ever remember him."[78]
If Bligh did always remember him, it was not an experience shared by
many other Britons. While he lived at Deptford, Maititi occasioned next
to no comment. Certainly his limited time in London explains some of
the silence, but, then, the stories of earlier New World visitors show that
many had been taken up in print and in society within the first fortnight.
One public record of Maititi's presence in Britain has survived: his death
was commemorated in the *Annual Register,* the best-known chronicler of
public events in the country. Its summation of the year 1793 included the
following note: "A native of Otaheite, lately brought over by capt. Bligh
in the Providence, died at his lodgings in Deptford . . . [He] had been
frequently ill during the voyage, and twice recovered from imminent
death, by the unremitting attention of his [British sailor] friends . . . His
native . . . manners had endeared him to all who knew him, and his death
is sincerely lamented by every individual engaged in the expedition."[79]
Thus, in the end, Maititi was not reviled for decadence or depravity. But
neither was he celebrated for becoming or promoting a better self. What
attention he did receive was due to the timeliness of his death, but even
this did not seem to elevate him over the radar beams of popular culture.

The common thread in the stories of Lebuu, Kualelo, and Maititi is
the decreasing level of British public interest in these visitors. They were
diminishing oddities to a people in the midst of a profound change in
priorities regarding expansion into the New World—something which
will be further explored in the next and final chapter. Bluntly, for now,
New World visitors had less to offer Britons struggling with questions
of best expansionist method than they had to earlier Britons debating
the propriety of expansion per se. Though they were still the best exemplars of "savagery" to Britons—following on from Mai and the generic
Native American before him—savagery itself now had a new relationship
to imperial rhetoric. As embodiments of an entirely alternate society,
savages had been a vital metaphor for discourse on Britain's own social
destiny. When discourse moved on to the ways in which social destiny
could be optimized within the now acknowledged bounds of empire, savages became less pertinent. Their radical difference was not the kind of
metaphor that an increasingly reformist public required. What savages

could offer in this later era was an exercise in pathos, but this required their observed and appropriate deaths, and even then they seemed eminently replaceable and only ever more so into the 1790s.

That said, no New World visitor of this era solicited the kind of harsh and dismissive remarks that Hawaiians in Hawaii had suffered in the concurrent eulogies to Cook. It took one further traveling savage to provoke this level of negation.

8.   Bennelong from *Res nullius*

The Decline of Savagery

In the same year that Maititi arrived in Britain, and just one year after the return of Kualelo to Hawaii, two visitors from the Australasian end of Oceania turned up in London. Australasia was, to many Britons, the latest version yet of the New World. Although its western and northern stretches had been long known to Europeans, the region acquired public prominence during the 1770s, after Cook announced his discovery of the eastern coast of what he termed "New South Wales."[1] New South Wales was linked to Oceania in the British imaginary at this time in the same way that Oceania was linked to the Americas. All three regions were understood as one unfolding New World, first, in terms of its political and economic promise, and second, in terms of its apparently savage inhabitants.

As the later Beauchamp Committee—charged in 1785 with considering a new site for British penal settlement—was no doubt delighted to hear, Cook believed he had found a land of rich and convenient fertility. It is "diversified with woods, Lawns, and Marshes," he opined from Botany Bay in May 1770, "the woods are free from under wood of every kind and the trees are at such a distance from one a nother that the whole Country or at least great part of it might be cultivated without being oblig'd to cut down a single tree." The soil, Cook claimed, was of equal merit: its lighter version "produceth a quant of good grass" while its darker version "we thought capable of produceing any kind of grain, at present it produceth besides timber as fine meadow as ever was seen."[2] His naturalist, Joseph Banks, was not quite as fulsome, though he too declared that the soil sustained "vast quantities of grass" and that further north the land was indeed "well wooded and looked beautiful as well as fertile."[3] Beyond the Beauchamp Committee, British officials gathered from such comments that New South Wales, like other New World sites before it, promised not only to feed a new colony but also provide additional sources of wealth to their greater imperial networks. Among the pundits, this view was entrenched by the mid-1780s. In 1786 a popular volume by Thomas Bankes, entitled *A New Royal Authentic and Complete System of Universal Geography*, announced that New South Wales was an "immense track [of] woods and lawns . . . well watered . . . [with] an abundance of fish."[4] The following year, the *St. James's Chronicle* assured that it was a place of "great plenty . . . undisturbed since the Creation."[5]

Cook's voyagers had been just as emphatic about the savagery of the local people they met in Australasia. Cook himself had no doubt that they were savages, from the simple fact of their simple practices. Their lack of "clothing [and] ornaments" clinched the matter for him, though he was careful to add that, while "they may appear to some to be the most wretched people upon Earth . . . in reality they are far more happier than we Europeans: being wholly unacquainted not only with the superfluous but the necessary Conveniences so much sought after in Europe, they are happy in not knowing the use of them. They live in a Tranquillity which is not disturb'd by the Inequality of Condition; The Earth and sea of their own accord furnishes them with all things necessary for life."[6] Banks was less sympathetic. He believed them "the most uncivilised savages perhaps in the world." They were to him "but one degree removed from the brutes": thinly grouped, completely naked, and extremely dirty.[7] Still in the 1770s, Britons could be mixed in their judgment of savagery's worth, but they were all sure that they knew what savagery was when they saw it. The Aborigines of New South Wales fitted perfectly within eighteenth-century conceptions of New World savage life—sometimes admirably, sometimes grotesquely, but always as instructive emblems of a radically alternate basic society.

When the Beauchamp Committee decided in 1786 that New South Wales would indeed best serve as Britain's latest colony, it was thus continuing a long-held vision of the New World as an optimal site for growth among a people of distinct simplicity. Somewhat ironically, this New World would realize its proper potential for Britain by resolving some of the problems that the previous New World now posed through its loss. First and immediately, it would help solve the problem of where to put the country's escalating numbers of convicts after losing American plantations. Second and more important, it would help solve the problem of how to supply the new trade routes that must form after losing American markets.[8] In this way, the settlement of New South Wales was a fresh take on an old model.

As Christopher Bayly has pointed out, though, New South Wales also soon became representative of another history entirely. When describing the difference in imperial practice in Britain after 1780, Bayly lit upon New South Wales as his most perfect example. Its quickly autocratic style of governance and rapidly essentializing view of culture appeared to him to be "imperial despotism in miniature"—far removed, that is, from any mode of expansionism ever practiced by Britons before.[9] New South Wales at the moment of settlement was simultaneously an extension of British conceptions and interactions with the New World *and* a harbinger of the profoundly different approach that Britons would undertake toward the New World into the nineteenth century.

RES NULLIUS

Once settlement had been decided, British officials moved relatively fast in organizing the first fleet of transportees. In less then nine months, Captain Arthur Phillip—a fifty-year-old war hero and farmer—found himself the commander of 11 ships, around 750 convicts, and nearly 400 crew and marines, all bound for Botany Bay. His instructions had been concise: establish good order, establish cultivation, and "endeavour by every possible means to open an Intercourse with the Natives and to conciliate their affections, enjoining all Our Subjects to live in amity and kindness with them."[10] On this last issue, Phillip was also told to punish any British offenders against the natives and to estimate as soon as possible the number of them in the vicinity.

Upon arrival at Botany Bay in the middle of a scorching January, Phillip was surely disappointed to find the land less promising than Cook or Banks had intimated. Phillip thought the water supply "indifferent" and the soil so stricken that it might not even "calculate for our numbers."[11] Felling the legion of hardwood eucalyptus turned out to be so backbreaking that "it was hardly possible [to give a] just idea" of the task.[12] Another officer complained pointedly that "the fine meadows talked of in Captain Cook's voyage, I could never see, though I took some pains to find them out."[13]

Far more worrying, however, were the kind and number of indigenous people encountered by the First Fleet. Though most officers believed and always maintained that the Aborigines were savages, they were disconcerted to find them neither as undeveloped nor as uncommon as they had been led to expect. Phillip mused that their "curiosity . . . gave me a much higher opinion of them than I had formed from [Banks]," and he noticed at once that they were "far more numerous than they were supposed to be."[14] After a few months he also conceded that they probably inhabited the "interior" as far west as could then be imagined.[15] Other officers shared the unfolding realization. "I am by no means of opinion," claimed one, "that they are the harmless, inoffensive race they have in general been represented to be."[16] Another thought the populousness of the Aborigines to be frankly "astonishing."[17]

The sophistication and sheer presence of the Aborigines did not just present a practical problem to a man trying to establish a new community 10,000 miles from home. Phillip knew that it also posed a legal problem. What the Beauchamp Committee had really been convened to decide was the best *legal* site for settlement. It had read up on all of Cook's comments about the savages in Australasia and brought in Banks himself to testify so that it could establish whether or not the land constituted *res nullius* (literally, "no one's property").

A version of the doctrine regarding *res nullius* had governed the English common law approach to colonization for over a century.[18] It stipulated that things that were empty or abandoned could be owned by the first taker. The definition of emptiness or abandonment—or rather of fullness and presence—was needless to say paramount in such a doctrine. By the late seventeenth century British governments had come more or less to understand fullness and presence in terms of sustained and prosperous cultivation: those that inhabited a space continuously and increasingly, and during that time forced it to turn them a living, were deemed to be true owners. Those that did not stay put long enough or densely enough to log, till, seed, or harvest were not. With such a view through the rest of the 1600s and into the 1700s, most Britons recognized that in America the natives were indeed genuine possessors of the lands in which they had been discovered. They consequently arranged to settle in American spaces via purchases or treaties, which may well have been "fraudulent" and "unintelligible," as many historians have pointed out, but which were nonetheless taken at the time to be within British law.[19] Even those that rejected the idea of Native American possession, still often behaved according to a recognition of ownership because they took the pragmatic view that purchases and treaties were far cheaper than physical removal.

By the 1780s, however, at the dawn of a newly systematic era regarding expansion, British officials were eager to see if *res nullius* could be obtained from the first instance. Emptiness and abandonment would make such an enormously risky and expensive enterprise that much more predictable, calculable, and profitable. In consequence, the Beauchamp Committee sought especially the views of those who could support this conclusion. It benefited greatly from the enhanced reputation during the 1780s of Cook, who had at one point admitted that, though possibly "happier" than Europeans, Australian Aborigines had not carved their imprint onto the land and had thus left it in a "pure state of nature."[20] The committee did even better out of Banks, who had in his survival after Cook replaced much of his playboy status with an aura of national authority about all things scientific. Banks believed not only that Australian Aborigines were of the simplest stage of humanity imaginable, but also that they were "very few" in number. Aborigines were so simple and unorganized, to Banks, that he thought that the question of purchase or treaty was moot anyway, for "there was nothing we could offer that they would take." With such a state of affairs, Banks was confident that the scattered groups that did exist in New South Wales "would speedily abandon the Country to [any] New Comers."[21]

But even with their stellar witnesses, the Beauchamp Committee evidently entertained a smidgeon of doubt about Australasia in the end. The wording of the instructions to Phillip betrays an important crack in its overall confidence: to countenance an intercourse or even a conciliation with others was in some sense to be prepared for a level of social development, and even plain demographic weight, that would crush Britain's legal claim to occupation. As far as can be ascertained, Phillip was not kitted with any specific sum or briefing to make a transaction with Aborigines upon his arrival—although he must have known that such processes had occurred in America before him on a promissory basis. He was, then, at once prepared and not prepared to follow older practices regarding British presence in the New World. In 1787, the government seemed to be leaning further toward an understanding of *res nullius* in New South Wales than it had in any previous New World land, but even then it maintained a shadow of concern. It was in that space between understanding and its shadow that Phillip's colony lived out its first five years. After about 1794, the British settlement at New South Wales behaved as if resolved on *res nullius*.[22] It never did broker a formal agreement about occupation with the indigenous inhabitants, and nor did the nation-state that grew out of it. But until that time, the paradox of being both a continuity and a discontinuity in history—of inviting both the familiar and the experimental—governed all relations between peoples in the place.

BENNELONG OF THE WANGAL

Nothing exemplified the tension between new determinations and old inclinations in New South Wales more than the relationship forged between Phillip and one particular Aborigine called Bennelong. Bennelong was about twenty-four years old when the First Fleet disembarked at its final stop in what is now called Sydney Harbour. He may have been among the scores of Aborigines who hollered "*woroo, woroo,* go away" that several officers observed on the shore, "brandish[ing] their spears as if vexed at the approach."[23] He was certainly by this time an initiated warrior of the Wangal—a clan that claimed territory further up the harbor's river but who freely associated among all Eora peoples in the vicinity.[24]

Bennelong did not, however, meet Phillip formally until November 1789. By that time, Phillip was near despair at ever achieving his order to establish communications with the Aborigines. Some ten months earlier, already in some degree of frustration, he had resolved to kidnap one by force. "It was absolutely necessary," he rationalized, "that we should . . . reconcile them by showing the many advantages they would enjoy by mixing with us."[25] The literary-minded marine Watkin Tench revealed the irony of their intention even more starkly. "Capturing some of them," he explained, "would induce an intercourse, by the report which our prisoners would make of the mildness and indulgence with which we used them."[26] The unfortunate candidate was a Guringai man called Arabanoo, who suffered many months of confinement before dying from smallpox in May 1789.[27]

After a short pause, Phillip resolved to try again. On 25 November 1789, several officers lured two Aboriginal men from their fishing boats and brought them shackled to the governor's house. Even the placatory Elizabeth Macarthur—one of the officer's wives—later admitted that the ordeal seemed to have induced the "Strongest marks of terror and Consternation" in the captives.[28] The ranking lieutenant on the scene stated simply that "It was by far the most unpleasant service I ever was ordered to execute."[29]

Bennelong was one of the captives, and the other was called Colebee. They presented together before Phillip in leg irons. This sorry start degenerated further when Colebee escaped after one week, still shackled. Bennelong, however, remained—presumably against his will for the first few weeks, but after only a couple of days following Colebee's escape officers noticed that he seemed calmer and more "lively."[30] By Christmas Bennelong appeared to be positively at ease: whether he had resigned himself to the situation or, more constructively, resolved to acquire some political leverage from it, Bennelong was now an active participant in his relationship with the colonists. From here, the irony of kidnapping an indigenous informant started to turn against the British.

Bennelong soon asserted his own priority in Government House: his leg irons came off in the new year but he chose to remain with Phillip; he loved the food and the wine and the fine clothes; and he was said by many to relish in revelry—he was intelligent, good-humored, and "scrupulous" in his observance of etiquette.[31] The officers appeared mostly to enjoy his company. Phillip was relieved finally to be making progress with at least one Aborigine and wrote eagerly to the home secretary that he "will soon be able to inform us of their Customs and Manners."[32] In those initial months, however, it was far more frequently Bennelong who dictated terms and gained information. Far from customs and manners, what Bennelong mostly communicated to Phillip was the devastation that the colonists' smallpox had delivered to his people.[33] What he communicated back to his own clansmen—with whom he had regular access—were stories of sufficient curiosity and useful warnings about British intentions that he quickly rose to a higher local status.[34] When extreme food shortages drove the colony into famine in April 1790, the officers' awkward dependence on Bennelong was made most apparent: Tench wrote that "every expedient was used to keep him in ignorance" of the shortages so that he would not reveal colonist failings to the other Aborigines. He was given his full allowance while others around him went hungry. Tench added nervously that "want of food has been known to make him furious, and often melancholy."[35]

Despite the attention given him and the advantages made by him in those early months, Bennelong still decided one day in early May 1790 to leave it all behind. Abruptly in the early morning, he took off his European clothes and jumped the fence back to his own kin.[36] The wobbly power relations between Phillip and his captive seemed to topple in on themselves with a single stroke. Upon discovery of abandonment, Phillip was woeful. "Our native has left us," he wrote in a letter to Banks, "& that at a time when he appeared to be happy & contended." Poignantly he noted that "I think that Mans leaving us proves that nothing will make these people amends for the loss of their liberty."[37]

Bennelong kept away from the British for over four months. Then, in September 1790, he reappeared as suddenly as he had vanished. Some officers sighted him at Manly Cove—far from his supposed territories and evidently now down on his luck. He looked emaciated and somewhat disfigured. The officers called for Phillip to join them and what followed appeared a spontaneous reconciliation. Historians have divided over whether Bennelong in fact managed the reunion or not. Bennelong's diminished physical state suggests that he was in no position to play politics, but the drama that subsequently unfolded surely points to a stage manager somewhere—and perhaps his straitened circumstances motivated more than hindered him. Briefly, events went like this: upon Phillip's approach toward Bennelong, twenty or so other Aborigines formed a neat circle around the pair; Bennelong was said then to gesture to one particular man and introduce him to Phillip as a "very intimate friend"; Phillip reached out to shake this friend's hand but in that time the man grabbed a long spear and launched it into the governor's shoulder. Bennelong mysteriously disappeared. When he met with the recovering governor again, some ten days later, Bennelong voiced strong disapproval of the spearing. Phillip believed him unconnected to the assault and issued no reprisals. Bennelong moved back into Government House.[38]

Bennelong's chief biographer, Keith Smith, is sure that his subject was the mastermind behind the whole affair. Not a random act of violence, Smith explains that the injury was rather a form of ritualized revenge. Bennelong was publically punishing the governor for kidnapping him the previous year and in so doing both erasing the historical slate between the two parties and regaining some of his apparently lost authority before kin peers.[39]

Smith's account certainly makes sense of the progress that Phillip now made with his native go-between. In his second period of residence at Government House, Bennelong started to bring in the benefits that Phillip had so long hoped for. Eora people from many different clans started to come in to Sydney Cove to mingle with the colonists from about October 1790. The two groups shared food, words, and manufactures in what has been called a true moment of peace and mutual advance.[40] Bennelong's Aboriginal elders saw in Phillip's refusal to retaliate that alliance with the British might have some advantages. For his part, Bennelong gained even further respect among the Eora—he was now not only an informer about British ways but also a clear master of British cultural politics. In addition, of course, he could resume his enjoyment of British victuals and merrymaking.

Peace did not make the fundamental ambiguity of the colony at New South Wales disappear completely. More than one officer started to grumble after October 1790 about the indulgences that the so-called incapable and apolitical savages were granted by Phillip. The "insolence" that Bennelong sometimes showed the governor, for instance, was an affront to Lieutenant John Hunter that, he pointed out, "would have been immediately punished in any other person".[41] Peace did not either ensure that all violence was at an end: skirmishes continued to break out for short periods between colonist and native through these early years. But it did mean that an "intercourse" was now established—a conversation had started that could be taken up again after a faltering. This in turn meant that between December 1790 and December 1792 at least the colony erred more toward older inclinations to treat for occupation than toward newer dictates simply to claim first ownership. Phillip's determination to follow through with his instructions had made the whole enterprise tip away from any easy assumption of *res nullius*. Further, it could not have been lost on men such as Phillip, or even Hunter, that with every instance of connection to the colonists—whether it was positive in the form of exchange and shared dining or whether it was negative in the form of altercation and armed conflict—Aborigines proved themselves to be a more and more complex people than once reckoned. In other words, they proved to be further and further removed from Banks's landless simpletons.

In this short-lived détente, one particular kind of Aboriginal person—other than Bennelong himself—played an especially active role. This kind was the teenaged male youth, soon approaching, or recently recovering from, warrior initiation. Scores of such young men were said to come and go frequently from Government House, serving as occasional servants and no doubt obtaining newly useful lessons in cross-cultural relations.[42] One of these youths was called Yemmerawanne. Also of Bennelong's Wangal clan, he was described by Tench as "slender . . . fine looking . . . good tempered and lively".[43] The governor's secretary, David Collins, later asserted that Yemmerawanne was "much attached" to Phillip, which may explain why he ended up with Bennelong accompanying Phillip to Britain when the governor retired in 1792. Alternatively, the youth may have made the journey because he was a favorite of Bennelong, or, indeed, because he was a kind of Bennelong-in-the-making, who gained a berth from his own entrepreneurial maneuverings.

However the arrangements were made for Yemmerawanne, Phillip had evidently planned for Bennelong's company many months in advance. In December 1791, he had written to Banks that "I think that . . . Bennillon will accompany me whenever I return to England and from him when he understands English much information may be obtained for he is very intelligent."[44] Plainly, Phillip was now fully committed to the idea of negotiation over declaration when it came to settling land rights in New

South Wales. He envisaged continuing his obligation to prepare for diplomacy even after formal retirement. Whether his fellow officers remaining in the colony or his superiors back in Whitehall felt the same at this point is less clear.

On a beautiful summer morning at the end of 1792, Phillip, Bennelong, and Yemmerawanne bid farewell to a large crowd gathered around the harbor heads. On board their vessel were also a couple of freed convicts, four kangaroos, and several dingoes. Though Collins noted that at the moment of their departure both Bennelong and Yemmerawanne had to field the "united distress of their wives, and the dismal lamentations of their friends," the Aboriginal travelers themselves seemed relaxed and cheerful. Collins believed they understood fully the maritime ordeal that lay ahead of them.[45] Considering the good condition of the ship, he thought a "speedy passage" would take six months. True to estimate, the voyagers disembarked at Falmouth on 19 May 1793.

BENNELONG IN BRITAIN

Within days, the party was in London. *Lloyd's Evening Post* announced the arrival in a lengthy paragraph:

> Governor Philip [sic] has brought home with him two natives of New Holland, a man and a boy, and brought them to town. The Atlantic has also on board four kangaroos, lively and healthy, and some other animals peculiar to that country. From the description given of the natives of Jackson's Bay they appear to be a race totally incapable of civilization, every attempt to that end having proved ineffectual . . . no inducement, and every means have been perseveringly tried, can draw them from a state of nature . . . They are cruel, particularly to their women, whom they beat in a most barbarous manner on every occasion. That instinct which teaches to propagate and preserve the species, they possess in common with the beasts of the field, and seem exactly on a par with them in respect to any further knowledge of, or attachment to kindred.[46]

Clearly the author of this piece took the more Banksian line on Australian savagery, which was not in itself insignificant. But in retrospect, the most startling aspect of the account was its singularity. Though repeated verbatim by the *Dublin Chronicle* a few days later, no other newspaper commented on the Aboriginals' presence in Britain for the next twenty-one months.

The movements of Bennelong and his fellow countryman while in Britain are best pieced together by the bill of expenses that Phillip tallied during their stay. It shows that the ex-governor arranged for them to lodge with the father of a First Fleet officer in Grosvenor Square for most of their time in London. It also tells of the many outings the Aborigines undertook about the city, their move in May 1794 to the small village of Eltham outside Greenwich on account of Yemmerawanne's failing health, the progress of the younger man's illness while in Eltham, and his eventual death, funeral, and burial.[47] Most of all, though, the bill shows that Phillip was a keen student of eighteenth-century New World visits to Britain. At every juncture, it seems that he expected his charges to be treated like previous travelers from the New World, such as Mai, Ostenaco, and the various others before them. Phillip believed that they would receive similar official attention and, whether he welcomed it or not, that they would suffer similar popular scrutiny. Such expectations probably flowed from his conviction that New South Wales, like previous New Worlds before it, would have to be treated for by the British after all, and that go-betweens like Bennelong would be not only crucial to the process but also, in consequence, intriguing to ordinary metropolitans. Whatever the rationale, all Phillip's predictions turned out in the end to be wrong.

The first expectation to fall was the assumption of a royal meeting. Perhaps knowing that most previous New World visitors in the century had met with the reigning monarch to initiate formal relations within weeks of arrival, Phillip had Bennelong and Yemmerawanne outfitted at a tailor's immediately upon settling in London. His purchases of silk stockings, blue- and buff-striped waistcoats and slate-colored ribbed breeches would have been more than fine enough for a king.[48] The apparel, however, never earned quite so lofty an audience. Though many historians have since claimed that Bennelong did meet with George III, no record of such an encounter exists in the extensive royal archive for 1793 and none of the court chroniclers—which in this decade included *The Times* and the *Annual Register*—even suggested it.[49] There is neither any record of Bennelong meeting other dignitaries such as bishops, bureaucrats, or even Phillip's friend Joseph Banks.

Second, Phillip seems to have been aware of the standard itinerary undertaken by most earlier New World envoys. His lodging of them in the same West End region that had housed the Iroquois and the Cherokee may have been a coincidence, but his resolve to make sure they saw St. Paul's Cathedral, the Tower arsenal, Woolwich docks, Exchange Alley, the Houses of Parliament, and all the theaters just like their predecessors was surely calculated. Phillip wanted the Aborigines to gain the same sense of power and organization in Britain's capital that previous escorts had wanted for their charges, and for the same pragmatic ends. The difference in the 1790s was that no one commented on these tourings. When earlier envoys had seen the same sites, the press had been full of accounts about the juxtapositions they supposedly made. In the 1790s, no one even discussed the piquancy of the Aborigines' visit to the Parkinson Museum, which famously housed artifacts from Cook's three Pacific voyages, or their presence at the trial of one-time imperial governor, Warren Hastings, which otherwise made the news for all 148 days of its progress.[50] Phillip's endeavor to impress Bennelong and Yemmerawanne with British achievement broke from tradition in the way their tours lacked the public buzz that had confirmed the significance of previous tours.

Third, like some more recent precursors, Phillip arranged for Bennelong and Yemmerawanne to receive language tuition during their stay.[51] He was determined to see through the realizing of possibilities of assistance from the Aborigines that he had mentioned to Banks. Unlike Mai's progress with English, however, their studies were not followed or debated in any public organ.[52] Rather more like Lebuu and Kualeleo's education, theirs went largely unobserved—encouraged only by a singular patron instead of a large official body.

Finally, Phillip may have braced himself for an outpouring of sentimental grief when Yemmerawanne died on 18 May 1794. He would have been acquainted with the gushing that had following Lebuu's demise only ten years before. But now it seemed that not even death gave savagery any resonance. Phillip organized a respectable funeral for Yemmerawanne at Eltham Parish Church and for his entry into Eltham Parish's burial registry. He also ensured that the Crown fund a modest tombstone in Eltham's churchyard.[53] Yet none of the trappings that had also been observed for Lebuu this time prompted the slightest response from metropolitan Britons. Emphatically still considered to be paradigmatic savages, these latest visitors from the New World no longer fascinated their hosts in any of the ways their predecessors had done for most of the century.

The 1790s were, of course, a particularly distracting decade in Britain. An argument could be made about the limits to British concentration when in the middle of counterrevolutionary wars: they were simply too busy to notice one more savage arrival.[54] But, then, most other New World envoys of the eighteenth century had also arrived in time of war. Moreover, Londoners in the 1790s were not so distracted that they ignored the four kangaroos that had come with Bennelong and Yemmerawanne.

Hundreds swarmed to view the one on display in the Lyceum Museum in the Strand. On show every day from eight in the morning till eight in the evening, for the not inconsiderable price of a shilling, the museum was hesitant to give too much away in its advertisement: "to enumerate [the animal's] extraordinary Qualities would far exceed the common Limits of a Public Notice. Let is suffice to observe that the Public in general are pleased, and bestow their Plaudits; the ingenious are delighted; the Virtuoso, and Connoisseur, are taught to admire!"[55] One reader of the *Gentleman's Magazine* was evidently tantalized to extremity. Unable to get to the Lyceum himself, he wrote a letter to the editor asking if he had "no kind friends . . . that will give you some account . . . of the *gamgarou*, the new animal just brought to England from South Wales by Governor Phillip[?] Certainly, Sir, it would give much satisfaction . . . to be informed of the . . . creature."[56]

The relative lack of interest in Bennelong and his compatriot was due rather to a shift in the purchase of so-called embodied savagery itself. It followed on from a decade of ever-lessening interest shown in New World visitors, as evidenced in the response to Lebuu in 1784, Kualelo in 1789, and Maititi in 1793. The shift reflected larger changes in metropolitan discourse regarding Britain's expansionist policies. As several historians have pointed out, and as the example of early New South Wales would so neatly testify, British officials determined on a new approach to overseas activity after the tumultuous events of the 1780s.[57] The British government's increasingly centralized view of authority in foreign territories and their noticeably narrowing opinion of those who got in the way was accompanied by a shift in general rhetoric from questions of *ought* to questions of *how*. In the move away from considerations about the propriety of creating imperial networks, the distinctive metaphor of savagery—with its connotations of everything opposite to expansionism—fell out of favor.

Though primarily now a less *useful* idea, savagery was after the 1780s also a less *flexible* idea. The increasing rigidity or one-sidedness of the evaluation of savagery into the nineteenth century was a direct effect of Britain's new order for imperial business. It was evident in the alacrity with which the Beauchamp Committee seized on Banks's condemnatory observations; it was evident in the grimness of the single-existing newspaper report of Bennelong's arrival in Britain; and it was evident in the move toward an assumption of *res nullius* in New South Wales after Phillip's departure. This narrower conception of savagery also contributed to its failing appeal in embodied form: savage visitors previously had gained wide popularity because their various appraisals by metropolitans meant they could be wielded for almost any position in the spectrum of views about expansion. They had been common vehicles for uncommon opinion. As embodiments now of what was mostly reviled or scorned, such visitors were lesser instruments for genuine debate. New World people in Britain from around Bennelong's era were both untimely and unamenable to contemporary metropolitan needs.

INCORRIGIBILITY

Bennelong was said to be anxious for a berth home after Yemmerawanne died.[58] It was probably Phillip who arranged for his passage on the next departing vessel, the HMS *Reliance*. Unfortunately, the *Reliance* was held up for over six months due to victualing problems, so Bennelong languished first at Chatham, then at Portsmouth, then at Plymouth. The highest ranking officer, John Hunter—who had come home with Phillip but who was now going out again to be the next governor of New South Wales—commented that "the surviving man, Benelong, is with me, but I think in a precarious state of health . . . [H]e has fondly look'd forward to . . . seeing again his native country . . . but so long a disappointment has much broken his spirit . . . I do all I can to keep him up, but still am doubtful of his living."[59]

Bennelong did survive the wait, and the journey back, but the colony to which he returned was markedly changed. One historian claims that by 1795 New South Wales was in fact "transformed" from what it had been under Phillip—its convicts were harder (and more reviled), its governance was harsher (and more "obscene"), and its attitude to Aborigines was tougher.[60] Others have not been as categorical, reminding us that the really rebellious convicts did not arrive until after the various mutinies and uprisings of 1796–97, which in turn did not prompt stricter punishments until nearer 1800, and that Aborigines were rather more avoided than ostracized until at least the 1820s.[61] Still, the trend toward Bayly's "imperial despotism" was in train with Hunter's arrival in 1795, and with it came the ever-greater likelihood of a legal consideration of *res nullius* for the land.

What Bennelong made of these changes is not transparent. At first he was probably too concerned with personal shifts to engage in colonial politics. In his absence, he discovered that his wife, Kurubarabulu, had taken up with another man and that other kin relations had also adjusted.

He was pleased to show off his new clothes and new ideas but, as with many a returning prodigal, his friends were only half listening. When he attempted a violent attack on his wife's lover, the ever-suspicious Colebee wanted to know "if he meant that kind of conduct to be a specimen of English manners?"[62]

His move back into Government House with Hunter had perhaps been planned while the two were still at sea. A letter dictated by Bennelong to his hosts in Eltham a few months after his return reveals both an upbeat and disquieted frame of mind. "Sir, I am very well," it began: "I hope you are very well. I live at the Governor's . . . I have not my wife; another black man took her away; we have had murry doings: he speared me in the back, but I better now . . . all my friends alive and well. Not me go to England no more. I am at home now. I hope Sir you send me anything you please Sir. Hope all are well in England . . . Bannolong."[63]

Home soon mutated for Bennelong, however. By 1797 he was straying away from Government House for longer and longer periods; within five years he rarely engaged with the colonists at all. His distancing from the colony may have resulted from personal reasons—his duties as a leader of the Wangal put increasing demands on his time. More likely, though, it was a response to the tenser atmosphere among the British. Bizarrely, few colonists interpreted Bennelong's retreat as an indictment, even as they freely admitted difficult times in the colony. David Collins for one described relations between indigenous and colonist by the late 1790s as nothing short of "open war." Yet he claimed to be amazed that Bennelong, "instead of making himself useful, or shewing the least gratitude for the attentions which he received from every one, [became] a most insolent and troublesome savage . . . Instead of living peaceably at the governor's house, as he certainly might always have done, [he] preferred the rude and dangerous society of his own countrymen."[64]

The enduring image of Bennelong as "the first Aboriginal drunk"—as a man who had walked onto the stage of history only to tumble off it in disgrace—stems from this first reversal of opinion in the late 1790s.[65] It certainly clung to the man for the remaining years of his life. In 1805, somewhat unexpectedly, *The Times* published a notice from Sydney Cove about the erstwhile doings of Britain's one-time visitor. That the newspaper assumed knowledge among its readership of Bennelong at all came from the centrality of his role in Collins's *Account of the English Colony at New South Wales*, which had become famous since its publication in 1798. *The Times* did not rely on any memory of Bennelong's own residence among metropolitans. Instead, it was conscious of providing the first mention of the event for most readers. "While BENNELONG the Botany Bay Chief, was in England," it began,

> he was treated with the distinction and favour which the fashionable world lavishes on every novelty . . . While in England he was presented to many of the principal nobility and first families in the kingdom, and received from many of them presents of cloth and other articles, which a savage of any other country would have deemed inestimable.

After this litany of a reception that never was, the report went on:

> It was not so, however, with BENNELONG; he was no sooner relanded in his own country, than he forgot, or at least laid aside, all the ornaments and improvements he had reaped from his travels, and returned with increased relish to his savage habits . . . He is, in truth, a savage beyond all hopes of amelioration by culture, and was . . . sent to Coventry as incorrigible.[66]

Bennelong's incorrigibility was sealed in the brief obituary published in the *Sydney Gazette* after his natural death in 1813.

> Bennelong died on Sunday morning last . . . His voyage to and benevolent treatment in Great Britain produced no change whatever in his manners and inclinations, which were naturally barbarous and ferocious. The principal officers of Government had for many years endeavoured, by the kindest of usage, to wean him from his original habits and draw him into a relish for civilised life; but every effort was in vain . . . In fact, he was a thorough savage, not to be warped from the form and character that nature gave him by all the efforts that mankind could use.[67]

In the space of fifteen years, Bennelong for those British observers who still cared to observe at all had gone from troublesome savage to incorrigible savage to immovable savage. It was a descent into an essential negativity that had been foreshadowed in the assessment of Cook's Hawaiian killers through the 1780s, in the doubts over Kualelo's ability to acquire any learning, and finally in the neglect shown Bennelong while visiting Britain. The lesser view of savagery went hand in hand with a general tendency to overlook the possibilities—the potential critiques, the latent lessons—of so-called savages themselves. In the popular imagination, the New World personification of radically distinct simplicity had become something of an "empty thing" as well.

. . .

In November 1790, even before Phillip first recorded his plans to take Bennelong to Britain, the ever-fanciful Watkin Tench reflected that he had already imagined his Aboriginal acquaintance to be one day "like a second Omai". He had envisaged Bennelong traveling to Britain like Cook's celebrated Polynesian voyager twenty years earlier, becoming "the gaze of the court and the scrutiny of the curious." Now, however, after only one month into Bennelong's reconciliation with Phillip, Tench sought to revise that opinion. After observing the Aborigine's "intrepid disregard of personal risque, nay of life," he had come to fear that Bennelong would never survive long enough to make the journey. He was sure that his "temerity" in the face of danger would kill him before opportunity arose.[68]

Tench proved to be halfway correct. Bennelong did not attain the notice of Mai, though he was able to manage his temper and he did withstand the ordeal of the passage to Britain. The failure of the response to Bennelong once arrived in London was due rather to a changed environment for New World exemplars. This changed environment was itself testimony to a new mode and conception of the British expansionist project.

Conclusion

British interest in eighteenth-century travelers from the New World re-emerged unexpectedly at the start of the new millennium. In 2001, Joshua Reynolds's 1775 portrait of Mai, *Omai*, sold for a record-breaking £10.3 million to an anonymous foreign buyer, which in turn prompted a public furor over its potential exportation and a consequent governmental bar against the work's removal from the country.[1] Curators, philanthropists, journalists, bureaucrats, and scholars all contributed to the case for keeping Reynolds's work. Various Tate Museum directors claimed it to be "an icon of the eighteenth century," while the Art Fund Charity, which helps British institutions acquire and keep their best treasures, issued a statement that the work was a "vivid testament to the open-minded way in which people in Britain, during the age of enlightenment, accepted . . . human beings from [other] worlds" and thus reminds us of how "art can bridge cultural divides."[2] The government's committee charged with justifying the bar went further when it declared that since Mai was "one of the first black visitors to be welcomed as an equal in English society," his image today shows "that Britain's historical response to other cultures and races could be positive."[3] In a television documentary on the controversy, the historian David Dabydeen even mused that the portrait "represents a great moment" because it helped to galvanize the abolition movement of the 1780s.[4]

Clearly, the concern over Reynolds's *Omai* in the twenty-first century turned around the historical significance of the subject rather than the greatness of the art. Despite the government's claim that the piece is discussed in "virtually every . . . [history] of British art," few Reynolds scholars ever rated it before 2001: the doyen of Reynolds studies, E. K. Waterhouse, neglected to mention it in his 1941 monograph, *Sir Joshua*

Reynolds; the editor of the volume that accompanied the major Reynolds exhibition of 1986, Nicholas Penny, only glossed it in his introduction; while David Mannings gave it half a column in his monumental 1,264-page Reynolds *catalogue raisonné.*[5] The emphasis on the subject over the art was confirmed when another Mai painting happened to go up for sale at the same time. William Parry's *Omai, Joseph Banks, and Dr Solander* (1776) has never enjoyed much critical appreciation, but when it was sold to an American buyer in 2002 for nearly £2 million, the government's Ministry of Culture halted this work's exportation too. In this case, the buyer soon withdrew interest and released the work back into the market, whereupon a consortium of British museums and galleries was able to get together and purchase the piece at the reduced price of £950,000.[6] One of its new owners, the National Portrait Gallery, explained that the group wanted the Parry because it was a "great historical portrait": painted "in an era when Britain was on the brink of considerable . . . intellectual expansion, it captures the desire for knowledge of these newly discovered lands and cultures."[7]

This latest manifestation of British interest, then, is not a neat repetition of history. First, it is a keenness for the representation of a phenomenon rather than for the phenomenon itself. And, more significant, it is marked by both a defensive tone and a remarkable degree of consensus about why the subject matter is so compelling. Original British fascination for Mai had been defined by its multiplicity of response—by, indeed, its very divisions. As such, the recent surge is really a third kind of reaction to New World travelers. For most of the eighteenth century, when Britain was expanding its global reach in new and unprecedented ways, New World visitors stirred a range of voices from multiple sectors to speak out about the benefits and ills of the very process which had enabled such arrivals. By the end of the eighteenth century, when Britain had consolidated its empire to a point of normalcy, New World visitors provoked little debate one way or the other. Suddenly, at the start of the new millennium, long after the dismantling of the British empire but while its legacies still generate some heated discourse, one New World traveler at least has revived his appeal, though now at one remove and in a much streamlined fashion. A more historical (and elitist) enterprise than the original, this modern form of interest has somewhat lower stakes but a noticeably more uniform motivation—which is to read the imperial past in a redeeming light against general accusations of former British aggression.

The irony here is that recent defenders of Britain's eighteenth century might have utilized the moment of Mai so much more convincingly if they had underscored the fierce debate about expansion that his visit occasioned, rather than reach implausibly for glimmers of "equality" or "racial tolerance" in his reception. These latter concepts would not have made much sense to ordinary Britons in 1775—at least not with the postcolonial overtones suggested by pundits in the recent *Omai* controversy. Arguments about the political, economic, and moral pitfalls of empire building, however, were familiar to Mai's hosts: their constant and constantly attacked airings during the two years of Mai's stay indicate that eighteenth-century Britons may not have had our modern ethical credentials but they were engaged in a genuine, bitter, and well-practiced dialogue over the potential outcomes of colonizing endeavors.

It remains to be said that this irony seems to pose no threat to the campaign to keep Reynolds's *Omai* (which is no doubt a good thing since greater numbers currently get to enjoy the piece than would if the campaign failed). The irony does not reverberate because few students of Britain's imperial past—either art pundits or historical scholars—concede the existence of a strong dialectic during its last 300 years at all. But the flurry of excitement that surrounded Mai in 1775—not to mention the several preceding envoys of similar stripe—indicate that until the 1780s at least empire was far from a given: debate over the savagery of New World peoples related directly to questions about the point, merit, and reach of Britain's relentless move away from savagery—into, that is, an ever more sophisticated, wealthy, and expansionist state. Significantly, this debate occurred at most levels of the public sphere; from the elite to the street.

Such a dialectic has been little recognized because the eventual triumph of expansionism has made the story of its emergence—even to it harshest critics—seem "primordial".[8] Even those historians who concentrate on the shift in imperial practice of the 1780s—notably, C.A. Bayly—are surprisingly taciturn about the corresponding shift in the rhetorical field concerning empire. In his cogent book *Imperial Meridian*, Bayly stated merely that after 1780 Britons found the "ideological will" necessary for their "more vigorous empire," and that the "classical fear that empire . . . corrupted civic virtue through luxury and decadence was already on the wane by the 1770s."[9]

Few phenomena revealed better the *experience* of both the prior debate and its later crucial waning than the periodic arrival of New World peoples through the eighteenth century. From the 1710s to the 1770s, these so-called savages proved amenable to Britons of varying backgrounds and political positions as a way of sparking off, thinking through, and then articulating their opinions about their nation's concurrent multilayered expansionist project. They enabled discourse at many levels about the problems and promises inherent in the increasing influence of monied interests, in the lessening role of the church, in the proliferation of military structures, in the plummeting depths of debt, and in the greater focus on sociability and public manners. Brought together, all these issues were connected via their respective relationships to imperial expansion overseas, especially into the New World. The increasingly fiscal-military culture of the British state during this time both created and then made necessary an insatiable reach into the resources of other lands and peoples. It was not just their place of origin that made eighteenth-century New World visitors pertinent to local debates. Specifically, it was their proclaimed savagery that was key to their amenability. Because savagery was taken, in its most elementary definition, to represent a radically simple society, its supposed embodiments stood for the precise opposite of everything Britain was moving toward: the equally fundamental characteristics of the savage state and the civilized or commercial (or imperial) state made them appropriate ideas with which to reflect upon each other.

In many ways, Mai was the apex of this phenomenon. His immense popularity demonstrated most dramatically how the appeal of embodied visiting savagery worked. While many of his legion of admirers shared Fanny Burney's breathless epiphany that Mai's "Nature" outshone and indeed shamed Britain's "Art," some, like Joseph Banks, believed that Mai's pure ways merely highlighted and endorsed through favorable comparison Britain's own increasing purity of intellect. At the same time, many popular squibs lambasted Mai for his shallow enjoyment of spas and parties in order primarily to criticize British culture's encroaching frivolity. Likewise, but for different ends, one of the numerous poets to discuss Mai, William Cowper, sneered at the visitor's laziness so that he might show by contrast Britain's worthier qualities. All positions on savagery were evident in the response to Mai, as were all positions on British society. And each came packaged in a different combination. Mai became a celebrity in the mid-1770s not because he appealed in the same way to everyone, but because he appealed differently to opposed types.

After Mai, New World peoples continued to arrive in Britain, though less and less often via officially encouraged means. The early-modern imperative to find potential go-betweens for use in later wranglings over trade and territory was fast diminishing in the face of a new confidence to declare the New World an empty place ripe for the taking. This confidence has been addressed in recent histories of the "imperial meridian"—explained with varying emphases on reactions to radicalism in America, France, and Asia.[10] Though less attention has been given to the concurrent change of mood about expansion at home, it can be vividly witnessed in the weakening appeal of "the savage visitor." Lebuu from Palau, Kualelo from Hawaii, Maititi from Tahiti, and Bennelong from New South Wales all followed similar itineraries to their New World predecessors; they all did similar things and were intimate with similar people. But they provoked less and less response. Britons were still interested in other ways in arrivals from their lands, but these were now either the flora and fauna of the New World, or, more likely, they were other Britons returning home from an adventure abroad. Indigenes of America or Oceania no longer represented a pertinent state for the discussion of British destiny because their fundamental associations no longer spoke to the dynamic of the debate. When imperial debate moved onto secondary questions of best practice over original questions of morality or legitimacy, radical otherness in the shape of savagery fell from rhetorical utility.

It is possible that the current interest in Reynolds's *Omai* may shift toward a greater understanding of the various ways the subject was handled in the eighteenth century. The work is still under export bar from the British government (making it the longest detained piece of art since such legislation existed), though in 2006 the owner was granted a *temporary* license to show it in the National Gallery of Ireland.[11] In this curious limbo between foreign private investment and British public treasure, Reynolds's *Omai* invites a deeper reading of what its subject generated in 1775. Neither a mascot for liberal tolerance nor a victim of racist brutality, Mai stirred instead a debate about the beginnings of an expansionist project that would only later conjure these kinds of extreme positions. A modern appreciation of the complexity surrounding early British imperialism may help illuminate why its history seems still so unresolved. It may also kick-start more nuanced accounts of the contexts of travelers like Mai, who have hitherto been seen simply as specimens of fleeting exotica.

Abbreviations

The following abbreviations are used throughout the notes:

BL	British Library, London
CO	Colonial Office
CSP	Colonial State Papers
CTP	Colonial Treasury Papers
DCMS	Department of Culture, Media and Sport
DNB	*Dictionary of National Biography* (Oxford, online prototype of the 2nd edition, 2003, consulted; current edition at www.oxforddnb.com)
DRCHSNY	*Documents Relating to the Colonial History of the State of New York*, ed. E. B. O'Callaghan and J. R. Brodhead (Albany, 1853–87)
HL	Huntington Library, San Marino
HRNSW	*Historical Records of New South Wales*, ed. F. Bladen and A. Britton (Sydney, 1892–1901)
ML	Mitchell Library, Sydney
NAA	National Archives of Australia
NLA	National Library of Australia, Canberra
OCRA	*Oxford Companion to the Romantic Age: British Culture, 1776–1832*, gen. ed. Iain McCalman (Oxford, 1999)
OHBE	*Oxford History of the British Empire*, gen ed. W. R. Louis, 5 vols. (Oxford, 1998–99)
PRO	Public Record Office (Kew)
SCHGM	*South Carolina Historical and Genealogical Magazine*
SPGFP	Society for Propagating the Gospel in Foreign Parts (est. 1701)

Notes

BOOK EPIGRAPH: J. G. A. Pocock, *Barbarism and Religion IV: Barbarians, Savages, and Empire* (Cambridge, 2005), p. 165.

INTRODUCTION

1. Until the twenty-first century, Mai was probably better known to British historians as Omai. It was Cook's one-time naturalist, Daniel Solander, who ruled his name, upon arrival in Britain, as Omai, repeating a common mistake among British voyagers of incorporating Tahitian's formal "O," meaning "it is," into proper names. See Eric McCormick, *Omai: Pacific Envoy* (Auckland, 1977), p. 94.

2. The most exhaustive account is McCormick's *Omai*. Some key earlier works include the relevant chapters in C. B. Tinker, *Nature's Simple Plan: A Phase of Radical Thought in the Mid-Eighteenth Century* (Princeton, 1922); H. N. Fairchild, *The Noble Savage: A Study in Romantic Naturalism* (New York, [1928] 1961); and T. B. Clark, *Omai: First Polynesian Ambassador to England* (Honolulu, 1941). See also Michael Alexander, *Omai: Noble Savage* (London, 1977); Neil Rennie, *Far-Fetched Facts: The Literature of Travel and the Idea of the South Seas* (Oxford, 1995), ch. 5; M. Hetherington, ed., *Cook & Omai: The Cult of the South Seas* (Canberra, 2001); Laura Brown, *Fables of Modernity: Literature and Culture in the English Eighteenth Century* (Ithaca, 2001), ch. 5; Anne Salmond, *The Trial of the Cannibal Dog: The Remarkable Story of Captain Cook's Adventures in the South Seas* (New Haven, 2003), chs. 10, 14, 15, 16; Harriet Guest, *Empire, Barbarism, and Civilization: Captain Cook, William Hodges, and the Return of the Pacific* (Cambridge, 2007), chs. 3, 6; and T. Fulford, D. Lee, and P. J. Kitson, *Literature, Science and Exploration in the Romantic Era* (Cambridge, 2004), ch. 2.

3. As Paul Turnbull says of Mai in his "Mai, the Other beyond the Exotic Stranger," in Hetherington, *Cook & Omai*, p. 43.

4. The term "good to think," coined by Claude Levi-Strauss, is deliberately

awkward, playing on the more common "good to eat." Levi-Strauss argued in *Totemisme* (1962) that certain things are chosen as totems not purely for utilitarian reasons—that they are good to eat, for instance—but because they fulfill larger cultural needs: they are instead "good to think" because they afford depth, breadth, and even potential transformation to a culture. See Claude Levi-Strauss, *Totemisme*, ed. Rodney Needham (Harmondsworth, 1963), p. 89.

5. Linda Colley, *Britons: Forging the Nation, 1707-1837* (New Haven, 1994), p. 61; Kathleen Wilson, "Empire, Trade, and Popular Politics in Mid-Hanoverian Britain: The Case of Admiral Vernon," *Past and Present* 121 (1988), p. 109. On this identity, see also Jack Greene, "Empire and Identity," in OHBE, vol. 2, pp. 208–31; Peter Marshall, *The Making and Unmaking of Empires: Britain, India, and America c.1750-1783* (Oxford, 2005); and David Armitage, *The Ideological Origins of the British Empire* (Cambridge, 2000), pp. 170–72.

6. Michael Leroy Oberg, "Between 'Savage Man' and 'Most Faithful Englishman': Manteo and the Early Indian-English Exchange," *Itinerario* 24 (2000), pp. 146–69. Kathleen Brown, "In Search of Pocahontas," in I. Steele and N. Rhoden, eds., *The Human Tradition in Colonial America* (Wilmington, 1999), pp. 71–96; Eric Hinderaker, "The 'Four Indian Kings' and the Imaginative Construction of the First British Empire," *William and Mary Quarterly*, 3rd ser. 53 (1996), pp. 487–526. (Note that each of these recent essays build upon some good older studies of particular episodes—see the discussions in chapters 1 and 2 of this volume.) See also Alden T. Vaughan, *Transatlantic Encounters: American Indians in Britain, 1500-1776* (Cambridge, 2006). Some other good general surveys include Carolyn T. Foreman, *Indians Abroad, 1493-1938* (Norman, 1943); Harald Prins, "To the Land of the Mistigoches: American Indians Travelling to Europe in the Age of Exploration," *American Indian Culture and Research Journal* 17 (1993), pp. 175–95; and Frances Karttunen, "Interpreters Snatched from the Shore: The Successful and the Others," in E. G. Gray and N. Fiering, eds., *The Language Encounter in the Americas, 1492-1800: A Collection of Essays* (New York, 2000), pp. 215–29.

7. Vaughan, *Transatlantic Encounters*, pp. 240, 244.

8. The later Oceanian travelers discussed in this book have really only been properly represented in Daniel J. Peacock, *Lee Boo of Belau: A Prince in London* (Honolulu. 1987); Nicholas Thomas, "The Pelew Islands in British Culture," in George Keate, *An Account of the Pelew Islands* (London, 1788 [5th ed. 1803]), ed. K. L. Nero and N. Thomas (London, 2002); and Jack Brook, "The Forlorn Hope: Bennelong and Yemmerrawannie go to England," *Australian Aboriginal Studies* 1 (2001). David A. Chappell has published *Double Ghosts: Oceanian Voyagers on Euro-American Ships* (Armonk, 1997), which covers a highly commendable spread but contains little on the experience or meaning of arrival. Slightly more discussions exist on nineteenth-century travelers: see particularly Roslyn Poignant, *Professional Savages: Captive Lives and Western Spectacle* (Sydney, 2004).

9. See Hayden White, "The Forms of Wildness" (1972), reprinted in his

Tropics of Discourse: Essays in Cultural Criticism (Baltimore, 1978); Stanley Diamond, *In Search of the Primitive: A Critique of Civilization* (New Brunswick, N.J., 1974); and Andrew Sinclair, *The Savage: A History of Misunderstanding* (London, 1977). Scholars who concentrate especially on the ancient pedigree include Anthony Pagden, *The Fall of Natural Man: The American Indian and the Origins of Comparative Ethnology* (New York, 1986); and Pocock, *Barbarism and Religion IV.* For the savage's medieval story, see Richard Bernheimer, *Wild Men in the Middle Ages: A Study in Art, Sentiment, and Demonology* (Cambridge, Mass., 1952). Scholars who trace the trajectory more often from the Renaissance alone, but who yet maintain a traditional intellectual-history method, include Fairchild, *The Noble Savage;* Margaret Hodgen, *Early Anthropology in the Sixteenth and Seventeenth Centuries* (Philadelphia, 1964); and Ter Ellingson, *The Myth of the Noble Savage* (Berkeley, 2001).

10. Note Richard Bernheimer's classic remark that "wildness meant more in the Middle Ages than the shrunken significance of the term would indicate today"; Bernheimer, *Wild Men in the Middle Ages,* p. 19. Bernheimer went on to argue that wildness, or savagery, instead meant in medieval times "everything that eluded Christian norms." This statement is perhaps too capacious for savagery after the fifteenth century.

11. Berkhofer finds this occurrence in many European languages simultaneously. Richard Berkhofer, *The White Man's Indian: Images of the American Indian from Columbus to the Present* (New York, 1978), pp. 13, 15.

12. See the *Oxford English Dictionary,* 3rd ed. See also Francis Jennings, *The Invasion of America: Indians, Colonialism, and the Cant of Conquest* (Chapel Hill, 1975), p. 74; and Roxann Wheeler, *The Complexion of Race: Categories of Difference in Eighteenth-Century British Culture* (Philadelphia, 2000), p. 67.

13. *Generydes,* c. 1450, ed. W. A. Wright, Early English Text Society, no. 55 (London, 1873), ll. 1344–45.

14. See Pagden, *The Fall of Natural Man,* ch. 2; and Kay Anderson, *Race and the Crisis of Humanism* (London, 2007), p. 38.

15. Hodgen, *Early Anthropology,* p. 23. Karen Kupperman is especially brilliant on early-modern descriptions of Native American cultural simplicity: see Karen Ordahl Kupperman, "Presentment of Civility: English Reading of American Self-Presentation in the Early Years of Colonization," *William and Mary Quarterly,* 3rd ser. 54 (1997), pp. 193–228.

16. Jonathan Lamb is eloquent on these "inventories of missing things" (see his "Fantasies of Paradise," in M. Fitzpatrick, P. Jones, C. Knellwolf, and I. McCalman, eds., *The Enlightenment World* [London, 2007], p. 527), as is Robert Berkhofer on the "description of deficiencies" (Berkhofer, *The White Man's Indian,* p. 27). For Shakespeare's Caliban in *The Tempest,* see Act 1, Sc. 2. For Columbus, see "Letter of Columbus," in *The Journal of Christopher Columbus,* ed. L. A. Vigneras (London, 1960), pp. 194–200. Vespucci, from his *Mundus novus* (1504–5), cited in Berkhofer, *The White Man's Indian,* pp. 8–9.

17. See Arthur Lovejoy, *The Great Chain of Being* (New York, 1960). See also William F. Bynum, "The Great Chain of Being After Forty Years: An Appraisal," *History of Science* 13 (1975), pp. 1–28; and Anderson, *Race and the Crisis of Humanism*, p. 37.

18. See Hodgen, *Early Anthropology*, p. 361. See also Sankar Muthu, *Enlightenment Against Empire* (Princeton, 2003), pp. 12, 37.

19. For citations of diatribes (mainly by the antiquarian William Camden [1551–1623] and the adventurer William Strachey [1572–1621]), see Hodgen, *Early Anthropology*, pp. 362–65; for citations of praises (mainly by the entrepreneur Walter Raleigh [1552–1618] and the navigator Francis Drake [1540–96]), see Richard Ashcraft, "Leviathan Triumphant: Thomas Hobbes and the Politics of Wild Men," in E. Dudley and M. Novak, eds., *The Wild Man Within: An Image in Western Thought from the Renaissance to Romanticism* (London, 1972), pp. 152–53.

20. See Arthur Lovejoy and George Boas, *Primitivism and Related Ideas in Antiquity* (Baltimore, 1935). See also Pocock, *Barbarism and Religion IV*, pp. 158–60; and Bernheimer, *Wild Men in the Middle Ages*, p. 112. Sankar Muthu has recently reminded that noble savagery from the early modern period was yet a "dehumanising" identification, which his apparent need to do both amazes and depresses; see *Empire Against Enlightenment*, pp. 3, 12, 13.

21. Ellingson, *The Myth of the Noble Savage*, p. xiii. See also Ronald Takaki, "The Tempest in the Wilderness: The Racialization of Savagery," *The Journal of American History* 79 (1992), p. 897; Nicholas Hudson, "From 'Nation' to 'Race': The Origin of Racial Classification in Eighteenth-Century Thought," *Eighteenth-Century Studies* 29 (1996), p. 249; Wheeler, *The Complexion of Race*, p. 67; and Anderson, *Race and the Crisis of Humanism*, p. 50. For a discussion about how other likely contenders did not prove to be as paradigmatic, see Kate Fullagar, "Reynolds' New Masterpiece: From Experiment in Savagery to Icon of the Eighteenth Century," *Journal of Cultural and Social History* 7 (2010), pp. 197–98, in which I argue that Eastern peoples, Celtic peoples, and African peoples, for examples, were often called "savage" but also associated first and more readily with some other quality, such as barbarism, bondage, or brutishness.

22. See Pocock, *Barbarism and Religion IV*, pp. 11–13, 157–58. See also David Bell, "Jumonville's Death," in C. Jones and D. Wahrman, eds., *The Age of Cultural Revolutions: Britain and France, 1750–1820* (Berkeley, 2002), p. 41.

23. Samuel Johnson, *A Dictionary of the English Language* (London, 1755). Ephraim Chambers, *Cyclopædia, or, An Universal Dictionary of Arts and Sciences* (London, 1728), vol. 2, p. 24. John Ash, *A New and Complete Dictionary of the English Language* (London, 1775), vol. 2, pp. 203–4.

24. Pocock, *Barbarism and Religion IV*, p. 175. Muthu, *Enlightenment Against Empire*, p. 12.

25. "The SAVAGE, occasioned by the bringing to Court a wild Youth taken in the Woods in Germany," *Miscellaneous Poems by Several Hands, published by David Lewis* (London, 1726).

26. Pagden's analysis of barbarism favors studying only those with such an attribute: *The Fall of Natural Man*, p. 25.

27. See especially Troy Bickham, *Savages within the Empire: Representations of American Indians in Eighteenth-Century Britain* (Oxford, 2005), pp. 3–7; and Stephanie Pratt, *American Indians in British Art, 1700–1840* (Norman, 2005), p. 68.

28. Hayden White, "The Noble Savage Theme as Fetish," in his *Tropics of Discourse*, p. 183.

29. Paul Langford, *A Polite and Commercial People: England 1727–1783* (Oxford, 1989), p. 2.

30. See here the sympathetic review by J. G. A. Pocock, which explains how John Brewer's modern-seeming fiscal-military state may plausibly exist alongside Jonathan Clark's portrayal of an *ancien régime:* review of *The Sinews of Power, Eighteenth-Century Studies* 24 (1991), pp. 270–72.

31. Norma Landau, "Eighteenth-Century England: Tales Historians Tell," *Eighteenth-Century Studies* 22 (1988–89), p. 218.

32. This general sense of "orderliness" and "harmony" (over "raucousness" or "riotousness") in eighteenth-century British history of the last twenty-five years has been superbly clarified by Paul Kleber Monod, "Are You Getting Enough Culture? Moving from Social to Cultural History in Eighteenth-Century Britain," *History Compass* 6 (2008), pp. 91–108. Monod notes how the "exploited labourers, angry rioters, and oppressed women who cried so loudly in traditional English social history" had become "pretty quiet" in books by Roy Porter, Jonathan Clark, Paul Langford, Dror Wahrman, Amanda Vickery, Linda Colley, and others. For works on the dominance of hegemony despite resistances, see, for example, works by Kathleen Wilson.

33. J. G. A. Pocock, *Virtue, Commerce, and History: Essays on Political Thought and History, Chiefly in the Eighteenth Century* (Cambridge, 1985), p. 33.

34. Though Pocock himself can hardly be defined as primarily an eighteenth-century scholar, his commentaries on eighteenth-century Britain have mostly been the consequences of his work on early modern political thought in toto. See *The Machiavellian Moment: Florentine Political Thought and the Atlantic Republican Tradition* (Princeton, 1975), part 3; *Virtue, Commerce and History* (1985); and, most recently, his series about Edward Gibbon's Enlightenment world entitled *Barbarism and Religion* (Cambridge, 1999–). Useful explications for social or cultural historians are given in Landau, "Eighteenth-Century England," and Steve Pincus, "Neither Machiavellian Moment nor Possessive Individualism: Commercial Society and the Defenders of the English Commonwealth," *American Historical Review* 103 (1998).

35. Pocock, *Virtue, Commerce, and History*, p. 32.

36. Ibid., pp. 32, 109.

37. See ibid., p. 71. Note also Pocock's polemical assertion (p. 111) that "we cannot tell [the history of eighteenth-century Britain] properly if we ignore the complex struggle between the two . . . or treat one as antique and the other as taking its place; both were formulations of the late seventeenth cen-

tury. There is, however, extremely strong pressure from the existing paradigms to take the triumph of 'liberalism' for granted. [Critics] of modern society appear to need the 'liberal' antithesis so badly . . . that they exaggerate its paradigmatic control while simplifying and antedating the history of its emergence."

38. See J.G.A. Pocock, "Nature and History, Self and Other: European Perceptions of World History in the Age of Encounter," in A.J. Calder, J. Lamb, and B. Orr, eds., *Voyages and Beaches: Pacific Encounters, 1769–1840* (Honolulu, 1999), p. 25. Also see *Virtue, Commerce and History*, p. 18, where he rather glibly claims to be interested in all utterances of the verbal and published but in practice, like most historians of thought, ignores large swathes of recorded literates.

39. Popular here is defined, following Kathleen Wilson, as both of the plebeian and middling sorts; see her *The Sense of the People: Politics, Culture, and Imperialism in England, 1715–1785* (Cambridge, 1995), p. 12. See also John Brewer, *Party Ideology and Popular Politics at the Accession of George III* (Cambridge, 1976), pp. 6–8.

40. Ironically, Pocock himself has devoted some study to the concept of savagery in eighteenth-century Britain, but his focus has only ever been on its use or attraction to the "polite man of commerce." He assumes that it held no value to "the patriot ideal." Savagery in Pocock is always just the synonym of nature, the state before history, "the passions not yet socialised." See *Virtue, Commerce and History*, p. 115; and *Barbarism and Religion IV*, pp. 171–75.

41. Vaughan, *Transatlantic Encounters*, pp. xvi–xvii, xx.

CHAPTER 1

I have chosen 1707, the Act of Union with Scotland, as the date after which it is most convenient to use the terms Britain and Britons. This chapter is concerned with activities in England, though it is intended—in admittedly broad style—to serve as a prehistory of my subject in Britain. It should also be acknowledged here that this chapter has benefited greatly from the primary research conducted by Alden T. Vaughan in his *Transatlantic Encounters: American Indians in England, 1500–1776* (Cambridge, 2006), chs. 1–6.

1. While there exist some tantalizing rumors of American Indians arriving in Europe in the twelfth century via Viking knars, they as yet remain unsubstantiated. See Harald E.L. Prins, "To the Land of the Mistigoches: American Indians Traveling to Europe in the Age of Exploration," *American Indian Culture and Research Journal* 17 (1993), pp. 177–78.

2. Richard Fabyan, *Great Chronicle of London*, ed. A.H. Thomas and I.D. Thornley (London, 1939), reproduced in David Quinn, ed., *New American World: A Documentary History of North America to 1612* (London, 1979), vol. 1, p. 103. In 1592, some ninety years after Fabyan's chronicle, the annalist John Stow began his account of the event thus: "This year were brought unto the king three men taken in the new found land, by Sebastian Cabot . . ."

Many scholars have interpreted this to mean that Cabot himself brought over the Indians, but Quinn has established that the reference to Cabot here is as finder of the new land.

3. Fabyan in Quinn, *New American World,* vol. 1, p. 103.

4. John Elliott, *The Old World and the New 1492–1650* (Cambridge, 1972); see also John Elliott, "Renaissance Europe and America: A Blunted Impact?" in F. Chiapelli, ed., *First Images of America; The Impact of the New World on the Old* (Berkeley, 1976), vol. 1, pp. 11–26. For a good overview of the debate on impact, see Karen O. Kupperman, "Introduction: The Changing Definition of America," in K. O. Kupperman, ed., *America in European Consciousness 1493–1750* (Chapel Hill, 1995), pp. 1–32.

5. Peter Burke, "America and the Rewriting of World History," in Kupperman, *America in European Consciousness,* pp. 33–51, esp. p. 35.

6. See David Armitage, "The New World and British Historical Thought: From Richard Hakluyt to William Robertson," in Kupperman, *America in European Consciousness,* pp. 52, 61.

7. Richard Hakluyt, *The Principal Navigations* (1589), ed. J. Masefield (London, 1907), vol. 8, p. 14.

8. Ibid., p. 14.

9. Ibid.

10. Ibid., pp. 201–2.

11. Cited in Sidney Lee, "The Call of the West: America and Elizabethan England," *Scribner's Magazine* 42 (1907), p. 318.

12. George Best, *A True Discourse of the Late Voyages of Discoverie, for the Finding of a Passage to Cathaya* (London, 1578), reprinted in the Hakluyt Society's *The Three Voyages of Martin Frobisher* (London, 1867), p. 74.

13. Best, *True Discourse,* p. 131. James McDermott also argues that Frobisher engaged in kidnapping in his *Martin Frobisher: Elizabethan Privateer* (New Haven, 2001), p. 191.

14. Best, *True Discourse,* p. 74.

15. Ibid.

16. Discussed in Vaughan, *Transatlantic Encounters,* p. 3; and in W. C. Sturtevant and D. B. Quinn, "This New Prey: Eskimos in Europe in 1567, 1576, and 1577," in C. C. Feest, ed., *Indians and Europe: An Interdisciplinary Collection of Essays* (Aachen, 1987), 61–140.

17. Vaughan, *Transatlantic Encounters,* p. 1. Sturtevant and Quinn also claim that, together with the 1577 Inuit, these travelers aroused a "remarkable amount of scientific and popular interest"; Sturtevant and Quinn, "This New Prey," p. 112.

18. Michael Lok, *Account of the First Voyage,* n.d., reprinted in the Hakluyt Society's *The Three Voyages of Martin Frobisher* (London, 1867), p. 87.

19. Best, *True Discourse,* p. 74.

20. An extended discussion of the images is in Sturtevant and Quinn, "This New Prey."

21. Lok, *Account of the First Voyage,* p. 87.

22. Ibid. Vaughan, *Transatlantic Encounters*, p. 3.

23. See the introduction to this volume and also the discussion of perception in Karen Ordahl Kupperman, "Presentment of Civility: English Reading of American Self-Presentation in the Early Years of Colonization," *William and Mary Quarterly*, 3rd ser. 54/1 (1997), pp. 193–228.

24. See Vaughan, *Transatlantic Encounters*, p. 5.

25. On the general term, see Simon Schaffer et al., eds., *The Brokered World: Go-Betweens and Global Intelligence* (Sagamore Beach, Mass., 2009).

26. William Adams, *Adams's Chronicle of Bristol* (Bristol, [1623] 1910), p. 115.

27. Ibid.

28. Postmortem report by Dr. Edward Dodding, 8 November 1577, reprinted in Quinn, *New American World*, vol. 4, pp. 216–18.

29. Ibid.

30. Ibid.

31. All these images are well discussed in Sturtevant and Quinn, "This New Prey." They are also reproduced in Stephen Greenblatt's *Marvelous Possessions: The Wonder of the New World* (Chicago, 1991), plates 7–8; and in P. H. Hulton and D. B. Quinn's *The American Drawings of John White, 1577–1590* (London, 1964), vol. 2, plates 114, 116. Neither of these sources provides much historical analysis, however.

32. Frederick, Duke of Wirtemberg, "A True and Faithful Narrative," in W. B. Rye, ed., *England as Seen by Foreigners in the Days of Elizabeth and James the First* (London, 1865), p. 18. Thomas Platter's *Travels in England, 1599*, trans. and ed. Clare Williams (London, 1937), p. 201.

33. Vaughan, *Transatlantic Encounters*, ch. 2; and Alden Vaughan, "Sir Walter Ralegh's Indian Interpreters, 1584–1618," *William and Mary Quarterly* 59 (2002).

34. Vaughan, *Transatlantic Encounters*, p. 40.

35. See Raphaell Holinshed et al., *The Chronicles of England, Scotland, and Ireland* (London, 1587), vol. 3, p. 1369.

36. On Harriot, see John W. Shirley, *Thomas Harriot: A Biography* (Oxford, 1983).

37. Lupold von Wedel, "Journey through England," in V. von Klarwill, ed., *Queen Elizabeth and Some Foreigners*, trans. T. H. Nash (London, 1928), p. 323.

38. "Bill to Confirm Raleigh's Patent," in D. B. Quinn, *The Roanoke Voyages, 1584–1590* (London, 1955), vol. 1, p. 127.

39. Vaughan, *Transatlantic Encounters*, p. 22.

40. For a negative view of Native Americans of this region, see Alexander Whitaker, *Goode Newes from Virginia* (London, 1613). For Barlowe's positive account, see Hakluyt's *Principal Navigations*, vol. 8, pp. 300, 305–6. Both sources are discussed in Robert Berkhofer, *White Man's Indian: Images of the American Indian from Columbus to the Present* (New York, 1978), pp. 17–19.

41. See also K. O. Kupperman, *Roanoke: The Abandoned Colony* (Totowa, N.J., 1984); and M. L. Oberg, "Between Savage Man and Most Faithful Englishman: Manteo and the Early American-Indian Exchange," *Itinerario* 24 (2000).

42. Vaughan, *Transatlantic Encounters*, pp. 30–39.

43. Ibid., pp. 31, 26.

44. My very broad sweep derives from Anthony Pagden, *Lords of All the World: Ideologies of Empire in Spain, Britain, and France, c. 1500–c. 1800* (New Haven, 1995), chs. 2–3. See also Patricia Seed, *Ceremonies of Possession in Europe's Conquest of the New World 1462–1640* (Cambridge, 1995), ch. 3; and Josep Fradera, "Spain: The Genealogy of Modern Colonialism," in Robert Aldrich, ed., *The Age of Empires* (London, 2007), pp. 44–67.

45. Cited in C. T. Foreman, *Indians Abroad 1493–1938* (Norman, 1943), p. 3.

46. Prins, "To the Land of the Mistigoches," p. 180. See also Margaret Hodgen, *Early Anthropology in the Sixteenth and Seventeenth Centuries* (Philadelphia, 1964), p. 111.

47. See Prins, "To the Land of the Mistigoches," p. 175. Also see Olive Dickason, *The Myth of the Savage and the Beginnings of French Colonialism in the America* (Edmonton, 1984), ch. 10; and Joyce Chaplin, "Race," in D. Armitage and M. J. Braddick, eds., *The British Atlantic World 1500–1800* (Basingstoke, 2002), p. 161.

48. On the Salamanca school, see Anthony Pagden, "Dispossessing the Barbarian: The Language of Spanish Thomism and the Debate over the Property Rights of the American Indians," in A. Pagden, ed., *The Languages of Political Theory in Early-Modern Europe* (Cambridge, 1987); and Andrew Fitzmaurice, "Moral Uncertainty in the Dispossession of Native Americans," in Peter Mancall, ed., *The Atlantic World and Virginia, 1550–1624* (Chapel Hill, 2007), pp. 383–409.

49. On the early English experience, see Pagden, *Lords of All the World,* ch. 3. And see Stuart Banner, *Possessing the Pacific; Land, Settlers, and Indigenous People from Australia to Alaska* (Cambridge, Mass., 2007), pp. 1–12. This claim does not try to engage with arguments about the different ideologies that *were* present among the English in America, for which see particularly Andrew Fitzmaurice, *Humanism and America: An Intellectual History of English Colonisation, 1500–1625* (Cambridge, 2003).

50. Cited in Ralphe Hamor, *A True Discourse of the Present Estate of Virginia* (London, 1615), p. 38.

51. On the Venetian and Spanish ambassadors, see Vaughan, *Transatlantic Encounters*, p. 46. For Jonson, see *Epicoene: Or, the Silent Woman,* ed., F. E. Schelling (Philadelphia, 2006).

52. See John Smith, *The Generall Historie of Virginia, New-England, and the Summer Isles* (London, 1624), pp. 67–68, 174–75. And see Whitaker, *Goode Newes from Virginia*, vol. 4, p. 1771.

53. Vaughan, *Transatlantic Encounters*, p. 49.

54. See P. L. Barbour, ed., *The Jamestown Voyages under the First Charter, 1606–1609* (London, 1969), vol. 1, p. 25.

55. See Christian F. Feest, "The Virginia Indian in Pictures, 1612–1624," *Smithsonian Journal of History* 2 (1967), pp. 6–13; and Christian F. Feest, "Virginia Indian Miscellany III," *Archiv fur Volkerkunde* 26 (1972), pp. 3–5. The

single copy of the company's broadside is housed by the Society of Antiquities in London.

56. James Rosier, "A True Relation of the Most Prosperous Voyage Made This Present Yeare 1606, by Captain G. Weymouth," reprinted in H. S. Burrage, ed., *Early English and French Voyages Chiefly from Hakluyt 1534–1608* (New York, 1906), p. 378.

57. Ibid., pp. 368, 379.

58. Ferdinando Gorges, *A Brief Narration of the Originall Undertakings of the Advancement of Plantations into the Parts of America* (1658), in J. P. Baxter, ed., *Sir Ferdinando Gorges and his Province of Maine* (Boston, 1890), vol. 2, p. 9. On the fortunes of these "Weymouth Five," also see Foreman, *Indians Abroad*, p. 16–17; and Vaughan, *Transatlantic Encounters*, pp. 63–65.

59. Gorges, *Brief Narration*, p. 9.

60. John Smith, "A Description of New England" (1616), cited in Prins, "To the Land of the Mistigoches," p. 186.

61. Foreman, *Indians Abroad*, p. 17.

62. This tale is convoluted in the sources and in many later histories. See Alexander Young, *Chronicles of the Pilgrim Fathers of the Colony of Plymouth from 1602 to 1625* (Boston, 1841), pp. 190–91; and George B. Cheever, *The Journal of the Pilgrims at Plymouth in New England in 1620* (New York, 1848), p. 144. For discussions, see Leonard A. Adolf, "Squanto's Role in Pilgrim Diplomacy," *Ethnohistory* 11 (1964), pp. 248, 257; Lee, "The Call of the West," p. 322; Foreman, *Indians Abroad*, pp. 20–21; and Vaughan, *Transatlantic Encounters*, pp. 67–76.

63. William Bradford in *A History of Plymouth Plantation*, ed. C. Deane (Boston, 1856), p. 95.

64. Smith, *The Generall Historie*, p. 205. See Vaughan, *Transatlantic Encounters*, p. 70.

65. Sir Hans Sloane, *A Voyage to the Islands Madera, Barbados, Nieves, S. Christophers and Jamaica* (London, 1707), vol. 1, pp. lxxvi–lxxviii.

66. See Vaughan, *Transatlantic Encounters*, p. 101; and Michael Olien, "The Miskito Kings and the Line of Succession," *Journal of Anthropological Research* 39 (1983), pp. 201–3.

67. For a sample of the different historical approaches to Pocahontas, see P. L. Barbour, *Pocahontas and Her World* (Boston, 1970); H. C. Porter, *The Inconstant Savage: England and the North American Indian 1500–1600* (London, 1979); Peter Hulme, *Colonial Encounters: Europe and the Native Caribbean* (London, 1986), pp. 141, 168; Karen Robertson, "Pocahontas at the Masque," *Signs* 21 (1996); Daniel Richter, *Facing East from Indian Country: A Native History of Early America* (Cambridge, Mass., 2001), p. 70; and Camilla Townsend, *Pocahontas and the Powhatan Dilemma* (New York, 2004).

68. Hamor, *True Discourse*, pp. 10–11. For the early life of Pocahonatas, see Smith, *The Generall Historie*, p. 49; Porter, *The Inconstant Savage*, pp. 400–401; and J. A. L. Lemay, *Did Pocahonatas Save Captain John Smith?* (Athens, Ga., 1992).

69. Letter of colonist Alexander Whitaker, June 1614, cited in Porter, *The Inconstant Savage*, p. 401.

70. Smith, *The Generall Historie*, p. 121.

71. See John Chamberlain, letter to Dudley Carleton (1616), cited in Vaughan, *Transatlantic Encounters*, p. 86.

72. Smith, *The Generall Historie*, p. 123.

73. For the images, see Barbour, *Pocahontas*, 232–35; and Robertson, "Pocahontas at the Masque," p. 570–73.

74. Chamberlain to Carleton (1616), cited in Vaughan, *Transatlantic Encounters*, p. 86.

75. See Barbour, *Pocahontas*, pp. 183, 273; and Samuel Purchas, *Hakluyt Posthumus* (London, 1625), vol. 4, p. 1774.

76. Townsend is particularly good on the trip's aftermath: *Pocahontas and the Powhatan Dilemma*, pp. 159–78.

77. Advertisement, dated c. 1670, in British Library scrapbook, shelfmark N. Tab. 2026/25.(2.).

78. Smith, *The Generall Historie*, p. 206. Retold in Gorges, *Brief Narration*, p. 20.

79. Trinculo's remark in Act II, Scene 2. Foreman, *Indians Abroad*, p. 17; Takaki, "The Tempest in the Wilderness: The Racialization of Savagery," *Journal of American History* 79 (1992), p. 897. Richard D. Altick, however, claims that Trinculo was referring to the ill-fated 1577 Inuit of Frobisher's second voyage; *The Shows of London* (Cambridge, Mass., 1978), p. 45; while Vaughan believes that he meant someone whose death was known, such as Namontuck; *Transatlantic Encounters*, p. 50.

80. Remark by the Porter in Act V, Scene 4. Lee, "The Call of the West," p. 322. Vaughan agrees: *Transatlantic Encounters*, p. 66. The *Oxford Companion to Shakespeare* (Oxford, 2001), p. 6, explains that the first folio edition of *All Is True* (c. 1620s) appeared under the title of *The History of King Henry VIII*, but Shakespeare himself knew it by the former title.

81. Altick, *The Shows of London*, p. 45. Frank Kermode, ed., *The Arden Shakespeare: The Tempest* (London, 1962), p. 62.

82. This is the ratio I estimated from the collections on early modern street ephemera mounted in British Library "scrapbooks"; viewed between Sept. and Dec. 2001. See those around shelfmark N. Tab. 2026/25.

83. For an account of freaks as the deformed or miraculous, see Altick, *The Shows of London*, ch. 3. Also see L. Daston and K. Park, *Wonders and the Order of Nature 1150–1750* (New York, 1998), ch. 5; and Henry Morley, *Memoirs of Bartholemew Fair* (London, c.1874), ch. 16.

84. For Strawe and Wampas, see Vaughan, *Transatlantic Encounters*, pp. 99, 105.

85. See discussions of port-life escalation in Peter Borsay, ed., *The Eighteenth-Century Town: A Reader in Urban History 1688–1820* (London, 1990), pp. 10, 47, 149.

86. See M. Dorothy George, *London Life in the Eighteenth Century* (New

York, 1965), ch. 3; and R. Visram, *Asians in Britain: 400 Years of History* (London, 2002), ch. 1.

87. See John Childs, *The Army of Charles II* (Toronto, 1976), p. 162. On noble "soldiers of fortune," see D. Chandler, ed., *The Oxford Companion to the British Army* (Oxford, 2003), pp. 32–33.

88. Smith, *The Generall Historie*, p. 204.

89. Vaughan, *Transatlantic Encounters*, pp. 106, 109. He guesses that of the 30,000–50,000 Native Americans traded as slaves in Britain's southern colonies between 1670 and 1715, some must have ended up in England itself.

90. See Vaughan, *Transatlantic Encounters*, pp. 106–7.

91. See Pagden, *Lords of All the World*, pp. 65–77. Also see Philip P. Boucher, "Revisioning the French Atlantic; or, How to Think about the French Presence in the Atlantic, 1550–1625," in Peter C. Mancall, ed., *The Atlantic World and Virginia, 1550-1624* (Chapel Hill, 2007), pp. 274–306; and K. J. Banks, *Chasing Empire across the Sea: Communications and the State in the French Atlantic, 1713-1763* (Montreal, 2002), pp. 14–22.

92. These sixteenth-century examples are discussed in Dickason, *The Myth of the Savage*, pp. 209–11.

93. This is according to Dickason's figures; see ibid.

94. Dickason follows John Elliott's thesis for France: ibid., chs. 1, 10.

95. Montaigne's essay on cannibals was inspired by his meeting with three Tupinamba at Rouen in 1562; on Hakluyt's polemic, see Armitage, "The New World and British Historical," pp. 52–78.

96. For an excellent account, see Michael Wintroub, "Civilizing the Savage and Making a King: The Royal Entry Festival of Henri II (Rouen 1550)," *Sixteenth-Century Journal* 29 (1998), pp. 465–94. Dickason deflects this example of interest by saying that the event spoke more about the French nobility's love of pageantry and exotica of any sort than about a French fascination for the New World; see *The Myth of the Savage*, p. 212. Certainly there appears to be little evidence of fascination from the sources of other visits.

97. See especially here David Armitage, *The Ideological Origins of the British Empire* (Cambridge, 2000), ch. 3. His discussion of eclecticism stems from Andrew Fitzmaurice, "The Civic Solution to the Crisis of English Colonization, 1609–1625," *The Historical Journal* 42 (1999), pp. 25–51.

98. See Pagden, *Lords of All the World*, pp. 65, 73. Also see Seed, *Ceremonies of Possession*, ch. 2; and Peter Cook, "Kings, Captains, and Kin: French Views of Native American Political Cultures in the Sixteenth and Seventeenth Centuries," in Mancall, ed., *The Atlantic World and Virginia*, pp. 307–41.

99. James Axtell, *The Invasion Within: The Contest of Cultures in Colonial North America* (New York, 1985), p. 23.

100. Citations in Dickason, *The Myth of the Savage*, p. 218.

101. Cited in ibid.

102. Some English Protestant missionaries set sail for the New World explicitly to attend to native children, but there is little evidence of reverse

transportation for juvenile education. See Roy Harvey Pearce, *Savagism and Civilization* (Berkeley, 1988), p. 9.

103. See Pagden, *Lords of All the World*, pp. 65–73; and Armitage, *Ideological Origins of the British Empire*, pp. 146–69.

104. See Banks, *Chasing Empire*, p. 27; and W. J. Eccles, *The French in North America, 1500–1765* (East Lansing, 1998), p. 80.

105. See M. J. Braddick, "The English Government, War, Trade, and Settlement, 1625–1688," in N. Canny, ed., OHBE (Oxford, 1998), vol. 1, pp. 286–308.

106. Banks, *Chasing Empire*, p. 28.

107. "Mr [John] Nelson's Memorial about the State of the Northern Colonies in America" (1696), in DRCHSNY, vol. 4, p. 208.

CHAPTER 2

1. "Mr [John] Nelson's Memorial about the State of the Northern Colonies in America" (1696), in DRCHSNY, vol. 4, p. 208.

2. For greater readability, I will henceforth refer to the four Native American visitors as "the Iroquois," without quotation marks but with due acknowledgment of the label's inadequacy.

3. Alongside his better-known argument that the Four Iroquois Kings were the first Native Americans "who were thought [by officials] to possess the authority of rulers" and as such helped to stimulate a new "language of empire" in Whitehall, Hinderaker proposed that what made this delegation *interesting* was the fact that they were *Indian kings*, or, as he implied later in his article, because they were *kingly Indians*. Eric Hinderaker, "The 'Four Indian Kings' and the Imaginative Construction of the First British Empire," *William and Mary Quarterly*, 3rd ser. 53 (July 1996), pp. 494, 497, 507.

4. In the middle of a controversial war, with a shaky government, and facing hordes of Rhinelander refugees together with violent urban riots related to the notorious Dr Sacheverell, Bond argues that the Iroquois appeared as magnificent novelties, "stimulating and restorative." Richmond P. Bond, *Queen Anne's American Kings* (Oxford, 1952), p. 15.

5. Some other significant studies of the Four Iroquois Kings include Carolyn T. Foreman, *Indians Abroad 1493–1938* (Norman, 1943); J. G. Garratt, ed., *The Four Indian Kings* (Ottawa, 1985); Stephanie Pratt, *American Indians in British Art, 1700–1840* (Norman, 2005); Troy Bickham, *Savages within the Empire: Representations of American Indians in Eighteenth-Century Britain* (Oxford, 2005); and Alden T. Vaughan, *Transatlantic Encounters: American Indians in Britain, 1500–1776* (Cambridge, 2006). These mostly duck the issue of appeal altogether or imply a general view that as savages, New World people are perennially popular with people who think themselves not-savage.

6. Daniel K. Richter rather vaguely dates the "coalescence" to "the sixteenth century" in his magisterial work, *The Ordeal of the Longhouse: The Peoples of the Iroquois League in the Era of European Colonization* (Chapel

Hill, 1992), p. 15. Elsewhere Richter claims that the political alliance started really to come into effect from the 1630s; "Native Peoples of North America and the Eighteenth-Century British Empire," in OHBE, vol. 2, p. 352. See also William N. Fenton, "Structure, Continuity, and Change in Iroquois Treaty Making," in F. Jennings et al., eds., *History and Culture in Iroquois Diplomacy: An Interdisciplinary Guide to the Treaties of the Six Nations and their League* (Syracuse, 1985), p. 16.

7. Francis Jennings, "Iroquois Alliances in American History," in Jennings, *History and Culture in Iroquois Diplomacy*, p. 41.

8. On the 1667 treaty and French Indian encroachment, see Richard Aquila, *The Iroquois Restoration: Iroquois Diplomacy on the Colonial Frontier, 1701–1754* (Detroit, 1983), p. 41. See also Bond, *Queen Anne's*, p. 18.

9. See Daniel K. Richter, *Facing East from Indian Country: A Native History of Early America* (Cambridge, Mass., 2001), pp. 147–49; and the glossary to Jennings, *History and Culture in Iroquois Diplomacy*, pp. 116–17.

10. For Iroquois participation in this war, see Thomas Elliot Norton, *The Fur Trade in Colonial New York, 1686–1776* (Madison, 1974), ch. 1.

11. Richter, "Native Peoples," p. 354; Bruce Lenman, "Colonial Wars and Imperial Instability, 1688–1793," in OHBE, vol. 2, p. 153.

12. Richter, "Native Peoples," p. 354; Bond, *Queen Anne's*, p. 19. See also Daniel K. Richter, "War and Culture: The Iroquois Experience," in P. Mancall and J. Merrell, eds, *American Encounters: Native and Newcomers from European Contact to Indian Removal, 1500–1850* (New York, 2007), pp. 427–54; and François Bigot, "The Rightness of the French and English to Fort Niagara Examined" (1727), DRCHSNY, vol. 9, p. 982.

13. On Vetch, see G. M. Waller, *Samuel Vetch: Colonial Enterpriser* (Chapel Hill, 1960); and the *Dictionary of Canadian Biography Online*.

14. For *Canada Survey'd*, see PRO, CSP America and West Indies, June 1708–9, no. 60. Vetch also submitted a copy to the Council for Trade.

15. See Aquila, *The Iroquois Restoration*, p. 86; Richter, *Ordeal of the Longhouse*, p. 226.

16. On the Onondagas and Senecas, see Richter, *Ordeal of the Longhouse*, p. 226. On the Iroquois' risk, see Aquila, *The Iroquois Restoration*, pp. 86–87. The precise enlistment included 443 warriors out of about 1500: see Richter, *Ordeal of the Longhouse*, p. 367; and Norton, *Fur Trade*, p. 13.

17. For this episode generally see G. G. Plank, *An Unsettled Conquest: The British Campaign against the Peoples of Acadia* (Philadelphia, 2001), ch. 2.

18. Vetch to Sunderland, 12 September 1709, Vetch Letter Book (privately owned), pp. 66–67: see Bond, *Queen Anne's*, p. 31.

19. Officers to Vetch, 2 September 1709, Vetch Letter Book (privately owned), pp. 70–71: see Bond, *Queen Anne's*, p. 32.

20. PRO, CSP America and West Indies, 1708–9, pp. 490–92.

21. Pratt, *American Indians*, p. 33. See also Vaughan, *Transatlantic Encounters*, p. 114.

22. Vaughan, *Transatlantic Encounters*, pp. 117–18; Bond, *Queen Anne's*,

pp. 39–40. See also Dean R. Snow, "Theyanoguin," in R. S. Grant, ed., *Northeastern Indian Lives, 1632–1816* (Amherst, 1996), pp. 208–26. For a history of Iroquois diplomacy, see Jennings, *History and Culture in Iroquois Diplomacy*. For the reluctance of Iroquois to travel overseas till now, see François Bigot, "The Rightness of the French," p. 983.

23. Vaughan, *Transatlantic Encounters*, p. 117; Bond, *Queen Anne's*, ch. 2.

24. Vetch to Sunderland, 9 January 1710, Vetch Letter Book (privately owned), p. 113, see Bond, *Queen Anne's*, p. 42.

25. Vetch to Sunderland, 10 February 1710, Vetch Letter Book (privately owned), pp. 115–16, see Bond, *Queen Anne's*, p. 43.

26. See Julian Hoppit, *A Land of Liberty? England 1689–1727* (Oxford, 2000), pp. 55, 426; and M. Dorothy George, *London Life in the 18th Century* (New York, 1965), chs. 2–3.

27. See, for examples and a discussion, Roy Porter, *London: A Social History* (Cambridge, Mass., 1998), p. 162.

28. On the "country persuasion," see Julian Hoppit, *A Land of Liberty*, p. 158.

29. For a similarly positive approach to these developments, along with explication, see Roy Porter, *The Creation of the Modern World: The Untold Story of the British Enlightenment* (New York, 2000), pp. 35–42.

30. See Hoppit, *A Land of Liberty*, pp. 285–86; and Linda Colley, *In Defiance of Oligarchy: The Tory Party 1714–60* (Cambridge, 1982), chs. 5–6.

31. Hoppit, *A Land of Liberty*, p. 283.

32. For a brief introduction to the 1709 Palatine refugees, see A. G. Roeber, *Palatines, Liberty, and Property: German Lutherans in Colonial British America* (Baltimore, 1993), ch. 1.

33. See Geoffrey Holmes, "The Sacheverell Riots: The Crowd and the Church in Early Eighteenth-Century London," *Past and Present* 72 (August 1976), p. 60.

34. See Hoppit, *A Land of Liberty*, p. 233.

35. For the rioters' targets, see Holmes, "The Sacheverell Riots," pp. 64–68.

36. On the peculiarly fraught nature of 1710, see Geoffrey Holmes, *The Making of a Great Power: Late Stuart and Early Georgian Britain 1660–1722* (Harlow, 1993), p. 334.

37. Although Thomas Arne the composer features in more than thirty biographical dictionaries before 1900, only two stories circulate about his father: one, that he was the host of the Four Iroquois Kings who visited Queen Anne, and two, that he was the infamous "political upholsterer" of Richard Steele's *Tatler* nos. 155, 160, 178, 180, and 232. The latter association, however, is not consistent. See *The British Biographical Index*, 7 vols. (1984). A broadside discovered by Richmond Bond reporting a fire in King Street in 1712 commented that the "House where the *Indian Kings* liv'd" had "usually several Gentlemen Lodgers"; see Bond, *Queen Anne's*, p. 96. Presumably Arne was simply a regular West-End landlord for temporary lodgers; as he was also an officeholder in the London Company of Upholsterers, he may have been an easy, reputable choice for government administrators in the city.

38. *The Four Kings of Canada* (London, 1710), pp. 6–7.

39. PRO, CTP, 1708–14, p. 176.

40. PRO, CO, 5/1049, no. 157. The speech went through many printings at the time, most popularly in the annalist Abel Boyer's *History of the Reign of Queen Anne* IX (London, 1711); and in the broadside *The Four Indian Kings' Speech* (London, 1710).

41. On moderate Toryism in this era, see Daniel A. Baugh, "Great Britain's 'Blue-Water' Policy, 1689–1815," *International History Review* 10 (1988), pp. 33–58; and David Hempton, "Contested Kingdoms 1688–1756," in P. Langford, ed., *The Eighteenth Century 1688–1815* (London, 2002), p. 42.

42. On the history of the Iroquois items, see the glossary in Jennings, ed., *History and Culture in Iroquois Diplomacy*, pp. 118–23; and Mary A. Druke, "Iroquois Treaties: Common Forms, Varying Interpretations," in Jennings, ed., *History and Culture in Iroquois Diplomacy*, pp. 88–90. For more on the exchange of gifts in 1710, see *Dublin Intelligence*, 29 April 1710; and Narcissus Luttrell, *A Brief Historical Relation of State Affairs from Sept 1678 to April 1714* (Oxford, 1857), vol. 6, p. 571.

43. See Luttrell, *Brief Historical Relation*, vol. 6, p. 571.

44. Ibid., p. 572; *The Evening Post*, 2–4 May 1710; *Dawks' News Letter*, 4 May 1710.

45. Boyer, *History*, p. 191; Luttrell, *Brief Historical Relation*, p. 572; *Dawks' News Letter*, 22 April 1710 and 4 May 1710; *Royal Strangers' Ramble* (London, 1710). *The Dublin Intelligence*, 6 May 1710. *The Evening Post* 2–4 May 1701. The visit to Montagu House, now the British Museum, was noted in a French dispatch of 2 May 1710, Archives des Affaires Estrangeres (Quai d'Orsay), vol. 230, fol. 152, cited in Bond, *Queen Anne's*, p. 101.

46. *Dawks' News Letter*, 29 April 1710. See also *Royal Strangers' Ramble*.

47. Boyer, *History*, p. 189.

48. *The Spectator*, 27 April 1711; *Dawks' News Letter*, 29 April 1710; and Arthur Murphy, *The Gray's-Inn Journal* 95 (10 August 1754), later collected in two volumes (London, 1756), vol. 2, p. 271.

49. *Dawks' News Letter*, 29 April 1710.

50. *The Spectator* 18 (1711); *Royal Strangers' Ramble*.

51. See playbills advertising the Four Iroquois Kings at theaters and shows, some reproduced in Bond, *Queen Anne's*, ch. 1. See also *Daily Courant*, 29 April 1710; and *The Flying Post*, 11–13 May 1710 (advertising a cockfight between one cock named Sacheverell and another named Burgess, after a well-known Dissenter).

52. *Royal Strangers' Ramble*; *The Tatler*, 27–29 April 1710; *Daily Courant*, 2 May 1710.

53. See the witty narrative of this event in Murphy, *The Gray's-Inn Journal*, vol. 2, p. 271.

54. See especially Bond, *Queen Anne's*, p. 5.

55. Saquainquaragton died within a few months of returning to Iroquoia,

some historians assuming that it was from diseases suffered while abroad: Vaughan, *Transatlantic Encounters,* p. 132.

56. Playbill reproduced in Garratt, *Four Indian Kings.*

57. See Verelst's obituary in the *Gentleman's Magazine,* June 1734. See also DNB. Verelst was paid the handsome sum of £100 for the commission: Stephanie Pratt, "The Four Indian Kings," in J. Hackforth-Jones, ed., *Between Worlds: Voyagers to Britain, 1700–1850* (London, 2007), p. 28.

58. See Pratt, *American Indians,* pp. 36–39.

59. A German traveler at the time confirms the position of the paintings: Zacharais von Uffenbach, *Travels,* in W. H. Quarrell and M. Mare, eds., *London in 1710* (London, 1934), p. 157.

60. Hinderaker, "The 'Four Indian Kings,'" p. 507.

61. Bruce Robertson, "The Portraits, an Iconographical Study," in Garratt, *Four Indian Kings,* pp. 145.

62. Roxann Wheeler, *The Complexion of Race: Categories of Difference in Eighteenth-Century British Culture* (Philadelphia, 2000), p. 174. Hayden White, *Tropics of Discourse: Essays in Cultural Criticism* (Baltimore, 1978), p. 191. Laura Brown endorses White's reading in *Fables of Modernity: Literature and Culture in the English Eighteenth Century* (Ithaca, 2001), p. 219.

63. David Bindman, *Ape to Apollo: Aesthetics and the Idea of Race in the 18th Century* (Ithaca, 2002), pp. 42–44.

64. Wylie Sypher, "The African Prince in London," *The Journal of the History of Ideas* 2 (1941), p. 237.

65. *The Four Kings of Canada* (London, 1710), pp. 5–8.

66. See Robertson, "The Portraits," p. 142; and Linda Colley, *Captives: The Story of Britain's Pursuit of Empire and How Its Soldiers and Civilians Were Held Captive by the Dream of Global Supremacy, 1600–1850* (New York, 2002), p. 163. See also Pratt, "Four Indian Kings," pp. 30–32.

67. See discussion in Robertson, "The Portraits," p. 144.

68. J. C. H. King, "North American Ethnography in the Collections of Sir Hans Sloane," in O. Impey and A. Macgregor, eds., *The Origins of Museums: The Cabinet of Curiosities in the Sixteenth and Seventeenth Centuries* (Oxford, 1985), pp. 232–36. King discusses the Native Americana contained and accessible in three different collections around 1710.

69. Karen Kupperman has written persuasively on the diversity of early English opinion about Native American self-presentation, but little scholarship has addressed either British re-presentations of dress or, more interestingly, Native American manipulations of foreign perceptions: see Karen Kupperman, "Presentment of Civility: English Reading of American Self-Presentation in the Early Years of Colonization" *William and Mary Quarterly,* 3rd ser. 54 (Jan. 1997), pp. 193–228.

70. See advertisements in *The Tatler* 250, 253, 256, 261, 267 (November–December 1710). David Bindman attests to the "wide-circulation" of the copies in *Ape to Apollo,* p. 42, as does Linda Colley in *Captives,* p. 162.

71. *The London Gazette,* 18 May 1710. Note also the contemporary Amer-

ican historian William Smith's assertion that "the arrival of the five [sic] *Sachems* in *England* made a great Bruit [noise] thro' the whole kingdom. The mob followed wherever they went, and small Cuts [prints] of them were sold among the People." William Smith, *The History of the Province of New-York* (London, 1757), p. 122.

72. *The Present State of Europe; or, the Historical and Political Monthly Mercury* 21 (London, 1710), pp. 158–59.

73. Ormonde had fought for James II in 1685 but supported William III in 1688; for his moderate Toryism by 1710 see his DNB entry; on Ormonde generally see T. Barnard and J. Fenlon, eds., *The Dukes of Ormonde, 1610–1745* (Woodbridge, 2000). Ormonde hosted the Four Iroquois at his country seat in Richmond twice before the parade in Hyde Park: both times were noted by an avid press: see *The Dublin Intelligence*, 2 May 1710; *Dawks' News Letter*, 27 April 1710; Luttrell, *Brief Historical Relation*, p. 574.

74. *The Present State of Europe*, pp. 158–59.

75. Boyer, *History*, p. 191.

76. DNB.

77. For Demaree's conviction, see *The Evening Post*, 25 April 1710; for Hearne's entry, see *The Remarks and Collections of Thomas Hearne*, ed., C. E. Doble (Oxford, 1886), vol. 2, p. 385.

78. On Anne's quiet sympathy for the Sacheverell cause, see Hoppit, *A Land of Liberty*, p. 234. On this event, see also Bond, *Queen Anne's*, pp. 10–11.

79. The last of the Stuarts, Anne herself retained much sympathy for the pre-revolution idea of monarchy in England. As a creature of the revolution, however, she represented a difficult concept for the debate over British destiny. See Hoppit, *A Land of Liberty*, ch. 9.

80. Richard Steele, *The Tatler* 171, 13 May 1711, ed. D. F. Bond (Oxford, 1989), p. 440.

81. On Steelite whiggism, see Porter, *Creation of the Modern World*, p. 196; and Lawrence E. Klein, "Sociability, Solitude, and Enthusiasm," in L. E. Klein and A. J. La Vopa, eds., *Enthusiasm and Enlightenment in Europe, 1650–1850* (San Marino, 1998), pp. 153–77.

82. Joseph Addison, *The Spectator* 50, 27 April 1711, ed., D. F. Bond (Oxford, 1965), vol. 1, p. 211–15. On Addison as a Shaftesburian New Whig , see Porter, *Creation of the Modern World*, pp. 194–97; J. G. A. Pocock, *The Machiavellian Moment: Florentine Political Thought and the Atlantic Republican Tradition* (Princeton, 1975), ch. 13; and L. E. Klein, *Shaftesbury and the Culture of Politeness: Moral Discourse and Cultural Politics in Early Eighteenth-Century Britain* (Cambridge, 1994).

83. Joseph Addison, *The Spectator* 69, 19 May 1711, ed. D. F. Bond (Oxford, 1965), vol. 1, p. 296.

84. For the posthumous life of this piece, see Bond, *Queen Anne's*, pp. 88–90; and Benjamin Bissell, *The American Indian in English Literature of the Eighteenth Century* (New Haven, 1968), p. 63.

85. Jonathan Swift, *Journal to Stella* (1711), ed., H. Williams (Oxford, 1948), vol. 1, p. 254.

86. See though especially Jonathan Swift, *The Intelligencer* 19 (1728), in H. Davis, ed., *Irish Tracts 1728-1733* (Oxford, 1955), pp. 54–61.

87. Ibid., p. 58.

88. On Swift's oppositionism, see Ian Higgins, *Swift's Politics: A Study in Disaffection* (Cambridge, 1994). See also Pocock, *Machiavellian Moment*, pp. 446–48.

89. DNB.

90. *Windsor-Forest* (1713) from Alexander Pope, *The Works of Alexander Pope, Esq* (London, 1736). Two days after its publication, Jonathan Swift wrote to his pupil Stella simply "read it"; *Journal to Stella*, vol. 2 p. 635. For an analysis, see Joseph Roach, *Cities of the Dead: Circum-Atlantic Performance* (New York, 1996), pp. 139–44.

91. *The Four Indian Kings Garland in Two Parts* (London, 1710). Hinderaker, "The 'Four Indian Kings,'" pp. 503–4. For the ballad's publication history, see Garratt, *Four Indian Kings*, pp. 36–76.

92. *Epilogue That Was Spoken before the Four Indian Kings at the Play-House* (London, 1710). Elkanah Settle, *A Pindaric Poem, on the Propagation of the Gospel in Foreign Parts. A work of piety so zealously recommended and promoted by her most gracious Majesty* (London, 1711).

93. Settle, *Pindaric Poem*, pp. iii, 1. On Settle as poet (and dunce), see Pat Rogers, *An Introduction to Pope* (London, 1975), p. 115.

94. *Royal Strangers' Ramble*. Although the satire mentioned India, this was probably a reference to the West-Indies, which itself could often stand for America. The anonymous author also referred in the piece to the "Iroquois breed" and their "wampum belts."

95. *A True and Faithful Account of the Last Distemper and Death of Tom Whigg, Esq.* (London, 1710), part 1, pp. 31–33.

96. For a fuller description of the artifacts, see Bond, *Queen Anne's;* and Hinderaker, "The 'Four Indian Kings.'".

97. Hinderaker, "The 'Four Indian Kings,'" p. 505, reiterating what most recent historians have assumed about the content of reaction to the visitors.

98. Boyer, *History,* p. 191; Luttrell, *Brief Historical Relation*, vol. 6, p. 577; *Calender of Treasury Books and Papers, 1708-14*, ed. J. Redington (London, 1879, republished Nendeln, 1974), p. 178.

99. "Conference of Governor Hunter with the Indians," 7 August 1710, DRCHSNY, vol. 5, pp. 217–29. For a cogent summary, also see Vaughan, *Transatlantic Encounters*, p. 130.

100. Barbara Silvertsen, *Turtles, Wolves, and Bears: A Mohawk Family History* (Bowie, 1996), pp. 62–66. See also Vaughan, *Transatlantic Encounters*, pp. 132–33; and Eric Hinderaker, *The Two Hendricks: Unravelling A Mohawk Mystery* (Cambridge, Mass., 2010).

101. See Bond, *Queen Anne's*, pp. 39–40; Vaughan, *Transatlantic Encounters*, p. 132.

102. For the Whig dismissal and Tory ascendancy, see Hoppit, *A Land of Liberty*, pp. 300–306. See also Bruce Lenman, *Britain's Colonial Wars 1688–1783* (Harlow, 2001), p. 34. For the official reneging, see Dartmouth in PRO, CSP America and West Indies, 1710–11, pp. 183–84.

103. In nice circularity, the striving Samuel Vetch was installed as the colony's first governor. The town of Port Royal was renamed Annapolis in somewhat over-generous honor of its patron. For more on this period in Acadian history, see Plank, *An Unsettled Conquest.*

104. See PRO, CSP America and West Indies, 1710–11, p. 47.

105. See DRCHSNY, vol. 5, p. 270.

106. The British Admiral Hoveden Walker withdrew his force in September after losing more than 800 men in the Egg Island storms. See Bond, *Queen Anne's*, p. 52.

107. See Richter, *Facing East*, p. 167.

108. See Vaughan, *Transatlantic Encounters*, p. 131.

109. See "Report of the Select Committee on the Six Nations of Indians," *Journal of the S. P. G.* (London, 1710), vol. 1, pp. 256–64.

110. But not before Iroquois leaders had sent a letter to the SPGFP to remind them of their promises: see letter dated 21 July 1710, in *Journal of the S. P. G.*, vol. 1, p. 122.

111. Andrews's letter to the Archbishop dated 9 March 1713, in ibid., vol. 8, pp. 143–47.

112. As a direct consequence of this disaster, the SPGFP entered a period of some pessimism regarding the convertibility of Native Americans: see Hoppit, *A Land of Liberty*, pp. 236–37; and F. J. Klingberg, "The Noble Savage as Seen by the SPFGP Missionary in Colonial New York, 1702–1750," *Historical Magazine of the Protestant Episcopal Church* (June 1939).

113. See for a good overview Daniel Statt, "The Case of the Mohocks: Rake Violence in Augustan London," *Social History* 20 (May 1995), pp. 179–99.

114. Modern scholars who doubt that the Mohocks ever existed include I. A. Bell, *Literature and Crime in Augustan England* (London, 1991); and Calhoun Winton, *John Gay and the London Theatre* (Lexington, 1993).

115. Daniel Defoe, *The Review* 153, 15 March 1712.

116. Joseph Addison, *The Spectator* 324, 12 March 1712. For historians who concur on the connection between the visitors and the gang, see Bond, *Queen Anne's*, p. 76; Winton, *John Gay*, p. 19; Hinderaker, "The 'Four Indian Kings,'" p. 524; Hoppit, *A Land of Liberty*, p. 439.

117. Swift, *Journal to Stella*, vol. 2, p. 509. Hearne, *Remarks and Collections*, vol. 3, p. 326.

118. *The Medley*, 24 March 1712. *Observator*, 15 March 1712.

119. See Robert Allen, *The Clubs of Augustan London* (Cambridge, Mass., 1933). The Hell-Fire Clubs of the 1720s and beyond were popularly known as affiliations of wealthy, libertine, young men: the Mohocks too, like the Scowrers of the 1690s before them, were also generally thought to be elitist, youth-

ful, and possibly homosexual rakes. See Statt, "The Case of the Mohocks," pp. 190, 195.

120. Richter's discussion of the "anglophiles" is cursory: *Ordeal of the Longhouse*, p. 227. Pratt, on the other hand, underscores their political significance: "Four Indian Kings," p. 24.

CHAPTER 3

1. J. H. Plumb, *The Growth of Political Stability in England: 1675–1725* (Harmondsworth, [1967] 1969). For some critiques, see Jeremy Black, "An Age of Political Stability?" in J. Black, ed., *Britain in the Age of Walpole* (London, 1984); Nicholas Rogers, "The Urban Opposition to Whig Oligarchy, 1720–1760," in M. Jacob and J. Jacob, eds., *The Origins of Anglo-American Radicalism* (London, 1984), pp. 132–47; C. Roberts, "The Growth of Political Stability Reconsidered," *Albion* 25 (1993); Kathleen Wilson, *The Sense of the People: Politics, Culture, and Imperialism in England, 1715–1785* (Cambridge, 1995), ch. 2; and Wilfrid Prest, *Albion Ascendant: English History 1660–1815* (Oxford, 1998), pp. 131–32.

2. Plumb, *The Growth of Political Stability*, p. 12; Geoffrey Holmes, *The Making of a Great Power: Late Stuart and Early Georgian Britain 1660–1722* (Harlow, 1993), p. 386.

3. See H. T. Dickinson, "Popular Politics in the Age of Walpole," in Black, ed., *Britain in the Age of Walpole*, pp. 64–66; Paul Langford, *A Polite and Commercial People: England 1727–1783* (Oxford, 1989), p. 46; Wilson, *Sense of the People*, pp. 101–35; Rogers, "The Urban Opposition to Whig Oligarchy"; and Michael Harris, "Print and Politics in the Age of Walpole," in Black, ed., *Britain in the Age of Walpole*, pp. 197–201.

4. Daniel Richter, *Facing East from Indian Country: A Native History of Early America* (Cambridge, Mass., 2001), pp. 151–52.

5. See Jacob M. Price, "The Imperial Economy, 1700–1776," in OHBE, vol. 2, p. 101.

6. For the weakness of Britain's opponents, see Bruce Lenman, *Britain's Colonial Wars 1688–1783* (Harlow, 2001), ch. 2; and Richter, *Facing East*, p. 164.

7. Though see William O. Steele, *The Cherokee Crown of Tannassey* (Winston-Salem, 1977). Also see V. W. Crane, *The Southern Frontier 1670–1732* (New York, [1928] 1981), p. 276; Carolyn T. Foreman, *Indians Abroad 1493–1938* (Norman, 1943); Barbara McRae, *Franklin's Ancient Mound* (Franklin, 1993), pp. 29–36; and Alden Vaughan, *Transatlantic Encounters: American Indians in Britain, 1500–1776* (Cambridge, 2006), pp. 137–50.

8. Charles C. Jones, Jr., *Historical Sketch of Tomo-Chi-Chi, Mico of the Yamacraws* (Albany, 1868); Helen Todd, *Tomochichi: Indian Friend of the Georgia Colony* (Atlanta, 1977); Julie Anne Sweet, "Bearing Feathers of an Eagle: Tomochichi's Trip to England," *Georgia Historical Quarterly* 87 (2002), pp. 339–71; and Julie Anne Sweet, "Will the Real Tomochichi Please Come Forward?"

The American Indian Quarterly 32 (2008), pp. 141–77. See also Foreman, *Indians Abroad;* and Vaughan, *Transatlantic Encounters,* pp. 151–60.

9. See Richter, *Facing East,* pp. 163–64, 169. Also see William L. Ramsey, *The Yamasee War: A Study of Culture, Economy, and Conflict in the Colonial South* (Lincoln, 2008), ch. 6; and Steven J. Oatis, *A Colonial Complex: South Carolina's Frontiers in the Era of the Yamasee War, 1680–1730* (Lincoln, 2004).

10. See Richter, *Facing East,* pp. 163–64, 169; and Ramsey, *The Yamasee War,* ch. 6. See also Tyler Boulware, "Native Americans and National Identity in Early North America," *History Compass* 4 (2006), pp. 927–32; and Tyler Boulware, "The Effect of the Seven Years' War on the Cherokee Nation," *Early American Studies: An Interdisciplinary Journal* 5 (2007), pp. 395–426.

11. Cuming has defied the descriptive powers of most serious historians. Richter names him "eccentric," while Vaughan calls him "extraordinary" and "remarkable." Richter, *Facing East,* p. 169; Vaughan, *Transatlantic Encounters,* pp. 139–40. Cuming appeared to have inherited a fatal speculating propensity: his father had been involved in the ill-fated Scottish Darien Scheme for the Panama Canal while Cuming himself had lost much family money in the South Sea Bubble of 1720. See Cuming's entry in the DNB and Crane, *Southern Frontier,* pp. 276–80.

12. See McRae, *Franklin's Ancient Mound,* p. 29; and Foreman, *Indians Abroad.*

13. Isaiah 28:21. Some accounts link Mount Perazim to the Valley of Gibeon, where David defeated the Philistines. See the Memorial Book of Sir Alexander Cuming (1767), BL Add. Mss. 39, 855, p. 1.

14. Crane assumes Cuming acted with a purely cynical heart: Crane, *Southern Frontier,* p. 276; and for an example of Cuming's pestering, see King George II, n.d., recorded September 1730, PRO CO 5/4 (47ii), p. 219. But see also Cuming's mania in his Memorial Book, pp. 1–3, 39. In this, Cuming explained his vocation in various ways: sometimes to teach Britons "a proper lesson" in the strength of faith required to build a successful nation; sometimes to clear the Carolinas for "Pagans and Jews" in order to convert them; sometimes to clear the Carolinas for debtors and other financial malfeasants in order to rid the British Isles of them; sometimes to "civilize the American savage"; but mostly to bring the "Savage Chiefs of the Cherokee Indians" under British rule so as to outmaneuver the French. Most of the Whitehall correspondence is still housed in the PRO; a deal of it also concerns Cuming's fight for a recommencement of his family's one-time royal allowance. Cuming claimed his father had saved the future George II from drowning during the course of allied fighting in Flanders in 1708. The Hanoverian Prince is said to have promised a royal annuity to his family, which apparently began sometime during his father's reign but was abruptly halted in 1721.

15. Colonists were also afraid of a new uprising by the Cherokee, rumored by the French around this time. See *The Political State of Great Britain* (London, 1730), vol. 40, p. 382. For Cuming's unfavorable reception in Charles Town, see Crane, *The Southern Frontier,* p. 276; and Tom Hatley, *The Dividing*

Path: Cherokees and South Carolinians through the Revolutionary Era (New York, 1995), pp. 67–68. For Grant, see Ludovic Grant, "Historical Relation," 12 January 1756, *South Carolina Historical and Genealogical Magazine* 10 (1909), pp. 54–66.

16. See Grant, "Historical Relation," p. 56; and Attakullakulla also recounted in SCHGM, pp. 65–66.

17. See *The Political State*, pp. 383–84; and Cuming, Memorial Book, p. 25. On eighteenth-century Cherokee society, see Hatley, *The Dividing Path*; and Gregory E. Dowd, *A Spirited Resistance: The North American Indian Struggle for Unity, 1745–1815* (Baltimore, 1992).

18. *The Political State*, p. 384.

19. Ibid., p. 385.

20. Ibid.

21. Their names are taken from the various reports of them in the British press also from the eventual *Articles of Friendship and Commerce* signed on 9 September 1730. See also Samuel C. Williams, *Dawn of Tennessee Valley and Tennessee History* (Johnson City, 1937), pp. 90–93; and Vaughan, *Transatlantic Encounters*, p. 141.

22. *The Political State*, p. 386. See also Attakullakulla's description of the same recounted in SCHGM, pp. 66–67. Because this seventh Cherokee did not have Moytoy's blessing, his name does not appear on the subsequent treaty.

23. Most accounts name Wiggan as the interpreter, noting his Cherokee nickname of "the Old Rabbit." Vaughan, however, argues that the interpreter was a Robert Bunning, also named "the Old Rabbit." The confluence of nicknames suggests these are the same person, with Wiggan as the most common appellation in southern histories. See Vaughan, *Transatlantic Encounters*, p. 304.

24. He freely admitted the unauthorized nature of his diplomacy in Cuming to King George II, 26 June 1730, PRO CO 5/361, folio 141. And see Cuming to Board of Trade, July–September 1730, PRO CO 5/361, folio 166.

25. *The Weekly Journal*, 27 June 1730.

26. *The Political State*, vol. 40, p. 386.

27. On Cuming's language, see Memorial Book, pp. 27, 33–39. On George II's approval, see *Daily Journal*, 8 August 1730; and *Daily Post*, 24 June 1730. It was perhaps George II's enthusiasm that prompted Whitehall to concede to Cuming's persistent requests for reimbursement. Cuming was repaid via South Carolina's Governor, Robert Johnson, later in 1730: see "Treasury Books and Papers: July 1730, 21–31," *Calendar of Treasury Books and Papers, Volume 1: 1729–1730* (1897), p. 426.

28. *The Daily Courant*, 3 August 1730. See also *The Universal Spectator*, 8 August 1730.

29. *Daily Post*, 12 August 1730.

30. Anonymous, *Royal Remarks; or the Indian King's Observations on the most fashionable follies now reigning in the Kingdom of Great Britain* (London, 1730).

31. See *St. James's Evening Post*, 29 August 1730; *The Daily Courant*, 13 August 1730; *Grub Street Journal*, 10 September 1730.

32. *Daily Post*, 28 August 1730. See also Foreman, *Indians Abroad*, p. 49.

33. See Peter Borsay, *The Image of the Georgian Town 1700–2000: Towns, Heritage, and History* (Oxford, 2000), p. 255. Also see Borsay's piece on "spas" in OCRA. The Cherokee visited both Sadlers' Wells and Richmond Wells. See, among many, *Daily Courant*, 12 August 1730; *Daily Journal*, 12 August 1730 and 20 August 1730; and *Daily Post*, 18 August 1730 and 20 August 1730.

34. See John Mullan and Christopher Reid, *Eighteenth-Century Popular Culture: A Selection* (Oxford, 2000), pp. 115–20. Also see Gillian Russell's piece on "fairs" in OCRA. The Cherokee were taken to Tottenham Court Fair, Croydon Fair, and St. Bartholomew's Fair. See *Grub Street Journal*, 10 September 1730; also see *Daily Journal*, 14 August 1730; and *Daily Courant* 14 August 1730.

35. See John Brewer, *Pleasures of the Imagination: English Culture in the Eighteenth Century* (London, 1997), pp. 39–50; and Roy Porter, *The Creation of the Modern World: The Untold Story of the British Enlightenment* (New York, 2000), pp. 36–38.

36. *Daily Courant*, 7 August 1730.

37. See *Daily Courant*, 14 August 1730; *The Universal Spectator*, 15 August 1730; *Daily Journal*, 4 September 1730.

38. *Daily Journal*, 12 August 1730; *Daily Courant*, 7 August 1730; *Daily Post*, 10 September 1730; *Grub Street Journal*, 10 September 1730; *Universal Spectator*, 12 September 1730.

39. *Daily Courant*, 1 August 1730.

40. Indeed, many scholars would claim it to be the greatest symbol yet of Britain's continued commercialization at this time. Buoyed by both a recent freeing up of the press and a new cultural imperative toward the exchange of current affairs, newspapers mushroomed during the early decades of the eighteenth century. By 1730 London sustained approximately a dozen dailies and a dozen monthlies. Some of these titles ran up to 2,000 copies per issue, each of which could be read by twenty readers or more given their chief distribution through coffeehouses and other sociable venues. With literacy rates up to 70 percent in urban men and 40 percent in urban women, newspapers now easily reached the majority of working people. See Harris, "Print and Politics"; Wilson, *Sense of the People*; Porter, *The Creation of the Modern World*, pp. 194–95; and Julian Hoppit, *A Land of Liberty? England 1689–1727* (Oxford, 2000), p. 181. See also Jeremy Black, *The English Press in the Eighteenth Century* (Beckenham, 1987); and Bob Harris, *Politics and the Nation: Britain in the Mid-Eighteenth Century* (New York, 2002).

41. *Grub Street Journal*, 2 July 1730. On the ambivalently critical position of this paper, see Black, *The English Press*, p. 149. On the "bed-tester's plot," see Paul Kleber Monod, *Jacobitism and the English People, 1688–1788* (Cambridge, 1993), p. 58.

42. *Grub Street Journal,* 30 July 1730.

43. *Fog's Weekly Journal,* 22 August 1730. For the Jacobitical leanings of *Fog's,* see Black, *The English Press,* p. 17.

44. *Daily Post,* 10 September 1730. See, again, for sense of this paper, Black, *The English Press,* p. 62.

45. Markham may have been the artist commissioned by the wealthy connoisseur Duke of Montagu: the Cherokee apparently sat for him three times: "Yesterday the Indian Kings sate a third time for their Pictures, at their Lodgings in Covent Garden," *Daily Courant,* 11 August 1730. Repeated in the *Daily Journal,* 7 August 1730; and *Fog's Weekly Journal,* 15 August 1730.

46. See DNB, which notes that his plagiarism of some flower prints in 1733 helped usher in some copyright protection laws for engravers.

47. See Bradford F. Swan, "Prints of American Indians, 1670–1775," in *Boston Prints and Printmakers, 1670–1775* (Boston, 1973), p. 262.

48. On painting genres, see Shearer West entry in OCRA, p. 466.

49. The Basire print has merited only one discussion by an art historian. Stephanie Pratt similarly finds that the subjects "connot[e] acquiescence in, if not submission to, Britain's colonial endeavors." But she also argues that the tattooing, hairstyles, and weaponry add a note of rupture and tension; they are "disturbing" and "awkward," and thus mar any final reading. While a valid reading, Pratt's neglect of the unusual heart symbol, together with a rather narrow appreciation of the meaning of savagery in the mid-eighteenth century, may grant too much leeway to the image. Stephanie Pratt, *American Indians in British Art, 1700–1840* (Norman, 2005), pp. 40–41. Also see Stephanie Pratt, "Reynolds' 'King of the Cherokees' and Other Mistaken Identities in the Portraiture of Native American Delegations, 1710–1762," *Oxford Art Journal* 21 (1998), p. 138.

50. PRO CO 5/400, 20 August 1730, folios 385–86.

51. Board of Trade to Newcastle: "they seem to expect it from us." PRO CO 5/400, 20 August 1730, folio 385.

52. James Adair, *The History of the American Indians* (London, 1775), p. 50.

53. For discussions about Cuming's power over the Cherokee, see *Daily Journal,* 30 September 1730.

54. Answer of the Indian Chiefs of the Cherokee Nation . . . , undated, PRO CO 5/4 (46ii), folio 215.

55. Articles of Friendship and Commerce proposed . . . to the Deputies of the Cherokee Nation, 7 September 1730, PRO CO 5/400. See the account attributed to Attakullakulla some twenty-six years later that insisted that no surrender of lands had occurred: "I am certain There was no such matter ever mentioned either by the Warriour in our Country or any of our people nor was it ever thought of, and I am equally certain that there was no Proposal of that kind made while we were in England either by the Great King George or any of his beloved men, nor had we power to agree to any Such Proposal, nor did I ever hear that question asked till now, I understand so much that if our Country had been given away then we could not have given it to you. I

remember the Talk we had in England perfectly well, that we would be one with the white people in War, That is if they assisted us in our wars against our Ennemies We would assist them against their Ennemies, but for our Lands they never would have been given." SCHGM, pp. 67–68.

56. Board of Trade to Cuming, 30 September 1730, PRO CO 5/361, folio 169. Cuming's plea is found in Cuming to Board of Trade, 30 September 1730, PRO CO 5/361, folio 168. The *Daily Journal* caught wind of the kerfuffle and reported Ouka's wish too: 3 October 1730. Cuming was furious at the Office's comeback, storming in his memoirs later that "Sir Alexander Cuming has laboured to be of real service to the Public [by] civilizing the American savage [and] adding 10 millions of subjects to the crown of Great Britain." For these labors, "Sir Alexander Cuming was refused every request and recognition and has become destitute of common necessities." Cuming, Memorial Book, pp. 33–39.

57. For the aftermath, see Samuel Carter, *Cherokee Sunset: A Nation Betrayed* (New York, 1976), p. 7; and John Oliphant, *Peace and War on the Anglo-Cherokee Frontier, 1756–63* (Baton Rouge, 2001), pp. 1–30.

58. Attakullakulla recounted in *The South Carolina Genealogical and Historical Magazine* 10 (1909), p. 65.

59. David H. Corkran, *The Creek Frontier, 1540–1783* (Norman, 1967), p. 83. On Tomochichi's age, see Sweet, "The Real Tomochichi," p. 156.

60. Corkran, *The Creek Frontier*, p. 83.

61. See Vaughan, *Transatlantic Encounters*, p. 152. See also Steven. C. Hahn, *The Invention of the Creek Nation, 1670–1763* (Lincoln, 2004), pp. 149–85; and Joshua Piker, "Colonists and Creeks: Rethinking the Pre-Revolutionary Southern Backcountry," *Journal of Southern History* 70/3 (2004), pp. 503–40.

62. James Oglethorpe, *A New and Accurate Account of the Provinces of South Carolina and Georgia* (London, 1733), pp. 27–28.

63. Oglethorpe, *New and Accurate Account*, p. 75. See also Keith Thomas, unpublished paper on James Edward Oglethorpe, 1696–1785, given in the Chapel of Corpus Christi College, Oxford, 5 October 1996, available at http://georgiainfo.galileo.usg.edu/jeo300/lecture.htm, accessed 29 March 2012; Karen O'Brien, "Poetry and Political Thought: Liberty and Benevolence in the Case of the British Empire, c. 1680–1800," in D. Armitage, ed., *British Political Thought in History, Literature and Theory, 1500–1800* (Cambridge, 2006), pp. 177–80; and Oglethorpe's entry in DNB.

64. See T. M. Harris, *Biographical Memoirs of General James Oglethorpe* (Boston, 1841), p. 89.

65. See Sweet, "Bearing Feathers," p. 347. And see *Gentleman's Magazine*, 30 October 1734.

66. See *Gentleman's Magazine*, 30 October 1734.

67. The attribution is made by many library catalogs, based on contemporary sources and like style. See for examples, those at the University of Virginia Library and the National Library of Australia.

68. Anonymous, *Georgia, a Poem. Tomo Chachi, An Ode. A Copy of Verses on Mr Oglethorpe's Second Voyage to Georgia* (London, 1736). Reprinted and

discussed in Jones, *Historical Sketch of Tomo-Chi-Chi,* pp. 59–63. It was printed to be bound with Samuel Wesley's popular *Georgia: A Poem* (1736).

69. Though one of the few scholars to discuss Tomochichi's visit to Britain, Julie Ann Sweet nevertheless reads the Fitzgerald ode as a jingoistic piece: Sweet, "The Real Tomochichi," p. 150.

70. *Edinburgh Caledonian Mercury,* 1 November 1734.

71. *Gentleman's Magazine,* October 1734, p. 571.

72. *Monthly Intelligencer,* August 1734, p. 447; and November 1734, p. 605.

73. Lack of clarity discussed in DNB, for Willem Verelst.

74. The trusteeship dissolved in 1752, after which the painting was given to Lord Shaftesbury. See web-published paper by Donald Panther-Yates, "Indians in the 'Trustees of Georgia' Painting" (2000); http://www.pantherslodge .com/indians.html, accessed 29 March 2012.

75. Julie Sweet points out that a bear was apparently brought with the envoy to give to George II but the inclusion of the animal in both father and son's portrayals is not, I believe, accidental. Sweet, "Bearing Feathers," p. 350.

76. See ibid., pp. 349–50.

77. *Manuscripts of the Earl of Egmont: Diary of the First Earl of Egmont (Viscount Percival) Volume II 1734–1738,* Historical Manuscripts Commission (London, 1923), pp. 114, 122.

78. See Robert G. McPherson, ed., *The Journal of the Earl of Egmont: 1732–1738* (Athens, Ga., 1962), p. 64.

79. *Edinburgh Caledonian Mercury,* 18 August 1734; and *London Magazine,* September 1734, p. 494.

80. *London Magazine,* September 1734, p. 494.

81. *Daily Journal,* 6 August 1734.

82. See the numerous theater notices made in W. V. Lennep, ed., *The London Stage, 1660–1800* (Carbondale, 1965–1979), vol. 3, pp. 409–10, 418–24.

83. See, for examples, *Daily Courant,* 7 and 19 October 1734.

84. *Diary of the First Earl of Egmont,* vol. 2, p. 122.

85. *Grub Street Journal,* 12 September 1734.

86. Sweet, "Bearing Feathers," pp. 347–48.

87. Robert G. McPherson, ed., *The Journal of the Earl of Egmont: 1732–1738* (Athens, Ga., 1962), p. 67.

88. See "America and West Indies: February 1735," *Calendar of State Papers Colonial, America and West Indies, Volume 41: 1734–1735* (1953), pp. 476, 477, 486.

89. *Gentleman's Magazine,* August 1734, p. 449.

90. *Daily Journal,* 16 July 1734.

91. *Diary of the First Earl of Egmont,* vol. 2, p. 117.

92. Ibid., p. 118.

93. *London Magazine,* August 1734.

94. See McPherson, *The Journal of the Earl of Egmont,* p. 61.

95. *London Magazine,* p. 447. See also *Diary of the First Earl of Egmont,* vol. 2, pp. 119–20.

96. See Sweet, "The Real Tomochichi," p. 165.

97. See ibid., p. 166.

98. For Creek relations with colonists in this period see the provocative Piker, "Colonists and Creeks," pp. 503–40.

99. Jones, *Historical Sketch of Tomo-Chi-Chi*, pp. 107–8.

CHAPTER 4

1. *Old England; Or, The Constitutional Journal*, 18 May 1745. See also worries by an anonymous pamphleteer in 1740 about how the "higher the [military] Debts of the nation are, the more must the power of the Minster increase," and by the oppositional MP Phillips Gybbon in 1741, who was concerned that his government was now ironically sending "men to fight for that liberty, of which we have deprived them." Both cited in Stephen Conway, *War, State, and Society in Mid-Eighteenth-Century Britain and Ireland* (Oxford, 2006), pp. 144–46, 154, 160, 228. See also Bob Harris, "'American Idols': Empire, War and the Middling Ranks in Mid-Eighteenth-Century Britain," *Past and Present* 150 (1996).

2. See John Brewer, *The Sinews of Power: War, Money, and the English State 1688–1783* (Cambridge, Mass., 1988), p. 30.

3. See Geoffrey Plank, *Rebellion and Savagery: The Jacobite Rising of 1745 and the British Empire* (Philadelphia, 2006), pp. 4–5. See also Frank McLynn, *The Jacobites* (London, 1985), ch. 7.

4. Brewer, *The Sinews of Power*, p. 30.

5. See for general comments, Daniel K. Richter, *Facing East from Indian Country: A Native History of Early America* (Cambridge, Mass., 2001), pp. 174–79; and John Oliphant, *Peace and War on the Anglo-Cherokee Frontier, 1756–63* (Baton Rouge, 2001), pp. 1–30.

6. See D. H. Corkran, *The Cherokee Frontier: Conflict and Survival, 1740–62* (Norman, 1962), pp. 142–78; Tom Hatley, *The Dividing Paths: Cherokees and South Carolinians through the Revolutionary Era* (New York, 1995), pp. 104–40; and Tyler Boulware, "The Effect of the Seven Years' War on the Cherokee Nation," *Early American Studies: An Interdisciplinary Journal* 5 (2007), pp. 395–426.

7. See John Oliphant, "The Cherokee Embassy to London, 1762," *The Journal of Imperial and Commonwealth History* 27 (1999), pp. 2–3. Oliphant's is the only history dedicated to this visit. See also Alden Vaughan, *Transatlantic Encounters: American Indians in Britain, 1500–1776* (Cambridge, 2006), pp. 165–75; and A. F. Rogers and B. R. Duncan, eds., *Culture, Crisis and Conflict: Cherokee British Relations 1756–1765* (Cherokee, 2009).

8. Henry Timberlake, *The Memoirs of Lieut. Henry Timberlake (who accompanied the three Cherokee Indians to England in the Year 1762)* (London, 1765).

9. In the mid-1750s Ostenaco had led numerous Cherokee forces in aid of Virginian skirmishes with other native peoples, including an important and successful battle against a Shawnee faction after which Virginia Colo-

nel George Washington noted that the Cherokee "are more serviceable than twice their number of white men. Their cunning and craft cannot be equaled. Indians are the only match for Indians." See D. M. Wood, "'I Have Now Made a Path to Virginia': Outacite Ostenaco and the Cherokee-Virginia Alliance in the French and Indian War," *West Virginia History: A Journal of Regional Studies*, new ser., 2 (fall 2008), pp. 31–60. Thomas Jefferson also noted in 1812 to John Adams that "I knew much [of Ostenaco], the warrior and orator of the Cherokees. He was always the guest of my father, on his journeys to and from Williamsburg": online at *From Revolution to Reconstruction: A Hypertext on American History from the Colonial Period until Modern Times*, Department of Humanities Computing and Department of American Studies University of Groningen, The Netherlands, http://www.let.rug.nl/usa/index.htm, accessed 3 March 2010.

10. Timberlake, *Memoirs*, p. 30.

11. See Timberlake's musings on this in ibid., pp. 72–73.

12. Ibid., p. 31.

13. Oliphant, "The Cherokee Embassy," p. 7.

14. Timberlake, *Memoirs*, pp. 97–111; quote on p. 111.

15. Ibid., p. 112.

16. Governor Fauquier to Board of Trade, 1 May 1762, PRO, CO 5/1330, folios 123–25.

17. See Duane King, "Mysteries of the Emissaries of Peace: The Story behind the *Memoirs* of Lt. Henry Timberlake," in Rogers and Duncan, eds., *Culture, Crisis and Conflict*, p. 140.

18. See Henry Howard, *A New Humourous Song, on The Cherokee Chiefs* (London, 1762); and Rogers and Duncan, eds., *Culture, Crisis and Conflict*, p. 1.

19. Letter from Jefferson to Adams, 1812, online at *From Revolution to Reconstruction*, accessed 3 March 2010.

20. Timberlake, *Memoirs*, p. 115.

21. See Oliphant, "The Cherokee Embassy," pp. 9–10. See also A. F. C. Wallace, *Jefferson and the Indians: The Tragic Fate of the First Americans* (Cambridge, Mass., 1999), pp. 24–25.

22. Timberlake, *Memoirs*, p. 116.

23. Egremont to Fauquier, 10 July 1762, PRO, CO 5/1345, folios 9–10.

24. *St. James's Chronicle*, 19 June 1762.

25. *The Royal Magazine* (July 1762), p. 16.

26. *London Chronicle*, 24 July 1762; *St. James's Chronicle*, 5 August 1762; Howard, *A New Humourous Song*.

27. See *The Public Register*, 20 July 1762; and citations in Carolyn T. Foreman, *Indians Abroad 1493–1938* (Norman, 1943), pp. 68–71.

28. Timberlake, *Memoirs*, p. 126.

29. Ibid., p. 118.

30. See F. F. Moore, *The Life of Oliver Goldsmith* (London, 1910), p. 239; John Forster, *The Life and Times of Oliver Goldsmith* (London, 1871), vol. 1, pp. 288–89; and Oliver Goldsmith, *Animated Nature* (London, 1774), vol. 1, p. 420.

31. *St. James's Chronicle*, 31 July 1762.

32. Ibid.; *The London Chronicle*, 27 July 1762; *The British Magazine*, 6 July 1762, cited in Foreman, *Indians Abroad*, p. 70; and Timberlake, *Memoirs*, p. 118.

33. *St. James's Chronicle*, 31 July 1762.

34. Advertisement in *London Evening Post*, 6 July 1762.

35. Advertisement in *Gazette*, 26 July 1762.

36. Advertisement in *Public Advertiser*, 10 July 1762.

37. Ibid., 6 August 1762.

38. *London Chronicle*, 24 August 1762.

39. Ibid., 31 August 1762.

40. Howard, *A New Humourous Song*. Note that the reference to "Canada Indians" is of course incorrect, but that the Four Iroquois Kings of 1710 were also sometimes called "Canada Indians." Also note that another broadside in the same pornographic, if less accusatory, style as the *Humourous Song* was *The Other Thing*, by George Rolls (London, 1762). *The Other Thing* was apparently a bunny, made to rhyme—a bit clumsily—with "cunny," given by Ostenaco to the Queen.

41. *St. James's Chronicle*, 5 August 1762. A further critique is evident in the *Royal Magazine* (1762), p. 83, where a correspondent, Z, compares the "jealousies . . . and undermining[s]" evident in Cherokee politics with those in British politics. See also the generally satiric print by Hogarth published in September 1762 called "The Times"—its picture of everyday chaos in London streets includes a poster of a Native American with the enticing words "Alive from America" written underneath. King, "Mysteries of the Emissaries of Peace," p. 157.

42. *Public Register*, 20 July 1762.

43. See John Brewer, *Party Ideology and Popular Politics at the Accession of George III* (Cambridge, 1976), p. 11.

44. See Brewer, *Party Ideology*, ch. 1; and Kathleen Wilson, *The Sense of the People: Politics, Culture, and Imperialism in England, 1715–1785* (Cambridge, 1995), ch. 4.

45. *St. James's Chronicle*, 21 August 1762.

46. *The Royal Magazine* 7 (August 1762).

47. Anonymous, *Without/Within* (London, July 1762).

48. Timberlake, *Memoirs*, p. 117.

49. *Gentleman's Magazine* 31 (1762), pp. 378–79.

50. *Annual Register for 1762* (London, 1763), p. 92. And see *Gazette or London Daily Advertiser*, 9 July 1762; Vaughan, *Transatlantic Encounters*, p. 170; and Oliphant, "The Cherokee Embassy," p. 12.

51. Timberlake, *Memoirs*, pp. 125–26.

52. *Public Register*, 20 July 1762.

53. *Annual Register*, p. 93.

54. Timberlake, *Memoirs*, pp. 119–21.

55. Cacanthropos is probably a version of an amalgam of *xaxos* (evil) and *anthropos* (man), though whether devised by Timberlake or another is unclear.

Duane King hazards that the pseudonym—fully "N. Cacanthropos"—referred to the loyalist acquaintance of Egremont, Nathan Carington: King, "Mysteries of the Emissaries of Peace," p. 156.

56. Timberlake, *Memoirs*, p.123. Also announced in *Public Advertiser*, 6 August 1762.

57. *Lloyd's Evening Post*, 28 July 1762.

58. Oliphant, "The Cherokee Embassy," p. 20.

59. *The Royal Strangers Ramble* (London, 1710).

60. *Jackson's Oxford Journal*, 10 July 1762.

61. *St. James's Chronicle*, 7 August 1762.

62. Troy Bickham, *Savages within the Empire: Representations of American Indians in Eighteenth-Century Britain* (Oxford, 2005), pp. 5, 7, 33, 67.

63. This point is developed further in chapter 5 in this volume, but see here Linda Colley, *Britons: Forging the Nation, 1707–1837* (New York, [1992] 1994), ch. 3.

64. Bickham, *Savages within the Empire*, pp. 5, 27, 30.

65. Ibid., p. 32.

66. Both these rough prints are reproduced in Stephanie Pratt, "Reynolds' 'King of the Cherokees' and Other Mistaken Identities in the Portraiture of Native American Delegations, 1710–1762," *Oxford Art Journal* 21 (1998), pp. 149–50.

67. Anonymous, *The Three Cherokees, Came Over from the Head of the River Savannah to London, 1762* (London, 1762).

68. Pratt, "Mistaken Identities," p. 149.

69. See DNB.

70. *British Magazine*, 6 July 1762, cited in Foreman, *Indians Abroad*, p. 70.

71. Pratt, "Mistaken Identities," p. 142.

72. See Pratt's concurrence in ibid., pp. 143–44.

73. Ibid., p. 145.

74. See Foreman, *Indians Abroad*, pp. 70–71; and DNB.

75. For McArdell, see DNB. Joshua Reynolds was said to be forever in McArdell's debt for making such sympathetic and popular mezzotints of his work. McArdell died in 1765.

76. It was acquired by the Marquis of Crewe sometime before 1830. How it came to be sold "by a New York dealer" in the 1940s to the Gilcrease Museum in Tulsa, Oklahoma, is unknown. See David Mannings, *Sir Joshua Reynolds: Complete Catalogue of His Paintings* (New Haven, 2000), vol. 1, p. 408, from files at the Gilcrease Museum, confirmed by recent correspondence. Pratt has given some explanation of Reynolds's odd title: she claims that Reynolds's notorious deafness may have mutated the Cherokee word for chief, "Skiagusta," to Scyacust and shortened the name Ostenaco (also commonly called Osteneca in Britain) to Ukah. Ukah, however, may also be a derivative of Ouka Ulah from 1730. See Pratt, "Mistaken Identities," pp. 145–47; and now also Pratt's *American Indians in British Art, 1700–1840* (Norman, 2005), pp. 57–58.

77. Joshua Reynolds, *Discourses on Art*, ed. R.R. Wark (New Haven, 1997), pp. 171, 235, 59. For helpful explications, see John Barrell, *The Political Theory of Painting from Reynolds to Hazlitt* (New Haven, 1986), ch. 1; and Susan Rather, "Stuart and Reynolds," *Eighteenth-Century Studies* 27 (1993).

78. On the irony that Reynolds himself worked mainly in portraiture instead of his theoretically favored history painting, see Richard Wendorf, *The Elements of Life: Biography and Portrait Painting in Stuart and Georgian England* (Oxford, 1990), p. 229. See also E.A. Bohls, "Disinterestedness and Denial of the Particular," in P. Mattick, ed., *Eighteenth-Century Aesthetics and the Reconstruction of Art* (Cambridge, 1993), pp. 16–51; and Reynolds, *Discourses*, pp. 70, 59, and see p. 200.

79. Interestingly, Reynolds made this argument in the 1770s with reference to a Cherokee: whoever would make a fuss about, or wish to suppress, his "yellow and red oker," Reynolds declared, is the barbarian. Such innocent "fashions" in fact promote a tolerance for difference—mostly national—which in turn, Reynolds implies, strengthens love of "universal rectitude and harmony." See Reynolds, *Discourses*, pp. 200, 137.

80. See Reynolds's third discourse in the *Discourses*, pp. 39–54; and Barrell, *Political Theory*, pp. 99–112.

81. Pratt hazards that it is a "pipe-tomahawk" as made in Europe (!) at the time or a "baton": "Mistaken Identities," pp. 145–46.

82. See Mannings, *Complete Catalogue*, vol. 1, p. 3.

83. *The Death of General Wolfe* (1771) is perhaps West's most famous painting, and also perhaps the most famous British image of a Native American. Leslie Reinhardt has recently tried to argue that West did in fact break new ground in the portrayal of Native Americans by individualizing them through the insertion of tribal paraphernalia like skins, tomahawks, and wampums. Ironically, Reinhardt even argued that West included such artifacts, although they were hardly representative of the experience of most Native Americans by the eighteenth century, because he was trying to recapture the "truth" of precolonial native culture. The idea that these artifacts were themselves clichés, possibly signifying the very opposite of individuality, never occurs in her article. Leslie Reinhardt, "British and Indian Identities in a Picture by Benjamin West," *Eighteenth-Century Studies* 31 (1998), pp. 283–305.

84. See *Public Advertiser*, 20 August 1762; *Royal Magazine* 7 (August 1762). For the cries of "detestation," see citation in Foreman, *Indians Abroad*, p. 78.

85. Egremont to Boone, 7 August 1762, PRO, CO 5/214, folios 228–29. Timberlake returned to Virginia separately in March 1763 with an English bride, Elinor Binel.

86. Boone to Egremont, 11 November 1762, PRO, CO 5/390, folios 1–5.

87. The post-visit lives of Stalking Turkey and Pouting Pidgeon are even harder to trace. Duane King attests that the latter, Woyi, died fighting with the revolutionaries. King, "Mysteries of the Emissaries of Peace," p. 159.

88. Cited in Pat Alderman, *Dragging Canoe: Cherokee-Chickamauga War Chief* (Johnson City, 1978), p. 38. See for this period generally: William Anderson, "The Cherokee World before and after Timberlake," in Rogers and Duncan, eds., *Culture, Crisis and Conflict*, pp. 4–14.

89. See R. E. Evans, "Notable Persons in Cherokee History: Ostenaco," *Journal of Cherokee Studies*, vol. 1, no. 1 (1976). This was the Treaty of Dewitt's Corner of 1777 into which most Cherokee were virtually forced.

CHAPTER 5

1. Henry Timberlake, *The Memoirs of Lieut. Henry Timberlake* (London, 1965), p. 152.

2. Ibid., pp. 152–53.

3. Ibid., p. 157.

4. Ibid., pp. 155–58.

5. Ibid., pp. 156–58.

6. See Duane H. King, "Mysteries of the Emissaries of Peace: The Story behind the *Memoirs* of Lt. Henry Timberlake," in A. F. Rogers and B. R. Duncan, eds., *Culture, Crisis and Conflict: Cherokee British Relations 1756-1765* (Cherokee, 2009), p. 142.

7. The Dutch side of the story is recounted in George R. Hammell, "Mohawks Abroad: The 1764 Amsterdam Etching of Sychnecta," in C. C. Feest, ed., *Indians and Europe: An Interdisciplinary Collection of Essays* (Aachen, 1987), pp. 175–94.

8. William Cobbett, ed., *The Parliamentary History of England, from the Earliest Period to the Year 1803* (London, 1806–20), vol. 16, pp. 50–52.

9. Cobbett, *Parliamentary History*, vol. 16, p. 52.

10. The term "humanitarianism" was not current until the early nineteenth century, but its concerns with "human" behavior as a requirement of one individual to another emerged in the latter half of the eighteenth century. For the emphasis on the individual at the centre of humanitarian discourses, see Thomas W. Laqueur, "Bodies, Details, and the Humanitarian Narrative," in Lynn Hunt, ed., *The New Cultural History* (Berkeley, 1989), p. 177.

11. Alden T. Vaughan, *Transatlantic Encounters: American Indians in Britain, 1500-1776* (Cambridge, 2006), pp. 179–232.

12. The three other examples that fit into this group include a coalition of Mohegans and Wappingers who came to protest land encroachments in 1766; a Mohawk brought over for unscrupulous display but quickly sent home by an embarrassed British government in 1774; and four Miskitos who came to offer an alliance against colonial rebels in 1774–75.

13. Occom was billed even before arrival as an "Indian unlike any . . . known before," *Ipswich Journal*, 9 March 1765. He was well versed in the classics and knew English as his first language. A prodigy of Eleazer Wheelock, he stayed with the evangelical George Whitefield when in London. He helped to solicit £12,000 during his two-year stay, which was apparently the largest

amount collected by any American institution in the colonial era. In the end he split from Wheelock when the latter gave most of those hard-earned funds to colonial students rather than Native American students at Dartmouth. See Margaret C. Szasz, "Samson Occom: Mohegan as Spiritual Intermediary," in M. C. Szasz, ed., *Between Indian and White Worlds* (Oklahoma, 1994), pp. 61–80; and L. B. Richardson, *An Indian Preacher in England* (Hanover, N.H., 1933).

For Brant, see *Annual Register* 27 (December, 1784). See also Carolyn T. Foreman, *Indians Abroad, 1493–1938* (Norman, 1943), p. 98, R. P. Bond, *Queen Anne's American Kings* (Oxford, 1952), p. 107; and Vaughan, *Transatlantic Encounters,* pp. 222–32. Brant took the name of his stepfather, Brant Canagaradunka, who was probably the son of Brant Saquainquaragton.

14. See also Troy Bickham's slightly narrower point in his *Savages within the Empire: Representations of American Indians in Eighteenth-Century Britain* (Oxford, 2005), p. 95: "the British public's rejection of the American Indian as candidate for the role of noble savage was more a dismissal of the idea of Indians fitting the image than of the concept itself."

15. See Linda Colley, *Britons: Forging the Nation, 1707–1837* (London, [1992] 1994), pp. 101–3; and Stephen Conway, *War, State, and Society in Mid-Eighteenth-Century Britain and Ireland* (Oxford, 2006), p. 227. For a concise tally of the victory, see Paul Langford, *A Polite and Commercial People: England 1727–1783* (Oxford, 1989), p. 350.

16. [William Burke], *An Examination of the Commercial Principles of the Late Negotiation between Great Britain and France* (London, 1762), p. 61.

17. Smollett in *The Briton,* 3 July 1762, pp. 33–34. See also Bob Harris, "'American Idols': Empire, War and the Middling Ranks in Mid-Eighteenth-Century Britain," *Past and Present* 150 (1996), p. 128; and Peter Miller, *Defining the Common Good: Empire, Religion, and Philosophy in Eighteenth-Century Britain* (Cambridge, 1994), p. 179.

18. Both examples cited in Colley, *Britons,* p. 102.

19. See Colley, *Britons,* p. 102; and Miller, *Defining the Common Good,* p. 157. See also Wilfrid Prest, *Albion Ascendant: English History, 1660–1815* (Oxford, 1998), p. 211.

20. William Pitt, cited in Eliga Gould, *The Persistence of Empire: British Political Culture in the Age of the American Revolution* (Chapel Hill, 2000), p. 106.

21. For a neat summary of the many other acts also introduced, see Langford, *A Polite and Commercial People,* p. 359.

22. Prest, *Albion Ascendant,* p. 213.

23. H. T. Dickinson, introduction to his *Britain and the American Revolution* (London, 1998), p. 7.

24. For an excellent overview of *later* popular controversies over American independence, see James E. Bradley, "The British Public and the American Revolution: Ideology, Interest, and Opinion," in Dickinson, *Britain and the American Revolution,* pp. 124–54.

25. Edmund Burke, speech on Declaratory Resolution, 3 February 1766, in Paul Langford, ed., *The Writings and Speeches of Edmund Burke* (Oxford, 1981), vol. 2, p. 46. Frances Brooke, *The History of Emily Montague* (London, 1769), cited and discussed in Carolyn S. Knapp, "The British Response to American Independence" (Ph.D. dissertation, University of California, Berkeley, 1998), pp. 52–59.

26. See Knapp, "The British Response," chs. 1–2.

27. Edmund Burke in 1774 cited in Kathleen Wilson, *The Sense of the People* (Cambridge, 1995), p. 252.

28. *The London Evening Post*, 10 January 1775. Anonymous, *The history of the old fring'd petticoat; a fragment: translated from the original MS. Greek of Democritus. With an epistle and dedication to Lord N——* (London, 1775), cited in Knapp, "The British Response," p. 134. Considering the vastness of the historiography on opinion about the American Revolution, amazingly little work has been done on its rhetorical forms.

29. William Robertson, *A History of the Discovery and Settlement of America* (London, 1777).

30. Robertson to [Sir Robert Murray Keith?], 8 March 1784, BL Add. MS 35350, cited in David Armitage, "The New World and British Historical Thought: From Richard Hakluyt to William Robertson," in K. O. Kupperman, ed., *America in European Consciousness 1493–1750* (Chapel Hill, 1995), pp. 69–70.

31. William Dampier to Admiralty, PRO Adm 2/1692, cited in Glyndwr Williams, *The Great South Sea: English Voyages and Encounters, 1570–1750* (New Haven, 1997), p. 119.

32. Daniel Defoe, *Essay on the South Sea Trade* (London, [1711] 1712), p. 37.

33. Daniel Defoe, *A New Voyage Round the World by a Course Never Sailed Before* (London, [1724] 1725), p. 178.

34. For brief general accounts, see Geoffrey Holmes, *The Making of a Great Power: Late Stuart and Early Georgian Britain 1660–1722* (Harlow, 1993), pp. 274–76; and Julian Hoppit, *A Land of Liberty? England 1689–1727* (Oxford, 2000), pp. 334–38.

35. John Campbell, ed., *Navigantium atque Itinerantium Bibliotecha: or, a Compleat Collection of Voyages and Travels* (London, 1744–48), vol. 1, cited in G. Williams, "The Pacific: Exploration and Exploitation," in OHBE, vol. 2, p. 554. Campbell's was a much revised edition of John Harris's work of the same name, published c. 1705: see Harris's entry in DNB.

36. This is the implicit thesis of the only major recent historian to chronicle early British activities in the Pacific, Glyndwr Williams in *Great South Sea*. See also Williams, "The Pacific," p. 555.

37. Admiralty instructions cited in Williams, *Great South Sea*, p. 271.

38. John Byron cited in ibid., p. 272.

39. Admiralty instructions cited in Helen Wallis, ed., *Carteret's Voyage Round the World 1766–1769* (Cambridge, 1965), vol. 2, p. 302.

40. Louis-Antoine de Bougainville, *Voyage autour du monde*, ed. M. Bideaux et S. Faessel (Paris, 2001), p. 219.

41. P. Marshall and G. Williams, *The Great Map of Mankind: British Perceptions of the World in the Age of Enlightenment* (London, 1982), p. 258. See also Bernard Smith, who calls it rather a "sensation" in his *European Vision and South Pacific* (Melbourne, [1968] 1989), p. 42.

42. John Callender, *Terra Australis Cognita* (London, 1766–68), 3 vols.

43. Both of Dalrymple's texts were published in London. On Dalrymple's influence, see Eric McCormick, *Omai: Pacific Envoy* (Auckland, 1977), p. 9.

44. "We have now got the Indian name of the Island, *Otahite*, so therefore for the future I shall call it": Joseph Banks, 10 May 1769, The Endeavour Journal of Joseph Banks, 25 August 1768–12 July 1771, vol. 1, p. 247, Mitchell Library, State Library of New South Wales. For a good general account on this first voyage, see Nicholas Thomas, *Cook: The Extraordinary Voyages of Captain James Cook* (New York, 2003), pp. 3–139.

45. Coke cited in Neil Rennie, *Far-Fetched Facts: The Literature of Travel and the Idea of the South Seas* (Oxford, 1995), p. 94. *General Evening Post*, 27 July 1771. For a good discussion of Pacific popularity in the 1770s, see Gillian Russell, "An Entertainment of Oddities: Fashionable Society and the Pacific in the 1770s," in K. Wilson, ed., *The New Imperial History* (Cambridge, 2004), pp. 48–70.

46. Thomas, *Cook*, pp. 140–41.

47. The piece was published in London by Thomas Becket despite a naval ban on unauthorized accounts. See discussion in McCormick, *Omai*, pp. 29–30.

48. *Monthly Review* 46 (1772), p. 212.

49. Alan Frost has discovered that it was the most popular title in the Bristol Library from 1773 to 1784, borrowed more than 200 times: "Captain James Cook and the Early Romantic Imagination," in W. Veit, ed., *Captain James Cook: Image and Impact* (Melbourne, 1972), vol. 1, p. 94. The work went into a second edition within six months; within 12 months there were French, Dutch, and German editions as well as separate English editions from Dublin and New York. See McCormick, *Omai*, p. 86.

50. Anonymous, *An Epistle from Mr. Banks, Voyager, Monster-hunter, and Amoroso, to Oberea, Queen of Otaheite* (London, c. December 1773). *An Epistle from Oberea, Queen of Otaheite to Joseph Banks, translated by T. Q. Z. Esq., Professor of the Otaheite Language in Dublin* (London, [1773] 3rd ed. 1774). Anonymous, *An Heroic Epistle from the Injured Harriot, Mistress to Mr Banks, to Oberea, Queen of Otaheite* (London, c. January 1774). For a succinct discussion of these texts, see McCormick, *Omai*, pp. 88–91.

51. *Public Advertiser*, 3 July 1773.

52. John Wesley, 17 December 1773, in N. Curnock, ed., *The Journal of the Rev. John Wesley* (London, 1909–16), vol. 6, p. 7.

53. Anonymous, *Otaheite: A Poem* (London, 1774).

54. [John Courtney], *Epistle (Moral and Philosophical) from an Officer at Otaheite* (London, 1774).

55. Cited and discussed in Rennie, *Far-Fetched Facts*, p. 102.

56. See William Guthrie, *A New Geographical, Historical, and Commercial Grammar* (London, 1770).

57. On the popular Leverian Museum's ethnographic collection—with fractionally more on Oceania than on Americana—see Bickham, *Savages within the Empire*, p. 40.

58. Mostly "savage" and "Indian" were used interchangeably among writers on Oceanian peoples. James Cook was notable for never using the word "savage," instead favoring "Indian": search Cook's complete journals at http://southseas.nla.gov.au/index_voyaging.html. He stands out among voyagers especially in this regard.

59. See R. L. Meek, *Social Science and the Ignoble Savage* (Cambridge, 1976), pp. 176–213. Bickham also makes a case for the popular profile of conjectural history: *Savages within the Empire*, pp. 172–75.

60. Dugald Stewart, *Account of the Life and Writings of Adam Smith* (first delivered as lecture in 1790), in W. Hamilton, ed., *The Collected Works of Dugald Stewart* (Edinburgh, 1854–60), vol. 10, pp. 33–34. On the question of why conjectural history flourished as it did where it did, see Mary Poovey's "intellectual confluence" argument in *A History of the Modern Fact: Problems of Knowledge in the Sciences of Wealth and Society* (Chicago, 1998), pp. 222–23. For Knud Haakonssen's more Scots-located rationale, see his introduction to David Hume, *Political Essays* (Cambridge, 1994), p. xvi.

61. Thomas Reid, *An Inquiry into the Human Mind* (1764), cited and discussed in Poovey, *History of the Modern Fact*, pp. 219–20.

62. H. M. Höpfl, "From Savage to Scotsman: Conjectural History in the Scottish Enlightenment," *Journal of British Studies* 17/2 (1978), p. 26. Margaret Hodgen shared Höpfl's skepticism: see her *Early Anthropology in the Sixteenth and Seventeenth Centuries* (Philadelphia, 1964), pp. 505, 510.

63. Various students' notes from the 1762–63 Glasgow lectures on Moral Philosophy, cited in Meek, *Social Science*, pp. 117–19. Smith appears to be the first British thinker to break the natural stages of society into four.

64. Adam Ferguson, *An Essay on the History of Civil Society*, 5th ed. (London, 1782), p. 133.

65. For Smith's concessions to potential problems in commercial society, see J. G. A. Pocock, *The Machiavellian Moment: Florentine Political Thought and the Atlantic Republican Tradition* (Princeton, 1975), p. 502; and Pocock, *Virtue, Commerce, and History* (Cambridge, 1985), pp. 79, 100, 121. For Smith's ultimate rejection of civic humanistic values and his views on the compensations of modern "justice," see Roy Porter, *The Creation of the Modern World: The Untold Story of the British Enlightenment* (New York, 2000), pp. 393–94.

66. Pocock argues that Ferguson was the "most Machiavellian" of the Scots theorists—by which he means the most republican-minded and thus the least well disposed toward modern commerce—but others have said that Ferguson plumped for progressive "civilization" in the final instance. Pocock, *The Machiavellian Moment*, p. 499, but see also Meek, *Social Science*, p. 155.

67. Ferguson, *Civil Society*, pp. 386, 312.

68. Ibid., p. 375.

69. "Rudest form" comes from William Robertson, cited in Meek, *Social Science*, p. 129.

70. *The Scots Magazine*, August 1777, p. 434. See also Bickham, *Savages within the Empire*, p. 184.

71. Students' notes of John Millar's lectures on government at Glasgow, cited in Meek, *Social Science*, p. 166. According to the DNB the course from which these lectures come started incorporating discussions of the four stages around 1767.

72. James Burnett (Lord Monboddo), *Of the Origin and Progress of Language* (Edinburgh, 1773), vol. 1, p. 231.

73. Henry Home (Lord Kames), *Sketches of the History of Man* (Edinburgh, 1774), cited and discussed in Marshall and Williams, *The Great Map*, p. 275.

74. See mostly Bickham, *Savages within the Empire*; and Stephanie Pratt, *American Indians in British Art, 1700–1840* (Norman, 2005). See also the review of both by Peter Silver in *William and Mary Quarterly* 67 (2010), pp. 145–54.

CHAPTER 6

1. Walpole to Horace Mann, *The Letters of Horace Walpole*, ed. P. Toynbee (Oxford, 1903–5), vol. 9, p. 16.

2. Modern scholarship on Mai has appeared in roughly three waves. The first was prewar and concentrated chiefly on the Rousseauist productions of his trip. See C. B. Tinker, *Nature's Simple Plan: A Phase of Radical Thought in the Mid-Eighteenth Century* (Princeton, 1922); H. N. Fairchild, *The Noble Savage: A Study in Romantic Naturalism* (New York, [1928] 1961); and T. B. Clark, *Omai: First Polynesian Ambassador to England* (Honolulu, 1941). The second wave occurred from the 1970s, and included as its centerpiece the exhaustive documentary biography by Eric McCormick, which remains at the heart of all Mai studies. McCormick's work was an instance of the new Pacific-centered scholarship emanating from Australasia at the time; it strove to highlight Mai's agency in his own story, arguing that "much of his success, it must be acknowledged, was due to qualities peculiar to himself." Eric McCormick, *Omai: Pacific Envoy* (Auckland, 1977), p. 132. Of this era, see also Michael Alexander, *Omai: Noble Savage* (London, 1977). The final wave began at the turn of the twenty-first century, claiming mostly to pursue more mutually constitutive elements of the encounter but continuing usually to follow McCormick's lead on agency. See the collection edited by Michelle Hetherington, *Cook & Omai: The Cult of the South Seas* (Canberra, 2001); and the television program *Portrait of Omai*, produced by Robin Dashwood for the Imagine Series at the BBC, broadcast in the UK on 16 July 2003. See also Neil Rennie, *Far-Fetched Facts: The Literature of Travel and the Idea of the South Seas* (Oxford, 1995), ch. 5; Laura Brown, *Fables of Modernity: Literature*

and Culture in the English Eighteenth Century (Ithaca, 2001), ch. 5; Harriet Guest, *Empire, Barbarism, and Civilization: Captain Cook, William Hodges, and the Return of the Pacific* (Cambridge, 2007), chs. 3 and 6; and T. Fulford, D. Lee and P. J. Kitson, *Literature, Science and Exploration in the Romantic Era* (Cambridge, 2004), ch. 2.

3. For Rousseauism in Britain, see Edward Duffy, *Rousseau in England: The Context for Shelley's Critique of the Enlightenment* (Berkeley, 1979), ch. 1.

4. See Daniel Solander to J. Lind, 19 August 1774 (after communicating with Mai in Tahitian); and E. S. C. Handy, *History and Culture in the Society Islands* (Honolulu, 1930), both cited and discussed in McCormick, *Omai,* pp. 1–3. See also D. L. Oliver, *Ancient Tahitian Society* (Canberra, 1974), vol. 2, pp. 750–53, 765–69; and Paul Turnbull, "Mai, the Other beyond the Exotic Stranger," in Hetherington, *Cook & Omai,* pp. 43–50. And see Sarah S. Banks, memorandums, August–November 1774, Papers of Sir Joseph Banks, NLA MS9, in which the naturalist's sister recounts much gossip about Mai, including his reputation as a priest in spite of his being actually "a more common man."

5. See, for one summary example, R. G. Crocombe, ed., *French Polynesia* (Suva, 1988).

6. James King cited in Turnbull, "Mai," p. 47. See also Sarah Banks, memorandums, where she mentions Mai's desire for guns no less than four times in her diary-of-sorts; and Solander to Lind, 19 August 1774.

7. Solander to Lind, 19 August 1774. James Burney, Journal 1772–1773, NLA MS3244.

8. McCormick, *Omai,* p. 11.

9. See Joseph Banks, *The Endeavour Journal of Joseph Banks 1768–1771,* ed., J. C. Beaglehole (Sydney, 1962), vol. 1, p. 305. See also Glyndwr Williams, "Tupaia: Polynesian Warrior, Navigator, High Priest—and Artist," in F. Nussbaum, ed., *The Global Eighteenth Century* (Baltimore, 2003), pp. 38–51; Vanessa Smith, "Banks, Tupaia, and Mai: Cross-Cultural Exchanges and Friendship in the Pacific," *Parergon* 26 (2009), pp. 136–60; and Nicholas Thomas, *Cook: The Extraordinary Voyages of Captain James Cook* (New York, 2003), pp. 80–81.

10. Thomas, *Cook,* p. 10.

11. Burney, Journal.

12. James Cook, *The Journals of Captain James Cook on his Voyages of Discovery,* ed. J. C. Beaglehole (Cambridge, 1955–67), vol. 2, p. 222. McCormick has dryly noted that "in eighteenth-century terms . . . this only meant that he was swarthy, plain, and of low birth—in which last respect, it may be remarked, he resembled the navigator himself": *Omai,* p. 53.

13. See Turnbull, "Mai," p. 47.

14. Cited in Greg Dening, "O Mai! This is Mai: A Masque of a Sort," in Hetherington, *Cook & Omai,* p. 52.

15. Sarah Banks, memorandums.

16. Frances Burney, 15 July 1774, in *The Early Letters and Journals of Fanny Burney,* ed. L. E. Troide (Montreal, 1990), vol. 2, p. 41.

17. See the philosopher G. C. Lichtenberg and the dramatist George Colman, both cited and discussed in McCormick, *Omai*, pp. 138, 155.

18. It was Daniel Solander who ruled his name as Omai: Solander to Lind, 19 August 1774.

19. Sarah Banks, memorandums.

20. *London Chronicle*, 21 July 1774.

21. Ibid.

22. Ibid. The report describing Mai's arrival as that of a savage exists: *London Chronicle*, 19 July 1774.

23. *General Evening Post*, 21 and 28 July 1774.

24. See John Dunmore, *French Explorers in the Pacific* (Oxford, 1965), vol. 1, p. 88; and W. B. Ober, *Boswell's Clap and Other Essays* (Carbondale, 1979), pp. 5–20.

25. See Peter Mancall, "Native Americans and Europeans in English America, 1500–1700," OHBE, vol. 1, pp. 328–50.

26. Banks in letter to Sandwich, cited in Alexander, *Omai*, p. 76; Sarah Banks, memorandums; *General Evening Post*, 25 August 1774.

27. See *General Evening Post*, 5 November 1774.

28. On the picturesque, see John Brewer, *The Pleasures of the Imagination: English Culture in the Eighteenth Century* (London, 1999), pp. 581, 615–19; and David Marshall, "The Problem of the Picturesque," *Eighteenth-Century Studies* 35 (2002), pp. 413–37.

29. Anonymous, "Letter from Leicester," *General Evening Post*, 24 September 1774.

30. Joseph Cradock, *Literary and Miscellaneous Memoirs* (London, 1828), vol. 1, pp. 27–28.

31. Richard Cumberland to George Cumberland, 10 October 1774, BL MS cited in McCormick, *Omai*, p. 117.

32. *General Evening Post*, 5 November 1774.

33. George Cumberland to Richard Cumberland, 18 October 1774, BL MS cited in McCormick, *Omai*, p. 117.

34. On Rousseauism as republicanism, see foremost J. G. A. Pocock, *Virtue, Commerce, and History* (Cambridge, 1985), p. 111.

35. Jean-Jacques Rousseau, *Emile* (Paris, 1762), trans B. Foxley, ed. P. D. Jimack (London, 1993), pp. 260–61. My appreciation of Rousseau's duality comes chiefly from Jean Starobinski, *Jean-Jacques Rousseau: Transparency and Obstruction* (Chicago, 1988).

36. Burney, *The Early Letters and Journals*, vol. 2, pp. 60–63. On Chesterfield, see P. D. Stanhope, *Lord Chesterfield's Letters* (London, 1774), discussed in Paul Langford, *A Polite and Commercial People: England, 1727–1783* (Oxford, 1989), p. 586.

37. See E. Smith, *The Life of Sir Joseph Banks* (London, 1911), pp. 41–43; and McCormick, *Omai*, p. 180.

38. Turnbull, "Mai," p. 43.

39. *St. James's Chronicle*, 4 August 1774.

40. Anonymous, *An Historic Epistle from Omiah to the Queen of Otaheite* (London, 1775), pp. 3, 11, 42–44.

41. *Gentleman's Magazine* 45 (1775), p. 132.

42. *London Magazine* 46 (1775), p. 497.

43. Gerald Fitzgerald, *The Injured Islanders; or, The Influence of Art upon the Happiness of Nature* (London, 1779), cited in McCormick, *Omai*, p. 303.

44. Anonymous, *Omiah: An Ode* (London, c.1776).

45. [William Preston], *Seventeen Hundred and Seventy Seven; or, A Picture of the Manners and Character of the Age. An Epistle from a Lady of Quality in England to Omiah at Otaheite* (London, 1777), p. 25.

46. See the images reproduced in McCormick, *Omai*, pp. 97, 104.

47. The foremost authority on Hodges is Guest; see her *Empire, Barbarism, and Civilization*.

48. See McCormick, *Omai*, pp. 119–21.

49. Ibid., p. 174.

50. I present a rather more complex reading of this work in Kate Fullagar, "Reynolds' New Masterpiece: From Experiment in Savagery to Icon of the Eighteenth Century," *Journal of Cultural and Social History* 7 (2010). See also my discussion of Reynolds's *Scyacust Ukah* in chapter 4 in this volume. For authoritative analyses of Reynolds's *Omai*, see Guest, *Empire, Barbarism, and Civilization*, ch. 3; David Mannings, *Sir Joshua Reynolds: Complete Catalogue of his Paintings* (New Haven, 2000), vol. 2, p. 357; Nicholas Penny, *Reynolds* (London, 1986), p. 272; and Caroline Turner, "Images of Mai," in Hetherington, ed., *Cook & Omai*, pp. 23–30.

51. Guest, *Empire, Barbarism, and Civilization*, pp. 74–78.

52. James Boswell, *The Life of Johnson*, ed. S. Roberts (London, 1949), vol. 1, pp. 273, 317, 464, 532; vol 2, pp. 33–34.

53. Ibid., vol. 2, p. 9.

54. Anonymous, *Omiah's Farewell* (London 1776). On this squib, see Fairchild, *The Noble Savage*, p. 73.

55. Anonymous, *Transmigration* (London, 1778), cited in Smith, *European Vision and the South Pacific* (Oxford, 1960), p. 47.

56. For D'Éon, see literature cited in McCormick, *Omai*, pp. 140–42. For Ray's murder, see the pretended letters between Ray and her murderer, James Hackman, *Love and Madness* (London, 1780), cited in Rennie, *Far-Fetched Facts*, p. 134.

57. Greg Dening, *Beach Crossings: Voyaging across Times, Cultures and Self* (Melbourne, 2004), p. 40. And see Kathleen Wilson, *The Island Race: Englishness, Empire, and Gender in the Eighteenth Century* (London, 2003), p. 63.

58. See McCormick, *Omai*, p. 117; and the "Expenses on Account of Omai" (1776), in The Papers of Sir Joseph Banks, NLA MS9.

59. Rod Edmond surveys the literature in chapter two of his *Representing the South Pacific: Colonial Discourse from Cook to Gauguin* (Cambridge, 1997). See also Wilson, *The Island Race*, pp. 59–69.

60. Anonymous, *A Letter from Omai, to the Right Honourable the Earl of* ******** [sic] (London, c.1780).

61. Seward, Anna, *Elegy on Captain Cook, to which is added an ode to the sun* (London, 1780), pp. 4, 9, 15–16. The *Elegy* went through four editions within a year: see Smith, *European Vision*, pp. 120–21. In June 1781 the *Gentleman's Magazine* published a poem thanking Seward for being the "comforter of the nation." On Seward generally, see Brewer, *Pleasures of the Imagination*, ch. 15.

62. William Cowper, *The Task, A Poem* (1785) (Boston, 1833), pp. 23–24. On Cowper himself, see Kevis Goodman, "The Loophole in the Retreat: The Culture of News and the Early Life of Romantic Self-Consciousness," *South Atlantic Quarterly* 102 (2003), pp. 25–52.

63. On the pantomime, see Iain McCalman, "Spectacle of Knowledge: *Omai* as Ethnographic Travelogue," in Hetherington, ed., *Cook & Omai*, pp. 9–15; Christa Knellwolf, "Comedy in the *Omai* Pantomime," in Hetherington, ed., *Cook & Omai*, pp. 17–21; Smith, *European Vision*, pp. 114–18; and McCormick, *Omai*, pp. 313–18.

64. See John O'Keeffe, *Omai; Or, A Trip Round the World*, in *The Plays of John O'Keeffe*, ed. F. M. Link (New York, 1981), pp. 4, 23. Note that historians generally name this text a "Cook play" rather than a piece in the "Omai cycle": see, for example, Wilson, *The Island Race*, p. 63.

65. For performance numbers, see Smith, *European Vision*, p. 115. For reviews, see *London Chronicle*, 20 December 1785; and *The Morning Chronicle*, 21 December 1785. On Cook's posthumous *Voyage to the Pacific Ocean*, see Edmond, *Representing the South Pacific*, p. 30. The Admiralty had helped to make it appear: at four and a half guineas, the first edition sold out in three days and soon found translation into all the major European languages.

66. See "Account of Presents Sent Out with Omai" (1776), in The Papers of Sir Joseph Banks, NLA MS9. See also Guest, *Empire, Barbarism, and Civilization*, p. 158.

67. For a brilliant description of the full return voyage, see Thomas, *Cook*, pp. 292–348. See also Anne Salmond, *The Trial of the Cannibal Dog: The Remarkable Story of Captain Cook's Adventures in the South Seas* (New Haven, 2003), pp, 351–85. The British officers are cited in Thomas, *Cook*, pp. 335, 348. See also Turnbull, "Mai," p. 47.

68. See William Bligh, *The Mutiny on Board HMS Bounty*, first pub. 1789 (New York, 1965), p. 92. Later voyagers learned variations on the same story: see journals of voyages from the 1790s to the 1840s, discussed in McCormick, *Omai*, ch. 11.

69. McCormick's vigorous research turned up little public commentary on Mai's death. The *Annual Register* for 1789 noted that "accounts have been received that Omai, of Otaheite, is dead; he did not chuse to live in his native island, and therefore settled in another, and soon squandered or gave away the greatest part of his property." *The Annual Register, or A View of the History, Politics, and Literature, for the Year 1789* (London, 1792), p. 230.

CHAPTER 7

1. C. A. Bayly, *Imperial Meridian: The British Empire and the World, 1780–1830* (London, 1989), p. 99. See also Linda Colley, *Britons: Forging the Nation, 1707–1837* (London, 1994); and Peter Marshall, *The Making and Unmaking of Empires* (Oxford, 2005).

2. Bayly, *Imperial Meridian*, pp. 99–154.

3. Ibid., p. 99. Elsewhere he noted but refrained from discussing the significance of the fact that the "classical fear that empire necessarily corrupted civic virtue through luxury and decadence was already on the wane by the 1770s": Ibid., p. 138.

4. Bernard Smith, *Imagining the Pacific: In the Wake of the Cook Voyages* (Melbourne, 1992), p. 227.

5. [John Rickman], *Journal of Captain Cook's Last Voyage to the Pacific Ocean* (London, 1781), p. 177.

6. See Gavin Kennedy, *The Death of Captain Cook* (London, 1978), pp. 91–94; and also Scott Ashley, "How Navigators Think," *Past and Present* 194 (2007), p. 118.

7. Rickman, *Journal*, pp. 328–29.

8. James Cook and James King, *A Voyage to the Pacific Ocean* (1784), vol. 63 of Historische Schifffahrt (Bremen, 2009), vol. 3, pp. 45–46.

9. Ibid., vol. 1, p. lxxxvii, and vol. 3, p. 26.

10. David Samwell, *Narrative of the Death of Captain Cook* (1786), ed. M. Fitzpatrick, J. Newell, and N. Thomas (Cardiff, 2007), pp. 82–83.

11. Ibid., pp. 75–76.

12. Ibid., p. 77.

13. Smith, *Imagining the Pacific*, p. 233. On Webber's painting, see also Rod Edmond, *Representing the South Pacific: Colonial Discourse from Cook to Gauguin* (Cambridge, 1997), pp. 30–37.

14. *Gentleman's Magazine*, January 1780, pp. 44–45.

15. William Fitzgerald, *Ode to the Memory of the Late Captain James Cook* (1780), cited in Bernard Smith, *European Vision and the South Pacific* (Oxford, 1960), p. 122.

16. Helen Maria Williams, *The Morai: An Ode* (1786), cited in full as the appendix to Andrew Kippis, *Captain Cook's Voyages with an Account of his Life* (1788) (New York, 1924), pp. 400–404.

17. Kippis, *Captain Cook's Voyages*, p. 352.

18. Hannah More, *Slavery: A Poem* (London, 1788), ll. 235–37.

19. Kippis, *Captain Cook's Voyages*, pp. 349–51. Martin Fitzpatrick notes that Kippis's biography went through nearly twenty editions before 1800 and "became the standard account . . . until the twentieth century": M. Fitzpatrick, "David Samwell: An Eventful Career," in Samwell, *Narrative of the Death*, p. 18.

20. For the anonymous squib *Letter from Omai*, see the discussion in chapter 6 of this volume.

21. Marshall Sahlins, *Islands of History* (Chicago, 1985), p. 131. Sahlins was elaborating a remark made earlier by Bernard Smith about Cook's being "[Adam] Smith's global agent": see *Imagining the Pacific*, p. 236. The other key recent scholar on Cook's death in Hawaiian culture, Gananath Obeyesekere, is no help in understanding its history in British culture. Although he was eager to explain the Hawaiians' killing of Cook in terms of "practical rationality" instead of cultural deification, Obeyesekere refused to see British action in the same light. In place of pragmatism, Obeyesekere painted a picture of such overdetermined behavior in Britons that they lost almost as much historical texture as Hawaiians did in the text—though for opposite reasons. Obeyesekere concluded simply that Britons heroized Cook because their superiority complex was a "structure of the long run in European culture and consciousness." Gananath Obeyesekere, *The Apotheosis of Captain Cook: European Mythmaking in the Pacific, with a New Afterword* (Princeton, [1992] 1997), p. 123.

22. Sahlins, *Islands*, p. 131. Sahlins's analysis was possibly unable to emphasize this advent because his structuralist anthropology in general does not admit of much division between cosmologies within a single culture at any one time.

23. The shipwreck's chief eighteenth-century historian, George Keate, comments that while the Spanish had been exploring parts of Micronesia since the 1690s, they probably did not sight Palauans until the 1720s, when missionaries thought them the fifth group of peoples of a larger set of islands. According to Keate, the Palauans were considered too "inhuman" to the Jesuits to warrant salvation and in consequence were "never since inquired after." George Keate, *An Account of the Pelew Islands* (London, 1788 [5th ed. 1803]), eds. K. L. Nero and N. Thomas (London 2002), pp. 49–51.

24. See Keate, *Account*, ch. 2. Keate surmises that "from . . . the great astonishment which the natives of Pelew discovered on seeing *white people*, it seems beyond doubt that the crew of the *Antelope* were the first Europeans who had ever landed on their islands," p. 51.

25. Keate, *Account*, pp. 77–78. The Malay-speaking crewman aboard the *Antelope* was called Tom Rose and said to be "a native of Bengal, calling himself Portuguese," p. 66.

26. Wilson, as well as Keate, took Abba Thule to be the "King of the Pelew Islands," when he was more like a chief of a province (today called Koror). His name is today rendered Ibedul. See K. L. Nero, "Keate's *Account of the Pelew Islands*: A View of Koror and Palau," in Keate, *Account*, pp. 7–27. As far as I can ascertain, no scholar has discovered any link between the favored rendition of Abba Thule's name and the ancient concept of Ultima Thule—the alleged land beyond the known world and sometimes associated with the "barbarian" Hyperboreans. There may well be none.

27. This other region, called Artingall by Keate, was really a rival province to Ibedul's own within the "Pelews."

28. The rebuilding of the *Antelope* and the British assistance in Ibedul's

wars takes up most of Keate's narrative: chs 4–19. See also a recent account, which mostly condenses Keate, by Daniel J. Peacock: *Lee Boo of Belau: A Prince in London* (Honolulu. 1987), ch. 7.

29. N. A. M. Rodger points out that though mutinies on merchantmen were not especially violent in this era, neither were they "infrequent" nor "unusual": see *The Wooden World: Anatomy of the Georgian Navy* (London, 1988), pp. 118, 185, 238.

30. Keate's account was based heavily on Wilson's own log; see Keate, *Account*, ch. 18, esp. p. 186.

31. Keate, *Account*, p. 199. The foremost authorities today on eighteenth-century Palau render Lee Boo's name as Lebuu: see N. Thomas and K. L. Nero, introduction to Keate, *Account*, p. 1.

32. In an unusually paranoid essay written in 1931, the novelist E. M. Forster insisted that Lebuu "was a hostage, though the word was never used . . . The Company's plan was to educate him in England, and send him back to rule the islands for us." E. M. Forster, "A Letter to Madan Blanchard" (1931), in his collection of essays, *Two Cheers for Democracy* (London, 1951), p. 307. Note also Paul Langford's remark that Lebuu was "exhibited in England as a curiosity and also treated as a living educational experiment": neither an exhibiting nor an experimenting spirit are evident in the sources. See Paul Langford, "The Eighteenth Century (1688–1789)," in K. O. Morgan, ed., *The Oxford Illustrated History of Britain* (Oxford, 1986), p. 414.

33. Greg Dening, *Beach Crossings: Voyaging Across Times, Culture, and Self* (Melbourne, 2004), p. 1. See also G. Irwin, *The Prehistoric Exploration and Colonization of the Pacific* (Cambridge, 1992); and B. Finney, *Voyages of Rediscovery: A Cultural Odyssey through Polynesia* (Berkeley, 1994). Scholars disagree about the original settlement of Palau—many Palauans have Polynesian origins that date from either the earlier migration or the later remigration; many also have Asian origins. Palauans are not considered to be "Micronesian" themselves, despite their locale. See John Unseem, "Structure of Power in Palau," *Social Forces* 29 (1950), pp. 141–48; and Nancy Barbour, *Palau* (Buffalo, 1995).

34. See William Bligh's journal of his second voyage to Tahiti, 9 July 1792: "it has been with no small trouble that I have resisted the sollicitations of [one particular Tahitian] to proceed to England with me. He has even considered himself slighted by my not permitting him" (cited in Douglas Oliver, *Return to Tahiti: Bligh's Second Breadfruit Voyage* [Melbourne, 1988], p. 227). See also David Chappell, *Double Ghosts: Oceanian Voyagers on Euroamerican Ships* (Armonk, 1997): "In 1787 Chief Ka'iana of Kaua'i boarded John Meare's [trading] *Nootka* amid a crowd of Hawaiians clamoring to go to 'Britanee, Britanee.' Ka'iana 'was alone received to embark with us, amid the envy of all his countrymen,'" p. 36. Chappell also claims, citing another merchant-ship officer of 1791, that "ever since Cook's visit, [Islanders] had ridden passing ships like taxis from island to island, saying 'Me ship, captain; me go Tahiti,'" p. 12.

35. N. Thomas, "The Pelew Islands in British Culture," in Keate, *Account*, pp. 1, 28.

36. On its publishing record see Thomas, "The Pelew Islands," p. 27.

37. See Philip Edwards, *The Story of the Voyage: Sea-Narratives in Eighteenth-Century England* (Cambridge, 1994), p. 13.

38. Keate, *Account*, p. 260.

39. See Philippe Ariès, *The Hour of Our Death* (New York, 1981), which discusses the romantic way of death in a chapter called "The Death of the Other," and lists among its features an intense affectiveness, a powerful ability to arouse pathos, the promise of a happy and unifying afterlife, and beauty: see ch. 10, and pp. 609–11.

40. Keate, *Account*, pp. 265–67.

41. Letter of 27 December 1784 cited in Keate, *Account*, p. 267.

42. See photograph of the tomb in Peacock, *Lee Boo*, p. 112.

43. S. T. Coleridge, "To a Young Lady with a Poem on the French Revolution" (1794), in *Complete Poetical Works*, ed. by E. H. Coleridge (Oxford, 1912), vol. 1, p. 64.

44. James C. McKusick, "That Silent Sea: Coleridge, Lee Boo, and the Exploration of the South Pacific," *The Wordsworth Circle* 24 (1993), p. 104.

45. William Lisle Bowles, "Abba Thule," published in the third edition of his minor *Sonnets, and Other Poems* (Bath, 1794). Bowles was "greatly admired" by Coleridge, Lamb, and Southey; see OCEL.

46. Joseph Cottle, "Lee Boo," published in the second edition of his *Poems* (Bristol, 1796).

47. See Ariès, *Hour of Our Death*, ch. 10.

48. Anonymous, *The Interesting and Affecting History of Prince Lee Boo* (London, 1789).

49. All these slightly different titles are in the National Library of Australia; none have specified authors. Paul Cuffee was a Native-American/African-American merchant abolitionist.

50. Anonymous, *The Adventures of Madiboo, a Native of the Pellew Islands* (London, 1809).

51. A copy of the engraving is in the NLA, RNK 1675, entitled *Prince Le Boo* and dated 1789. A copy of the jigsaw puzzle is also in the NLA, PIC 6176, entitled *The History of Lee Boo* and dated 1822. On children's jigsaws, see M. A. Norcia, "Puzzling Empire: Early Puzzles and Dissected Maps as Imperial Heuristics," *Children's Literature* 37 (2009), pp. 1–32.

52. Both OCEL and OCRA identify the 1740s–1750s as the time of take-off for children's literature.

53. Keate, *Account*, pp. 260, 264.

54. See Richard D. Altick, *The Shows of London* (Cambridge, Mass., 1978), p. 85.

55. For an array of press commentary, see excerpts in Duncan Sprott, *1784* (London, 1984), esp. pp. 220–26; *Public Advertiser*, 13 and 14 September 1784;

and *Bristol Journal*, 18 September 1784. For a discussion of this general "wonder of the world," see D. K. Cameron, *London's Pleasures, from Restoration to Regency* (Thrupp, 2001), ch. 11.

56. Keate, *Account*, p. 264, Keate's italics.

57. Ibid., pp. 260, 264. Keate does not relate which Academy he attended; probably a free, or endowed grammar, school for the sons of seafarers. Peacock has speculated that it might have been Peter Hill's school, which fits this description and was situated nearby the Wilson's home: *Lee Boo of Belau*, p. 95. Lebuu's church was the local Anglican, St. Mary's.

58. Keate, *Account*, p. 267.

59. For radical educational theorists, see Brian Simon, *Studies in the History of Education, 1780–1870* (London, 1960), ch. 1. For moralists trying to stem the tide of "national deterioration and depravity," see T. W. Laqueur, *Religion and Respectability: Sunday Schools and Working-Class Culture, 1780–1850* (New Haven, 1976), pp. 4–5.

60. Alongside the massive growth of Sunday Schools in the period, Laqueur notes that endowed grammar, or "free"/public, schools increased from 255 in 1760 to 298 in 1780 to 334 in 1800: see *Religion and Respectability*, p. 3.

61. See Laqueur on increased membership to Dissenting churches in *Religion and Respectability*, p. 3; see R. K. Webb, "Religion," in OCRA, for the rise and changing definition of evangelicalism.

62. See Peacock's *Lee Boo of Belau* (1987).

63. See the appendix to E. S. Dodge, *Beyond the Capes: Pacific Exploration from Captain Cook to the Challenger, 1776–1877* (London, 1971), pp. 403–6. Dodge's list indicates that from Wilson's 1783 voyage to 1803, exactly twenty British vessels sailed: incidences are a bit more heavily sprinkled around 1788–89 and a bit less apparent in the war years after 1793.

64. This record comes from the best account of Kualelo's British odyssey, Archibald Menzies's log of his voyage on Vancouver's *Discovery*, which was the vessel that returned Kualelo in 1791: see entry for 4 March 1792, BL MS 32641. Note that most eighteenth-century sources called him Towereroo; scholars today favor Kualelo: see Chappell, *Double Ghosts*, p. 79 *passim*. See also Nicholas Thomas, *Islanders: The Pacific in the Age of Empire* (New Haven, 2010), introduction.

65. One nineteenth-century Pacific-voyaging captain noted that by now, "no one ought to attempt a voyage through the South Seas without carrying an extra crew of [Islanders]": cited in Chappell, *Double Ghosts*, p. xvi. Menzies rather simply thought that "Mr Duncan's motive for taking [Kualelo] on board was his lively & sprightly appearance & his own voluntary offer," 4 March 1792, BL MS 32641.

66. Menzies, 4 March 1792, BL MS 32641.

67. Ibid.

68. According to the British Library Newspaper Catalogue, this was the only title operating at the time: the BL holds a microfilm of the originals, which are housed at the West Country Studies Library, Exeter, UK.

69. Menzies, 4 March 1792, BL MS 32641.

70. George Vancouver, *A Voyage of Discovery to the North Pacific Ocean and around the World, 1791–1795*, ed. The Hakluyt Society (London, 1984), vol. 1, pp. 307, 420. See also Vancouver's DNB entry. Menzies recounts how "Toworero [eventually] expressed a desire of returning home to his native country. This was made known to Sir Joseph Banks . . . who readily procured the youth a passage in the *Discovery*" [Menzies, January 1792, BL MS 32641]. For Banks's role as advisor to the Vancouver expedition, see Edward Smith, *The Life of Joseph Banks* (London, 1911), pp. 142–43.

71. Vancouver, *Voyage of Discovery*.

72. See ibid., vol. 1, p. 448. Vancouver relates that Kualelo "had formed an attachment with the daughter of . . . the chief of Matavai": p. 420. Menzies relates that "the punishment . . . suffered for his imprudence . . . was far too severe," 23 January 1793, BL MS 32641.

73. A study in the 1960s remarked that "though at first the inhabitants of the British West Indies were slow in acquiring a taste for the fruit, it has long since become an integral part of their diet." Cited in Oliver, *Return to Tahiti*, pp. 259–60. Note that the mutiny on Bligh's *Bounty* of 1789 had caused a frenzy of interest in Britain, manifested in the demand for literature on the subject as well as in the assembly of huge crowds to watch the execution of the eventually captured mutineers. This frenzy was another example of the new public interest in tales of Britons rather than Oceanians in Oceania. See Greg Dening, "Fatal Histories," in his *Mr Bligh's Bad Language: Passion, Power, and Theatre on the Bounty* (Cambridge, 1992), pp. 35–54.

74. Bligh's log of the *Providence*, 9 July 1792, cited in Oliver, *Return to Tahiti*, p. 227.

75. Bligh cited in ibid., p. 227. Scholars today would render Bligh's approximation as Maititi (ibid.).

76. See Bligh's log cited in Ida Lee, *Captain Bligh's Second Voyage to the South Sea* (London, 1920), pp. 127, 215. For the name of Jacket, see the discussion in Oliver, *Return to Tahiti*, p. 259.

77. See Rosemary Hunter, "Surviving the Pacific," *Pacific Islands Focus* 1 (1989), pp. 27, 40. A special thanks to Dr. Hunter for sending this article to me, a complete stranger.

78. Cited in Lee, *Captain's Bligh's Second Voyage*, p. 219. According to the present-day Pitcairn Island Study Group, Bligh arranged for a headstone to be laid at St. Paul's but it never eventuated until the group itself organized the funds to complete the task in 1998. The then Bishop of Polynesia, Jabez Bryce, performed the dedication in Deptford on 2 August 1998, before a congregation that included the great-great-great-grandson of William Bligh. Information from Timothy John Waters's website: http://www.printerspie.co.uk/CloseLook/01-20a.html, accessed 18 March 2010 (no longer available).

79. *The Annual Register* (1793), p. 37.

CHAPTER 8

1. Dutch and English traders had sighted these parts variously during the first quarter of the seventeenth century. Cook first sighted the eastern coast in April 1770. See G. Schilder, "New Holland: The Dutch Discoveries," and G. Williams, "New Holland to New South Wales: The English Approaches," both in G. Williams and A. Frost, eds., *Terra Australis to Australia* (Melbourne, 1988), chs. 3 and 4.

2. Cited in Williams, "New Holland to New South Wales," p. 147.

3. Cited in ibid., pp. 147, 150.

4. Thomas Bankes, *A New Royal Authentic and Complete System of Universal Geography* (London, 1786), pp. 5–11.

5. *St. James's Chronicle*, 16 January 1787.

6. James Cook, *The Journals of Captain James Cook*, ed., J.C. Beaglehole (Cambridge, 1955–68), vol. 1, p. 399. See also Williams, "New Holland to New South Wales," p. 147.

7. See Williams, "New Holland to New South Wales," p. 150. See also Banks's Journal of 1768–71, cited in Alan Moorehead, *The Fatal Impact: An Account of the Invasion of the South Pacific 1767–1840* (Honolulu, 1966), pp. 114–18; and Banks's testimony to the Beauchamp Committee, May 1785, PRO HO 7/1.

8. Britain did not lose as much commerce from American independence as was feared. See Linda Colley, *Britons: Forging the Nation, 1707–1837* (New Haven, 1994), p. 149.

9. C.A. Bayly, *Imperial Meridian: The British Empire and the World, 178-1830* (London, 1989), p. 207. This goes against, for example, the argument of Glyn Williams, who claims that New South Wales represented "eighteenth-century government at its best"—that is, the apex of a long history of thought and practice. Bayly rather believes that centralization and social rigidity were new processes. See G. Williams, "The Pacific: Exploration and Exploitation," in OHBE vol. 2, pp. 566–67.

10. Taken from facsimile at website of the National Archives or Australia (NAA): http://www.foundingdocs.gov.au/. The NAA points out with interest that a draft version of the instructions, dated 20 April 1787, had originally contained "Savages," but this was crossed out in favor of "Natives": see CO 201/1 ff 29–45v, website accessed 26 March 2010.

11. See Phillip to Sydney (secretary of the Home Office), 15 May 1788, reproduced in HRNSW, vol. 1, part 2, pp. 122–23.

12. Cited in G. Williams and A. Frost, "New South Wales: Expectations and Reality," in Williams and Frost, eds., *Terra Australis to Australia*, p. 170.

13. Officer John White, cited in Williams and Frost, "New South Wales," p. 169.

14. See Phillip to Sydney, 15 May 1788 and 9 July 1788, reproduced in HRNSW, vol. 1, part 2, pp. 129, 153.

15. Cited in Williams and Frost, "New South Wales," p. 186.

16. Major Robert Ross, letter to Phillip, 22 August 1788, cited in Williams and Frost, "New South Wales," p. 188.

17. Lieutenant William Bradley, cited in ibid., p. 181.

18. On *res nullius* generally—its content and era of influence—see Stuart Banner, *Possessing the Pacific: Land, Settlers, and Indigenous People from Australia to Alaska* (Cambridge, Mass., 2007), pp. 10–12, 18; and Andrew Fitzmaurice, "The Genealogy of Terra Nullius," *Australian Historical Studies* 38 (2007), pp. 1–15.

19. See Anthony Pagden, *Lords of All the World: Ideologies of Empire in Spain, Britain, and France, c. 1500–c.1800* (New Haven, 1995), p. 83.

20. Cited in Williams and Frost, "New South Wales," p. 166. Cook's conclusion was that "the Industry of Man has had nothing to do with it."

21. Joseph Banks, testimony to the Beauchamp Committee, 10 May 1785, PRO HO 7/1.

22. The early 2000s witnessed heated debate in Australia about this issue, much of it foundering on the minor point that those who insisted Britons behaved as first takers believed New South Wales was thus regarded a *terra nullius*. As the doubters remarked, *terra nullius* was not in common legal use until the early twentieth century: on this ground they wished to argued that Britons did not therefore behave as first takers. Plainly, *terra nullius* derives from the five-hundred-year-old concept of *res nullius*, and is thus, as Fitzmaurice concludes, simply a "synecdoche"—hardly grounds for refuting the historical evidence of behavior. See Andrew Fitzmaurice on ABC Radio "Terra Nullius—The History Wars," 16 August 2004, available under http://www.abc.net .au, accessed 31 March 2010. See also Henry Reynolds, *The Law of the Land* (Camberwell, [1987] 2003), ch. 2; Bain Attwood in *The Financial Review*, 11 June 2004; and Christopher Pearson, *The Australian*, 25 June 2004. A recent review of British imperial law is Lisa Ford, *Settler Sovereignty: Jurisdiction and Indigenous People in America and Australia, 1788–1836* (Cambridge, Mass., 2010).

23. Philip Gidley King, in John Hunter's *The Historical Journal of the Transactions at Port Jackson, Including the Journals of Governors Phillip and King* (London, 1793), p. 406. Robert Brown, 26 January 1788, reproduced in HRNSW, vol. 1, part 2, p. 407.

24. On Bennelong generally, and on the Eora, see first Keith Vincent Smith, *Bennelong* (Sydney, 2001), esp. p. 5. See also Grace Karskens, *The Colony: A History of Early Sydney* (Sydney, 2009), pp. 32–60.

25. Phillip to Sydney, 12 February 1790, reproduced in HRNSW, vol. 1, part 2, p. 298.

26. Watkin Tench, *Sydney's First Four Years* (1789–93), ed. L. F. Fitzhardinge (Sydney, 1979), p. 138.

27. See Smith, *Bennelong*, p. 37; and Karskens, *The Colony*, p. 372.

28. Macarthur to Kingdon, 7 March 1791, HRNSW, p. 502.

29. William Bradley, cited in Inga Clendinnen, *Dancing with Strangers* (Melbourne, 2003), p. 105.

30. Newton Fowell, 31 July 1790, HRNSW, p. 373.

31. See Tench, *Sydney's First Four Years*, pp. 159–61. See also Philip Gidley King, Journal, 9 April 1790, MS C115, Mitchell Library.

32. Phillip to Sydney, 13 February 1790, HRNSW, p. 309.

33. See ibid.

34. Smith, *Bennelong*, pp. 46–48.

35. Tench, *Sydney's First Four Years*, p. 167.

36. See Smith, *Bennelong*, p. 51.

37. Phillip to Banks, 26 July 1790, PRO reel CY300 2/89–93.

38. Tench, *Sydney's First Four Years*, p. 179. For accounts, see Smith, *Bennelong*, pp. 52–59; Karskens, *The Colony*, pp. 383–85; and Philip Jones, *Ochre and Rust: Artefacts and Encounters on Australian Frontiers* (Adelaide, 2007), pp. 41–42.

39. Smith, *Bennelong*, pp. 57–59. Note that Clendinnen also made this point, though two years after Smith, in *Dancing with Strangers*, pp. 110–32.

40. See Smith, *Bennelong*, p. 67; and Karskens, *The Colony*, p. 385. Clendinnen calls this period between 1790 and 1793 the "days of hope": *Dancing with Strangers*, p. 272.

41. John Hunter, cited and discussed in Isadore Brodsky, *Bennelong Profile: Dreamtime Reveries of a Native of Sydney Cove* (Sydney, 1973), pp. 50–53.

42. See Isabel McBryde, *Guests of the Governor: Aboriginal Residents of the First Government House* (Sydney, 1989).

43. Tench, *Sydney's First Four Years*, pp. 185, 202. Smith conjectures that Yemmerawanne may have introduced himself with the words: "jam-ora wanne," meaning "my country is wanne [wangal]": *Bennelong*, pp. 97–98.

44. Phillip to Banks, 3 December 1791, cited in John Kenny, *Bennelong: First Notable Aboriginal* (Sydney, 1973), p. 53.

45. David Collins, *Account of the English Colony at New South Wales* (London, 1978), vol. 1, p. 211.

46. *Lloyd's Evening Post*, 29 May 1793.

47. The bill is found in the Treasury Board Papers, PRO, T1/733. From July 1793 to October 1793 and then again from November 1793 to May 1794 the Aboriginals boarded with William Waterhouse—father of Lieutenant Henry Waterhouse of the First Fleet—in Mount Street, Grosvenor Square: thanks to Keith Smith for pointing me to this residential information.

48. TBP, PRO, T1/733.

49. It is perhaps the single commonest statement made in today's cursory one-liners about Bennelong's travels that he "was taken to London to see the King." See, for example, Clendinnen, *Dancing with Strangers*, p. 264. The first Bennelong historian to question the royal meeting was Brodsky, *Bennelong Profile*, 65. My own hunt confirms the absence of reports. Brodsky believes that the historical consensus arose from a claim made in a soldier's 1803 published account. If so, it gained currency without acknowledging the part that such a claim served in the soldier's broader argument about the willfulness of Bennelong to return to savagery despite all the "comforts" of civilization

shown him. See George Bond, *A Brief Account of the Colony at Port Jackson* (Southhampton, 1803), p. 6.

50. Brook offers a neat exegesis of the Aboriginals' touring from the bills of expenses extant in the PRO. See Jack Brook, "The Forlorn Hope: Bennelong and Yemmerawannie go to England," *Australian Aboriginal Studies* 1 (2001), pp. 38–41.

51. TBP, PRO, T1/733.

52. See Eric McCormick, *Omai: Pacific Envoy* (Auckland, 1977), pp. 165, 258, 290.

53. TBP, PRO, T1/733.

54. Hiatt offers this argument in "Bennelong and Omai," *Australian Aboriginal Studies* 2 (2004), pp. 88–89.

55. Lyceum Museum Broadside, Mitchell Library, reproduced in Williams and Frost, "New South Wales," p. 201.

56. *Gentleman's Magazine* (1973), p. 531.

57. See Bayly, *Imperial Meridian*, and my discussion in chapter 7 in this volume.

58. Missive carried on the *Surprize*, reported in Collins, *Account*, vol. 1, p. 331.

59. Hunter to Under-Secretary King, 25 January 1795, reproduced in HRNSW, vol. 2, p. 281.

60. Clendinnen, *Dancing with Strangers*, pp. 242, 244, 247, 260.

61. Bayly, *Imperial Meridian*, p. 207; Karskens, *The Colony*, p. 443.

62. Colebee cited in Collins, *Account*, vol. 1, p. 390. Karskens gives a nice narrative of Bennelong's return in general: *The Colony*, p. 422.

63. Bennelong to Phillips, 29 August 1796, Rex Nan Kivell Collection, NLA. "Murry doings" translates to "major happenings" or "big issues". Thanks to Keith Smith.

64. Collins, *Account*, vol. 2, pp. 49, 96.

65. For a compelling account of Bennelong's reputation from 1800 to the present, see Emma Dortins, "The Many Truths of Bennelong's Tragedy," *Aboriginal History* 33 (2009), pp. 53–75.

66. *The Times*, 29 October 1805. I thank Judy Barbour and the late Les Hiatt for alerting me to his article, which they located after a long search for all London reports of Bennelong.

67. *Sydney Gazette*, 9 January 1813. For Bennelong's status among his own people at the time of his death, see Keith Smith, "Bennelong among his People," *Aboriginal History* 33 (2009), pp. 7–30.

68. Tench, *Sydney's First Four Years*, p. 203.

CONCLUSION

1. Reynolds had never sold the portrait, keeping it in his studio always as a showpiece. By the time of his death in 1792, however, the fashion for its subject was well and truly over. It was sold by Reynolds's executors in 1796 to a dealer, who quickly sold it on to one of Reynolds's old friends, Lord Carlisle of Castle

Howard: see Martin Postle, *Sir Joshua Reynolds: The Subject Pictures* (Cambridge, 1995), p. 277. The Howards retained the work for over 200 years, but found it necessary to sell it in 2001 for financial reasons. In 2001, the piece sold for £10.3 million, which at the time was the highest price ever paid for a Reynolds by a good £8 million, and the second highest price ever paid for a British work of art. (The highest had been for John Constable's *The Lock* in 1990, at £10.7 million.) In 2003, when the work was still in abeyance, the late John Paul Getty offered £12.5 million to get the work back, though this price was and remains rejected. See, for an extended musing on this episode, Kate Fullagar, "Reynolds' New Masterpiece: From Experiment in Savagery to Icon of the Eighteenth Century," *Journal of Cultural and Social History* 7 (2010), pp. 191–212.

2. Serota quoted in Department of Culture, Media and Sport (DCMS), *The 49th Report of the Reviewing Committee on the Export of Works of Art* (London, 2003), p. 50; Deuchar cited in *The Guardian*, 24 Dec. 2002. Art Fund Charity, "Noble Savage," at www.artfund.org. See also "Anonymous Donor Steps In To Help Acquire Omai," Tate News, 26 March 2003.

3. See DCMS, *The 49th Report*, pp. 50–53. See also *The Guardian*, 8 February 2003, and DCMS, *The 48th Report of the Reviewing Committee on the Export of Works of Art* (London, 2002), p. 57.

4. BBC1 documentary, *Imagine . . . Portrait of Omai*, prod. Robin Dashwood (London, 2003).

5. DCMS, *The 49th Report*, p. 52; E. K. Waterhouse, *Sir Joshua Reynolds* (London, 1941); Nicholas Penny, ed., *Reynolds* (London, 1986), pp. 27. David Mannings, *Sir Joshua Reynolds: Complete Catalogue of His Paintings* (New Haven, 2000), vol. 1, p. 357.

6. Sold by another strapped family for £1.8 in 2002, the Parry eventually went to the National Portrait Gallery, the Captain Cook Memorial Museum, and the National Museums and Galleries of Wales for £950,000. See Maev Kennedy, "Galleries Plead for Omai Portrait," *The Guardian*, 27 March 2002; and Maev Kennedy, "Galleries Buy Omai Portrait at Discount," *The Guardian*, 6 August 2003. See also the press release from the National Portrait Gallery: http://www.npg.org.uk/about/press/portrait-of-omai-secured.php, accessed 18 February 2011.

7. National Portrait Gallery press release, http://www.npg.org.uk/about/press/portrait-of-omai-secured.php.

8. See J. G. A. Pocock, *The Machiavellian Moment: Florentine Political Thought and the Atlantic Republican Tradition* (Princeton, 1975), p. 32.

9. C. A. Bayly, *Imperial Meridian: The British Empire and the World, 1780–1830* (London, 1989), pp. 99, 138.

10. See Bayly, *Imperial Meridian*. See also Linda Colley, *Britons: Forging a Nation, 1707–1837* (New Haven, 1992).

11. See Martin Bailey, "Owner of Reynolds' Portrait," *The Art Newspaper* 171 (2006), and *The Guardian*, 5 February 2005, in which a government spokesperson declares that no *permanent* export license will be granted "in the foreseeable future." The temporary license ran out in 2011.

Index

LIBRARY, UNIVERSITY OF CHESTER

Lightning Source UK Ltd.
Milton Keynes UK
UKOW052229220213

206664UK00001B/64/P